A Brief Introduction to Western Literature

西方文学

（修订版）

主　编　左金梅
副主编　李旭奎　张德玉　乔国强

中国海洋大学出版社
·青岛·

图书在版编目(CIP)数据

西方文学＝A Brief Introduction to Western Literature/左金梅主编；—修订本.—青岛：中国海洋大学出版社，2006.9(2016.8 重印)

ISBN 978－7－81067－877－3

Ⅰ.西…　Ⅱ.左…　Ⅲ.文学史－西方国家－高等学校－教材－英语Ⅳ.I109

中国版本图书馆 CIP 数据核字(2006)第 049473 号

西方文学(修订版)

左金梅　主编

出版发行	中国海洋大学出版社
社　　址	青岛市香港东路 23 号　　邮政编码 266071
网　　址	http://www.ouc-press.com
订购电话	0532－82032573　82032573(传真)
责任编辑	李夕聪
电子信箱	xicongli@yahoo.com.cn
印　　制	日照报业印刷有限公司
版　　次	2006 年 9 月第 1 版
印　　次	2016 年 8 月第 3 次印刷
开　　本	850 mm×1168 mm　1/32
印　　张	12.75
字　　数	420 千字
定　　价	25.00 元

前　言

　　近些年来我国高等院校英语专业陆续开设了西方文学方面的新课程,但到目前为止有关方面英文版本的教材还很少。本书是根据作者近些年从事西方文学教学的经验和学生的实际需要、基于 2001 年出版的《西方文学纲要及选读》而修订的一本专业教材。

　　本书分古代、中世纪、文艺复兴、古典主义、浪漫主义、现实主义和自然主义、现代主义七部分,每部分又分为历史背景、文学流派及特点、杰出代表人物及作品、经典作品选读和思考题,系统全面地简述了西方文学的发生、发展历史,并重点概述了现代主义和后现代主义的各个分流派:象征主义、未来主义、表现主义、存在主义、荒诞派戏剧、超现实主义、意识流、黑色幽默、新小说、新现实主义。内容翔实新颖,条理层次分明,重点突出,语言通俗易懂,便于学生在较短的时间内系统地掌握西方文学方面的知识。

　　《西方文学》与本人主编的《美国文学》、《英国文学》和《当代西方文论》已成为有关西方文学方面的比较完整的系列教材,在我校英语专业已使用过数届,并被列为我校英语专业外国语言学和英语语言文学研究生入学考试的参考书,也有其他兄弟院校开始陆续使用。

左金梅

2006 年 8 月 8 日

Contents

Introduction

The Western literature has gone through seven phases since its beginning, which includes the Ancient World, the Middle Ages, the Renaissance, Neo-classicism, Realism, Romanticism, and Modernism.

The Ancient World began from the 8th century B C and ended at the 5th century A D. Its literature contains two aspects — the Biblical and the classical, which have exerted the greatest influence on the Western literature. The *Bible* is a collection of religious writing comprising two parts: the *Old Testament* and the *New Testament*. The former is about God and the laws of God; the latter, the doctrine of Jesus Christ. The classical mainly refers to the ancient Greco-Roman literature. The achievement of Greek literature lies in its poetry and drama. The great poet,

Homer, left us two great epics — the *Iliad* and the *Odyssey*. The *Iliad* deals with the war against the city of Troy. The heroes are Hektor on the Trojan side and Achilles and Odysseus on the Greek. In the final battle, Hektor was killed by Achilles and Troy was burned by the Greeks. The *Odyssey* deals with the return of Odysseus after the Trojan war to his home island of Ithaca. It describes many adventures Odysseus runs into on his sea voyage and how he is finally reunited with his faithful wife Penelope. The greatest Greek playwrights of tragedy are Aeschylus, Sophocles, and Euripides, and the greatest playwright of comedy is Aristophanes. Among the most renowned Greek tragedies are Sophocles' *Oedipus Rex* and Aeschylus' *Prometheus Bound*.

The greatest of Latin poets is Virgil. He wrote the great epic, the *Aeneid*. It tells the story of Aeneas, one of the princes of Troy, who escaped from the burning city when it fell to the Greeks, to carry on the Trojan cause in a new place, Rome. Aeneas stood at the head of a race of people who were to found first the Roman Republic and then the Roman Empire. He was a truly tragic hero because to fulfill his historic mission he had to sacrifice his own happiness. With the Greco-Roman achievements in literary creation emerged a number of forerunners of Western literary criticism and theory, of whom Plato, Aristotle, Horace and Longinus are the greatest.

The classical literature ended with the fall of the Roman Empire in the 5th century, and then the Western literature entered the phase of the Middle Ages, which lasted till the 14th century. During the Medieval times, there was no central government to keep the order. The only organization that seemed to unite Europe was the Christian Church. Christianity took the lead in politics, law, art, and learning for hundreds of years. Religion shaped people's lives.

The medieval literature can be divided into three categories — religious writings, romance, and vernacular writings. The greatest achievement of religious literature was made by the greatest Italian poet, Dante. His masterpiece, the *Divine Comedy*, is the greatest Christian poem with a profound vision of the Medieval Christian world. It expresses humanistic ideas which foreshadowed the spirit of the Renaissance. With regard to romance, the most well-known are the adventures of King Arthur and his knights of the Round Table. The vernacular literature of this time tends to be realistic and satirical. The greatest works of this kind are Boccaccio's *Decameron* and Chaucer's *The Canterbury Tales*. *Decameron* is a collection of about one hundred tales told by seven young ladies and three younger gentlemen on their way to escape the Black Death of 1348. The tales are witty, licentious, full of praises of true love and wisdom and also satire on the hypocrisy of the priest and the aristocratic. *The Canterbury Tales* is also a collection of tales, which were told by thirty pilgrims on their way to the saint place, Canterbury. The tales are a true-to-life picture of the medieval England, in which Chaucer sang of man's energy, intellect, quick wit, and love of life, and at the same time, Chaucer exposed and satirized the evils of his time such as the corruption of the church.

Against the theology of the Middle Ages arose the intellectual movement, Renaissance, which sprang first in Italy in the 14th century and gradually spread all over Europe. The movement had two striking features. One was the thirsting curiosity for classical literature, and the other was the keen interest in human beauty and human activities, which are in sharp contrast with Medieval theology. The greatest novel of this period is Cervantes' *Don Quixote*, which is a parody satirizing a very popular type of literature, the romance of chivalry. Don Quixote is a poor country gentleman who has read too many chivalric romances. He, together with another peasant, sets forth on a series of adventures, which are put against the reality of the 17th century Spain. Don Quixote is an idealist. When his ideals are in conflict with reality and can not be realized, the idealist turns into an absurd, comic character. The other writers giving full expressions to the humanist ideals of the Renaissance include Shakespeare and Marlowe (playwrights), Bacon and More (essayists), and Spenser and Milton (poets). The literary criticism and theory of the Renaissance is the summation of the views and creations of these great Renaissance writers. The outstanding British critic of this period is Sir Philip Sidney.

The Renaissance is romantic in nature, for it stresses the liberation of the human mind. To restrain the liberal mind arose a new literary movement, Neo classicism, which began in France in the late 17th century and flourished in other European countries in the mid-18th century. Often in contrast with Realism and Romanticism, Neoclassicism places emphasis upon qualities of the classical literature: clear, direct, simple expressions of ideas in balanced and well-proportioned form; restraint of motion and passion; an ability to think and to communicate objectively rather than subjectively. These qualities are apparent in the works of

Molière, the best representative dramatist of French classical comedies, and of Pope, the greatest English poet and critic of Neo classicism.

As a reaction to the restraints and rules imposed by classicists, Romanticism came into being in the late 18th century. Romanticists looked to the Middle Ages and emphasized individual freedom, pure sentiments and ideal beauty. Romanticism brought forth a full flowering of literary talents. The leading Romantic writers include Blake, Wordsworth, Coleridge, Scott, Byron, Shelly, and Keats in England; Goethe and Schiller in Germany; Hugo and Sand in France; and Irving, Whitman, Poe, Emerson, and Hawthorne in America. Most of these writers also contribute to literary criticism.

Against the sentimentality of Romanticism emerged Realism, which began in France in the 1850's and prevailed in Europe and the United States until the early years of the twentieth century. Realism centered in the novel and put emphasis on fidelity to actual experience. At the end of the 19th century, Realism developed into Naturalism, which applied determinism to literature and held that the fate of human beings were determined by environment and heredity. The representative realistic writers are Stendhal, Balzac, Flaubert, Maupassant in France; Turgenev, Dostoyevsky, Tolstoy in Russia; Dickens, Hardy in England; Mark Twain, Henry James, and Lowells in the United States. The renowned realistic dramatists are Shaw in England, and Ibsen in Norway. Among these writers, those who can be also regarded as great critics are Balzac, Tolstoy, and Henry James.

At the beginning of the twentieth century, the Western literature entered the phase of Modernism. Modernism, as a literary movement, is a very complicated term to define. It has been made up of many facets including surrealism, symbolism, existentialism, expressionism, stream of consciousness, Black Humor, the Theatre of the Absurd, and other minor trends.

Symbolism rose in the late 19th century as opposed to Realism. Symbolists of this era tried to suggest life through the use of symbols and images. Ezra Pound and Yeats are among the representatives of symbolism.

Surrealism sprang up in France at the end of World War I. Influenced by Freudianism and horrified by the brutality of war, it stresses the subconscious or the nonrational aspects of man's existence. Writers of this school tend to present imagery in disorderly array, much like the random sequence of events or recollections experienced in dreams.

Existentialism is normally applied to writings that emphasize man's responsibility for forming his own nature and stress the prime importance of personal decisions, personal freedom, and personal goals. The most important existentialist of the century is Sartre, French philosopher and writer, whose principal theory is that life has no meaning and purpose.

Expressionism appeared at the beginning of the 20th century and reached its climax in Germany and the United States in the 1930s. It stresses the subjective, intuitive and conscious aspects of man, and presents reality in symbolism, abstraction, or even distortion. The expressionistic tendency is notable in the plays of Eugene O'Neill and Tennessee Williams.

Stream of consciousness is a manner of writing in which the

character's perceptions and thoughts are presented as occurring in random form. This method of writing was employed by such writers as James Joyce and Virginia Woolf.

Black Humor is a term used to refer to some Western, especially American writers after World War Ⅱ. Black Humor is a kind of desperate humor. It is the laughter at tragic things. To black humorists, the world is meaningless; man's fate is decided by incomprehensible powers; we can't do anything about it, and there we may as well laugh. Joseph Heller's *Catch*-22 has been considered the major work of Black Humor.

The Theatre of the Absurd refers to the works of some European, particularly French, playwrights of the 1950's and 1960's. In their plays, these playwrights attempted to convey the idea that human existence is purposeless and meaningless, and that in this world man feels constantly bewildered, troubled and threatened. Samuel Beckett's *Waiting for Godot* has been remembered as one of the most famous Absurd drama.

Chapter I   The Ancient World

1. Historical Introduction

The ancient world represents the most significant area and period of ancient man's development. The area is the Mediterranean basin, and the period is roughly from 500 B C to 400 A D. In this place and time ancient man laid the intellectual and religious foundations of the modern Western outlook. The literature of the ancient world was written in three languages — Hebrew, Greek, and Latin. The peoples who spoke these languages created their civilizations independently in place and time, but the development of the Mediterranean area into one economic and political unit brought these civilizations into contact with each other and produced a fusion of their typical attitudes which has become the basis of all subsequent Western thought.

The territory of the Hebrews was Palestine which was of no particular strategic importance. In their period of independence, from their beginning as a pastoral tribe to their high point as a kingdom with a splendid capital in Jerusalem, the Hebrews achieved little of note in the military spheres and their later history was a bitter and unsuccessful struggle for freedom against a series of foreign masters — Babylonian, Greek, and Roman. They left no drama nor epic poetry but religious literature, probably written down between the 8th and 2nd centuries B C, which was later called the *Old Testament*.

Greek literature began with two masterpieces the *Iliad* and the *Odyssey*, which were created by the blind poet Homer on the basis of the legends passed down by many generations of singers before him. The production of the two epics are roughly dated between the 11th and 9th centuries B C, the time when the clan system began to disintegrate and the slavery was on its way to come in Greek society. In the 7th and 6th centuries B C, Greece entered the slave society. With the increasing conflict between commercial and aristocratic slave owners arose the classical Greek tragedy, with the three great tragedians — Aeschylus, Sophocles and Euripides taking the lead. At the same time, Greek comedy came into being. The only comic poet of the 5th century whose work has survived is Aristophanes. As a result of the political and economical development and the great literary achievements in poetry and drama, the ancient Greek literary criticism prospered. The greatest Ancient Greek literary critics are Plato and Aristotle, who opened the history of Western literary criticism.

The Romans looked to Greek models for their literature. Greek literature began before the Greeks as a people had any political importance. The Romans, on the other hand, had conquered half the world before they began to write. They began to do so only when, in the 3rd century B C, they dominated Greece and discovered Greek literature. The first real example of a literary work in Latin is a translation of Homer's *Odyssey*. In spite of the imitation, the finest Roman accomplishments in literature, as in other aspects of art and life, were seen in the reign of the first of Rome's emperors, Augusts Caesar (27 B C-14 A D). The great works of the Augustan Age was Virgil's *Aeneid*, Horace's satirical lyrics, Ovid's *Metamorphoses*, and the *New Testament*. The critical works, based on these literary creations, are Horace's *The Art of Poetry* and Longinus' *On the Sublime*.

2. Literary Giants and Works

Bible is a collection of writings known as the *Holy Scriptures*, the sacred writings of the Christian religion. Of the two chief parts, the *Old Testament* consists of the sacred writings of the ancient Hebrews, and the *New Testament* of writings of the early Christian period. The *Old Testament*, written in ancient Hebrew at various times in the pre-Christian era, includes four collections — *The Law*, *The History*, *The Writings*, and *The Prophets*, dealing with God's creations, ancient Jewish legends, law and doctrines. The *New Testament*, written in the Greek dialect of Mediterranean countries at the time of Christ, includes *The Gospel*, *The Letters*, and *The Revelation*, concerning Jesus Christ's birth, youth, teachings, trial and crucifixion. The *Bible* is partly in prose and partly in verse and exploits various literary types — short story, biographical narrative, love lyric, battle ode, epigram, psalm, elegy, letter, and dramatic philosophical poem. The *Bible* is the most quoted, the most influential and powerful book of all literature. Great Western authors commonly show a familiarity with it.

Iliad describes the events of a few weeks in the ten-year siege of Troy. The war was fought by the Akhaians against the Trojans for the recovery of Helen, the wife of the Akhaian chieftain Menelaos, who had been taken away by the Prince of Troy.

The particular subject of the poem is the anger of Achilles, the bravest of the Akhaian chieftains encamped outside the city. Achilles is a man who lives by and for violence, who is creative and alive only in violent action. The great champion of the Trojans is Hektor, who fights bravely, but reluctantly. War, for him, is a necessary evil, and he thinks nostalgically of the peaceful past, though he has little hope of peace to come. The two heroes stand for the two poles of the human condition, war and peace, with their corresponding aspects of human nature, the destructive and the creative. The poem begins with Achilles' anger and ends with Hektor's funeral.

Odyssey is concerned with the peace which followed the war, and in particular with the return of the heroes who survived. Its subject is the long drawn-out return of one of the heroes, Odysseus, who had come farther than most (all the way from western Greece) and who was destined to spend ten years' wandering in unknown seas before he returned to his rocky kingdom. Odysseus' voyage home, full of trials of physical obstacles and temptations, is the symbol of life, for which Odysseus is struggling. Odysseus' outstanding quality is a probing and versatile intelligence, which, combined with long experience, keeps him safe and alive through the trials and dangers of twenty years of war and seafaring. He finds in the end the home and peace he has fought for, his wife faithful, a son worthy of his name ready to succeed him, and the knowledge that the death which must come at last will be gentle.

Prometheus Bound is one of Aeschylus' greatest tragedies. It deals with Prometheus' defiance against tyranny and his love of mankind. According to Greek myth, Prometheus stole fire from heaven and taught men how to use it. For this he was punished by Zeus, the supreme god, who chained him to a rock on Mt. Caucasus, where during the daytime a vulture fed on his liver, which was restored each succeeding night. The figure of Prometheus has been symbolic of those noble-hearted who devote themselves to the good of mankind and suffer great pains at the hands of tyrants.

Oedipus Rex is Sophocles' masterpiece of tragedy. Here Sophocles used for his tragedy a well-known legendary story handed down from generation to generation. Oedipus is the son of the king and queen of Thebes. Before his birth, Apollo has predicted that he will kill his father and marry his mother. When he is born, his parents have their shepherd desert him in a deep valley. But out of compassion, the shepherd gives the boy to another shepherd in another kingdom, in which Oedipus becomes the foster son of the king and queen. When he grows up, Oedipus learns his dreadful fate from Apollo's prediction and leaves his foster parents. On his way, he meets with a group of strangers and kills one of them, who is none other than his father by birth. Then he reaches Thebes, where he is made king for his bravery of getting rid of the Sphinx and marries the ex-king's wife, his mother. When the truth is made known, Oedipus, in remorse, puts out his eyes and his mother commits suicide. Through the tragedy of Oedipus, the playwright implies the inadequacy of the human intellect and gives a warning that there is a power in the universe which humanity cannot control, nor even fully understand.

Medea, one of Euripides' masterpieces, was produced in 431 B C. It is a tragedy of devotion, desertion and revenge. Medea, the daughter of king, falls in love with Jason, who has come to her kingdom to get his uncle the gold wool in exchange of the throne his uncle robbed of his father. Devoted to her lover, Medea helps Jason get the wool and elopes with him to Greece even at the cost of her brother. In Greece Medea also helps Jason kill his uncle because his uncle has broken his promise and killed Jason's father. Driven away by his cousin, Jason and Medea come to live in another kingdom, where Jason is attracted to the king's daughter and determines to marry her. In rage, Medea has her two sons burn the king's daughter and then kills her own sons for the revenge of her husband. The play dramatizes disorder, not just the disorder of the family of Jason and Medea, but the disorder of the universe as a whole. It is a world full of the senseless fury and degradation of permanent violence.

Aeneid, the great epic of Rome, was written by Rome's greatest poet, Virgil. It is about both war and the struggles of Aeneas. Aeneas was predestined by Fate to come from Troy to Italy. According to legend he was a Trojan, who, after the Trojan war, escaped from his defeated city, piously carrying his old father on his shoulders. After long years of various hardships and delays, he at last arrived in Italy. There he married Lavinia, the daughter of king Latinos, thus uniting the Trojan people with the native Latin people to found the Roman race. Aeneas is not an individual. He is the prototype of the ideal Roman ruler. His qualities are the devotion to duty and the seriousness of purpose which were to give the Mediterranean world two centuries of ordered government.

Metamorphoses, essentially a narrative of twelve thousand lines in Latin hexameter, is divided into fifteen books. It recounts two hundred legends and myths arranged chronologically. In these stories, as the title suggests, Ovid chose for his theme the changes of state commonly experienced by divine and human actors. Two examples are the transformation of Zeus into the bull that carried off the maiden Europa, and Daphne, who became a tree to ward off the lusty embrace of Apollo. Ovid's keen eye for natural beauty and his power to bring to life the fantastic world of gods, demigods, and heroes has made the *Metamorphoses* one of the most delightful writings produced in the ancient world.

Aristophanes (450-388) was the greatest representative of ancient Greek comedy, and the one whose works have been preserved in the greatest quantity. His major plays include *Acharnians*, *Knights*, *Clouds*, *Wasps*, *Peace* and *Birds*. These comedies are notable for their bold fantasy, merciless invective, outrageous satire, licentious humour, and marked freedom of political criticism. Among his special satirical targets were contemporary Athenian society, its fashionable philosophies and literature, and the aggressive foreign policy of Athens during the Peloponnesian War. His plays are still produced on the 20th-century stage in numerous translations that attempt to make the playwright's puns, witticisms, and topical allusions accessible to modern audiences.

Plato (427-347 B C), the great philosopher and thinker of idealism, was also a great critic. His literary criticism, like his

西方文学

philosophical thoughts, was presented in the form of dialogue. Plato wrote more than forty dialogues, which were collected in one book called *The Dialogues of Plato*. His dialogues, with his teacher, Socrates, as the leading speaker, cover many aspects — politics, philosophy, law, ethics, education, and artistic criticism. His critical ideas of art mainly center in such pieces as *The Republic* and *The Ion*, in which he first raised these issues: the place of the poet in society; the effect of literature upon its audience; the proper function of literature; the nature of artistic process; and the nature of artistic imitation. In terms of artistic imitation, Plato held that art imitates reality. But his reality has two levels — the world we know and a world of perfect ideas. For him, the world of matter is the imitation of the world of ideas, and the world of art is the imitation of the world of matter. Thus art becomes the shadow's shadow. Under the guidance of this idealism, Plato developed his other idealistic ideas of art such as the concept of creative inspiration and genius, which, in nature, denied the truth and value of art. Plato's ideas were criticized by Aristotle, but their great influence on later critics can not be denied.

Aristotle (384-322 B C), in addition to having made enormous contributions to the fields of ethics, politics, physics, and rhetoric, was also the Western world's first important literary critic and his views on poetic and dramatic forms stated in his *Poetics* continue to be influential to the present. In *Poetics* Aristotle sought not only to define the nature of the forms of the epic, tragedy and comedy, but also to produce a kind of manual for writers who wished to write in these forms. He was also, in a sense, answering his former master Plato, who thought that poetry, with its dangerous effects on emotions, ought to be banished from the ideal republic. For Aristotle, poetry is actually superior to history, because poetry deals with the general and the philosophical, whereas history treats the particular. All poetry, for Aristotle, is an imitation of life, but this imitation involves not merely the realistic copying of a "slice of life" but the condensation of life into a form, with a beginning, a middle and an end resulting in both pleasure and self knowledge for the audience. For Aristotle, tragedy, because it portrays people as better than they actually are, and because its form is the most cohesive, is superior to both comedy and epic. Indeed, most of the *Poetics* concerns tragedy.

Longinus was the great literary critic in about the 3rd century of Rome. His work *On the Sublime* reflects his view on literary art. For Longinus, sublimity refers to both the heightened mind of the writer and the lofty style of the work. Longinus listed the five sources of the sublime — power of great conceptions; strong and impetuous passion; the proper handling of figures of diction and thoughts; noble phraseology including choice of words and use of tropes and of elaboration; and dignified and spirited composition. Longinus held that the first two constituents of sublimity are in most cases native-born, and so sublimity is the note which rings from a great mind. For him, the artist should pursue sublimity, for artistic sublimity evokes ecstasy, heightens emotional response, and lightens a subject under inquiry.

Horace (65-8 B C), the great poet of the Augustan Age, was also interested in literary criticism and theory. In *The Art of Po-*

etry, Horace formulated the basic tenet for Roman poets: poetry must be both pleasing and useful. The poem should combine patriotic, moral, or philosophical messages with sensuous beauty of rhythm and language. Besides, Horace's literary views include: literary creation is the combination of poetic inspiration and painstaking labor; art does not only mean the imitation of reality, but the imitation of the Greek models; and the artist should pay attention to the representativeness in character creation. All of these play an important part in critical debate and form the Horatian tradition in English literary criticism.

St. Augustine was born in North Africa in 354 A D, the time when the Roman Empire with its Christianity was about to go down to destruction. Augustine, one of the men responsible for the consolidation of the church in the West, was not converted to Christianity until he had reached middle life. The lateness of his conversion and his regret for his wasted youth were among the sources of the energy which drove him to assume the intellectual leadership of the Western Church and to guarantee, by combating heresy on the one hand and laying new ideological foundations for Christianity on the other, the Church's survival through the dark centuries to come. In Augustine are combined the intellectual tradition of the ancient world at its best and the religious feeling which was characteristic of the Middle Ages. The transition from the old world to the new can be seen in his famous *Confessions*, the first authentic ancient autobiography. In this book, Augustine set to Christianity. Throughout the book Augustine talks directly to God, in humility, yet conscious that God is concerned for him personally, and at the same time he comes to an understanding of his own feelings and development as a human being which marks his *Confessions* as one of the great literary documents of the Western World.

3. Readings

THE OLD TESTAMENT
Genesis 4. [The First Murder]

4. And Adam knew Eve his wife; and she conceived, and bare Cain, and said, I have gotten a man from the Lord. And she again bare his brother Abel. And Abel was a keeper of sheep, but Cain was a tiller of the ground. And in process of time it came to pass, that Cain brought of the fruit of the ground and offering unto the Lord. And Abel, he also brought of the firstlings of his flock and of the fat thereof. And the Lord had respect unto Abel and to his offering. But unto Cain and to his offering he had not respect. And Cain was very wroth,[1] and his countenance fell. And the Lord said unto Cain, Why art thou wroth? And why is they countenance fallen? If thou doesn't well, shalt thou not be accepted? And if thou does not well, sin lieth at the door. And unto thee shall be his desire, and thou shall rule over him.[2] And Cain talked with Abel his brother: and it came to pass, when they were in the field, that Cain rose up against Abel his brother, and slew him.

And the Lord said unto Cain, Where is Abel thy brother? And he said, I know not: Am I my brother's keeper? And he said, What hast thou done? The voice of thy brother's blood crieth unto me from the ground. And now art thou cursed from the earth, which hath opened her mouth to receive thy brother's blood from thy hand; When thou tillest the ground, it shall not henceforth yield unto thee her strength; a fugitive and vagabond shalt thou be in the earth. And Cain said unto the Lord, My punishment is greater than I can bear. Behold; thou has-driven me out this day from the face of the earth; and from thy face shall I be hid; and I shall be a fugitive and a vagabond in the earth; and it shall come to pass, that every one that findeth me shall slay me. And the Lord said unto him, Therefore whosoever slayeth Cain, vengeance shall be taken on him sevenfold. And the Lord set a mark upon Cain, lest any finding him should kill him.

Notes

1. wroth: angry.
2. an obscure sentence. It seems to mean something like: "It (i. e. , sin) shall be eager for you, but you must master it. "

Genesis 6—9. [The Flood]

6. .... And God saw that the wickedness of man was great in the earth, and that every imagination of the thoughts of his heart was only evil continually. And it repented the Lord that he had made man on the earth, and it grieved him at his heart. And the Lord said, I will destroy man whom I have created from the face of the earth; both man, and beast, and the creeping thing, and the fowls of the air; for it repenteth me that I have made them. But Noah found grace in the eyes of the Lord.

These are the generations of Noah: Noah was a just man and perfect in his generations, and Noah walked with God. And Noah begat three sons, Shem, Ham, and Japheth.

The earth also was corrupt before Cod, and the earth was filled with violence. And God looked upon the earth, and; behold, it was corrupt; for all flesh had corrupted his way upon the earth.

And God said unto Noah, The end of all flesh is come before me; for the earth is filled with violence through them; and, behold, I will destroy them with the earth. Make thee an ark of gopher[1] wood; rooms shalt thou make in the ark, and shalt pitch it within and without with pitch. And this is the fashion which thou shalt make it of: The length of the ark shall be three hundred cubits,[2] the breadth of it fifty cubits, and the height of it thirty cubits. A window[3] shalt thou make to the ark, and in a cubit shalt thou finish it above; and the door of the ark shalt thou set in the side thereof; with lower, second, and 3 stories shalt thou make it. And, behold, I, even I, do bring a flood of waters upon the earth, to destroy all flesh, wherein is the breath of life, from under heaven; and every thing that is in the earth shall die. But with thee will I establish my covenant; and thou shalt come into the ark, thou, and thy sons, and thy wife, and thy sons' wives with thee. And of every living thing of all flesh, two of every sort shalt thou bring into the ark, to keep them alive with thee; they shall be male and female. Of fowls after their kind, and of cattle after their kind, of every creeping thing of the earth after his kind, two of every sort shall come unto thee, to keep them alive. And take thou unto thee of all food that is eaten, and thou shalt gather it to thee; and it shall be for food for thee, and for them. Thus did Noah; according to all that God commanded him, so did he.

7. ... And Noah was six hundred years old when the flood of waters was upon the earth. And Noah went in, and his sons, and, his wife, and his sons' wives with him, into the ark, because of the waters of the flood. Of clean beasts, and of beasts that are not clean,[4] and of fowls, and of everything that creepeth upon the earth, There went in two and two unto Noah into the ark, the male and the female, as God had commanded Noah. And it came to pass after seven days, that the waters of the flood were upon the earth. In the six hundredth year of Noah's life, in the second

month, the 17th day of the month, the same day were all the fountains, of the great deep broken up, and the windows of heaven were opened. And the rain was upon the earth forty days and forty nights, In the selfsame day entered Noah, and Shem, and Ham, and Japheth, the sons of Noah, and Noah's wife, and the three wives of his sons with them, into the ark; They, and every beast after his kind, and all the cattle after their kind, and every creeping thing that creepeth upon the earth after his kind, and every fowl after his kind, every bird of every sort. And they went in unto Noah into the ark, two and two of all flesh, wherein is the breath of life, And they that went in, went in male and female of all flesh, as God had commanded him, and the Lord shut him in. And the waters prevailed, and were increased greatly upon the earth; and the ark went upon the face of the waters, And the waters prevailed exceedingly upon the earth; and all the high hills, that were under the whole heaven, were covered, Fifteen cubits upward did the waters prevail; and the mountains were covered. And all flesh died that moved upon the earth, both of fowl, and of cattle, and of beast, and of every creeping thing that creepeth upon the earth; and every man: all flesh died that moved upon the earth, both of fowl, and of cattle, and of beast, and of every creeping thing that creepeth upon the earth; and every man: All in whose nostrils was the breath of life, of all that was in the dry land, died. And every living substance was destroyed which was upon the face of the ground, both man, and cattle, and the creeping things, and the fowl of the heaven; and they were destroyed from the earth, and Noah only remained alive, and they that were with him in the ark. And the waters prevailed upon the earth a hundred and fifty days.

8. and God remembered Noah, and every living thing, and all the cattle that was with him in the ark: and God made a wind to pass over the earth, and the waters assuaged; The fountains also of the deep and the windows of heaven were stopped, and the rain

from heaven was restrained; And the waters returned from off the earth continually: and after the end of the hundred and fifty days the waters were abated. And the ark rested in the 7th month, on the 17th day of the month, upon the mountains of Ararat[5]. And the waters decreased continually until the 10th month: in the 10th month, on the first day of the month, were the tops of the mountains seen.

And it came to pass at the end of forty days, that Noah opened the windows of the ark which he had made: And he sent forth a raven, which went forth to and fro, until the waters were dried up from off the earth. Also he sent forth a dove from him, to see if the waters were abated from off the face of the ground; But the dove found no rest for the sole of her foot, and she returned unto him into the ark, for the waters were on the face of the whole earth: then he put forth his hand, and took her, and pulled her in unto him into the ark. And he stayed yet another seven days; and again he sent forth the dove out of the ark: And the dove came into him in the evening; and, lo, in her mouth was an olive leaf plucked off: so Noah knew that the waters were abated from off the earth, And he stayed yet other seven days; and sent forth the dove; which returned not again unto him any more.

And it came to pass in the six hundredth and first year, in the first month, the first day of the month, the waters were dried up from off the earth: and Noah removed that covering of the ark, and looked, and, behold, the face of the ground was dry. And in the second month, on the seven and 20th day of the month, was the earth dried.

And God spake unto Noah, saying, Go forth of the ark, thou, and thy wife, and thy sons, and thy sons' wives with thee every living thing that is with thee, of all flesh, both of fowl, and of cattle, and of every creeping thing that creepeth upon the earth; that they may breed abundantly in the earth, and be fruitful, and multi-

西方文学

ply upon the earth. And Noah went forth, and his sons, and his wife, and his sons' wives with him: Every beast, every creeping thing, and every fowl, and whatsoever creepeth upon the earth, after their kinds, went forth out of the ark. And Noah builded an altar unto the Lord: and took of every clean beast, and of every clean fowl, and offered burnt offerings on the altar. And the Lord smelled a sweet savour; and the Lord said in his heart, I will not again curse the ground any more for man's sake; for the imagination of man's heart is evil from his youth; neither will I again smite any more every thing living, as I have done. While the earth remaineth, seedtime and harvest, and cold and heat, and summer and winter, and day and night shall not cease.

9. And God blessed Noah and his sons, and said unto them, Be fruitful, and multiply, and replenish the earth. And the fear of you and the dread of you shall be upon every beast of the earth, and upon every fowl of the air, upon all that moveth upon the earth, and upon all the fishes of the sea; into your hand are they delivered. Every moving thing that levity shall be meat for you; even as the green herb have I given you all things. But flesh with the life thereof, which is the blood thereof, shall ye not eat.[6] And surely your blood of your lives will I require; at the hand of every beast will I require it, and at the hand of man; at the hand of every man's brother will I require the life of man. Who so sheddeth man's blood, by man shall his blood be shed, for in the image of God made he man. And you, be yet fruitful, and multiply; bring forth abundantly in the earth, and multiply therein.

And God spake unto Noah, and to his sons with him, saying, And I, behold, I establish my covenant with you, and with your seed after you; And with every living creature that is with you, of the fowl, of the cattle, and of every beast of the earth with you; from all that go out of the ark, to every beast of the earth. And I will establish my covenant with you; neither shall all flesh be cut off any more by the waters of a flood; neither shall there any more be a flood to destroy the earth. And God said, This is the token of the covenant which I make between me and you and every living creature that is with you, for perpetual generations: I do set my bow in the cloud, and it shall be for a token of a covenant between me and the earth. And it shall come to pass, when I being a cloud over the earth, that the bow shall be seen in the cloud: And I will remember my covenant, which is between me and you and every living creature of all flesh; and the waters shall no more become a flood to destroy all flesh. And the bow shall be in the cloud; and I will look upon it, that they may remember the everlasting covenant between God and every living creature of all flesh that is upon the earth. And God said unto Noah, This is the token of the covenant, which I have established between me and all flesh that is upon the earth.

Notes

1. gopher: cypress.
2. cubits: a Hebrew measure of length about one and a half feet.
3. window: The text is obscure; it may refer to a skylight in the roof.
4. not clean: Certain animals were forbidden food to the Hebrews. For a list of them see Leviticus 11.
5. Ararat: a mountain in the eastern part of Asia Minor.
6. This sentenee refers to the dictary, laws: blood was drained from the slaughtered animal.

THE ILIAD
Book XXII [The Death of Hektor]
by Homer

Once in the town, those who had fled like deer
wiped off their sweat and drank their thirst away,
Leaning against the cool stone of the ramparts,
Meanwhile Akhaians with bright shields aslant
come up the plain and nearer. As for Hektor,
fatal destiny pinned him where he stood
before the Skainan Gats, outside the city.
Now Akhilleus heard Apollo calling
Back to him:

                     "Why run so hard, Akhilleus,
mortal as you are, after a god?
Can you not comprehend it? I am immortal.
you are so hot to catch me, you no longer
think of finishing off the men you routed.
They are all in the town by now, packed in
while you were being diverted here. And yet
you cannot kill me; I am no man's quarry,"

Akhilleus bit his lip and said:

"Archer of heaven, deadliest
of immortal gods, you put me off the track,
turning me from the wall this way. A hundred
might have sunk their teeth into the dust
before one man took cover in Ilion!
You saved my enemies with ease and stole
my glory, having no punishment to fear.

I'd take it out of you, if I had the power."

Then toward the town with might and main he ran,
Magnificent, like a racing chariot horse
that holds its form at full stretch on the plain.
So light-footed Akhilleus held the pace.
And aging Priam was the first to see him
sparkling on the plain, bright as that star
in autumn rising, whose unclouded rays
shine out amid a throng of stars at dusk —
the one they call Orion's dog[1], most brilliant,
Yes, but baleful as a sign: it brings
great fever to frail men. So pure and bright
the bronze gear blazed upon him as he ran.
The old man gave a cry. With both his hands
thrown up on high he struck his head, then shouted,
groaning, appealing to his dear son. Unmoved,
lord Hektor stood in the gateway, resolute
to fight Akilleus.

                              Stretching out his hands,

old Priam said, imploring him:

                                        "No, Hektor!

Cut off as you are alone, dear son,
don't try to hold your ground against this man,
or soon you'll meet the shock of doom, borne down
by the son of Peleus. He is mere powerful
by far than you, and pitiless. Ah, were he
but dear to the gods as he is dear to me!
Wild dogs and kites would eat him where he lay
within the hour, and ease me of my torment.
Many tall sons he killed, bereaving me,
or sold them to far islands. Even now

I cannot see two sons of mine, Lykaon
and Polydoros[2], among the Trojans massed
inside the town. A queen, Laothoe[3],
conceived and bore them. If they are alive
amide the Akhaian host, I'll ransom them
with bronze and gold: both I have, piled at home,
rich treasures that old Altes,[4] the renowned,
gave for his daughter's dowry. If they died,
if they went under to the homes of Death,
sorrow has come to me and to their mother.
But to our townsmen all this pain is brief,
unless you too go down before Akhilleus.
Come inside the wall, child; here you may
fight on to save our Trojan men and women.
Do not resign, the glory to Akhilleus,
losing your own dear life! Take pity, too,
on me and my hard fate, while I live still.
Upon the threshold of my age, in misery,
the son of Kronos will destroy my life
after the evil days I shall have seen
my sons brought down, my daughters dragged away,
bedchambers ravaged, and small children hurled
to earth in the atrocity of war,
as my sons' wives are taken by Akhainans'
ruinous hands. And at the end, I too —
when someone with a sword-cut or a spear
has had my life — I shall be torn apart
on my own doorstep by the hounds
I trained as watchdogs, fed from my own table.
These will lap my blood with ravenous hearts
and lie in the entranceway.

                                    Everything done

to a young man killed in war becomes his glory,
once he is riven by the whetted bronze:
dead though he be, it is all fair, whatever
happens then. But when an old man falls,
and dogs disfigure his gray head and cheek
and genitals, that is most harrowing
of all that men in their hard lives endure. "

The old man wrenched at his gray hair and pulled out
hanks of it in both his hands, but moved
Lord Hektor not at all. The young man's mother
wailed from the tower across, above the portal,
streaming tears, and loosening her robe
with one hand, held her breast out in the other,
saying:

"Hektor, my child, be moved by this,
and pity me, if ever I unbound
a quieting breast for you. Think of these things,
dear child, defend yourself against the killer
this side of the wall, not hand to hand.
He has no pity. If he brings you down,
I shall no longer be allowed to mourn you
laid out on your bed, dear branch in flower,
born of me! And neither will your lady,
so endowed with gifts. Far from us both,
dogs will devour you by the Argive ships. "

With tears and cries the two implored their son,
and made their prayers again, but could not shake him.
Hektor stood firm, as huge Akhilleus neared.
The way a serpent, fed on poisonous herbs,
coiled at his lair upon a mountainside,
with all his length of hate awaits a man

and eyes him evilly: so Hektor, grim
and narrow-eyed, refused to yield. He leaned
his brilliant shield against a spur of wall
and in his brave heart bitterly reflected:
"Here I am badly caught. If I take cover,
slipping inside the gate and wall, the first
to accuse me for it will be Poulydamas,
he who told me I should lead the Trojans
back to the city on the cursed night
Akhilleus joined the battle. No, I would not,
would not, wiser though it would have been.
Now troops have perished for my foolish pride,
I am ashamed to face townsmen and women.
Someone inferior to me may say:
'He kept his pride and lost his men, this Hektor!'
So it will go. Better, when that time comes,
that I appear as he who killed Aknilleus
man to man, or else that I went down
before him honorably for the city's sake.
Suppose, though, that I lay my shield and helm
aside, and prop my spear against the wall,
and go to meet the noble Prince Akhilleus,
promising Helen, promising with her
all treasures that Alexandros brought home
by ship to Troy — the first cause of our quarrel —
that he may give these things to the Atreidai?
Then I might add, apart from these, a portion
of all the secret wealth the city owns.
Yes, later I might take our counselors' oath
to hide no stores, but share and share alike
to halve all wealth our lovely city holds,
all that is here within the walls. Ah, no,

why even put the question to myself?
I must not go before him and receive
no quarter, no respect! Aye, then and there
he'll kill me, unprotected as I am,
my gear laid by, defenseless as a woman,
No chance, now, for charms[5] from oak or stone
in parley with him — charms a girl and boy
might use when they enchant each other talking!
Better we duel, now at once, and see
to whom the Olympian awards the glory,"

These were his shifts of mood, Now close at hand
Akhilleus like the implacable god of war
came on with blowing crest, hefting the dreaded
beam of Pelican ash on his right shoulder,
Bronze light played around him, like the glare
of a great fire or the great sun rising,
and Hektor, as he watched, began to tremble,
Then he could hold his ground no more, He ran,
leaving the gate behind him, with Akhilleus
hard on his heels, sure of his own speed,
When that most lightning — like of birds, a hawk
bred on a mountain, swoops upon a dove,
the quarry dips in terror, but the hunter,
screaming, dips behind and gains upon it,
passionate for prey, Just so, Akhilieus
murderously cleft the air, as Hektor
ran with flashing knees along the wall,
They passed the lookout point, the wild figtree
with wind in all its leaves, then veered away
along the curving wagon road, and came
to where the double fountains well, the source
of eddying Skamander. One hot spring

flows out, and from the water fumes arise
as though from fire burning; but the other
even in summer gushes chill as hail
or snow or crystal ice frozen on water.
Near these fountains are wide washing pools
of smooth-laid stone, where Trojan wives and daughters
laundered their smooth linen in the days
of peace before the Akhaians came. Past these
the two men ran, pursuer and pursued,
and he who fled was noble, he behind
a greater man by far. They ran full speed,
and not for bull's hide or a ritual beast
or any prize that men compete for: no,
but for the life of Hektor, tamer of horses.
Just as when chariot-teams around a course
go wheeling swiftly, for the prize is great,
a tripod or a woman, in the games
held for a dead man, so three times these two
at full speed made their course round Priam's town,
as all the gods looked on. And now the father
of gods and men burned to the rest and said:

"How sad that this beloved man is hunted
around the wall before my eyes. My heart
is touched for Hektor; he burned thigh flesh
of oxen for me often, high on Ida[6],
at other times on the high point of Troy.
Now Prince Akhilleus with devouring stride
is pressing him around the town of Priam.
Come, gods put your minds on it, consider
whether we may deliver him from death
or see him, noble as he is, brought down
by Peleus' son, Akhilleus."

Gray-eyed Athena
said to him:

"Father of the blinding bolt,
the dark stormcloud, what words are these? The man
is mortal, and his doom fixed, long ago.
Would you release him from his painful death?
Then do so, but not all of us will praise you."

Zeus who gathers cloud replied:

"Take heart,
my dear and honored child. I am not bent
on my suggestion, and I would indulge you.
Act as your thought inclines, refrain no longer."
So he encouraged her in her desire,
and down she swept from ridges of Olympus,
Great Akhilleus, hard on Hektor's heels,
kept after him, the way a hound will harry
a deer's fawn he has startled from its bed
to chase through gorge and open glade, and when
the quarry goes to earth under a bush
he holds the scent and quarters[7] till finds it;
so with Hektor: he could not shake off
the great runner, Akhilleus. Every time
he tried to sprint hard for the Dardan gates
under the towers, hoping men could help him,
sending missiles down, Akhilleus loomed
to cut him off and turn him toward the plain,
as he himself ran always near the city.
As in a dream a man chasing another
cannot catch him, nor can he in flight
escape from his pursuer, so Akhilleus
could not by his swiftness overtake him,
nor could Hektor pull away. How could he

run so long from death, had not Apollo
for the last time, the very last, come near
to give him stamina and speed?"

                                    Akhilleus

shook his head at the rest of the Akhaians,
allowing none to shoot or cast at Hektor —
none to forestall him, and to win the honor.
But when, for the 4th time, they reached the springs,
the Father poised his golden scales.

                                    He placed

two shapes of death, deather prone and cold, upon them,
one of Akhilleus, one of the horseman, Hektor,
and held the midpoint, pulling upward. Down
sank Hektor's fatal day, the pan went down
toward undergloom, and Phoibos Apollo left him.
Then came Athena, gray-eyed, to the son
of Peleus, falling in with him, and near him,
saying swiftly:

                                    "Now at last I think

the two of us, Akhilleus loved by Zeus
shall bring Akhaians triumph at the ships
by killing Hektor — unappeased
though he was ever in his thirst for war.
There is no way he may escape us now,
not thought Apollo, lord of distances[8],
should suffer all indignity for him
before his father Zeus who bears the stormcloud,
rolling back and forth and begging for him.
Now you can halt and take your breath, while I
persuade him into combat face to face."
These were Athena's orders. He complied,
relieved, and leaning hard upon spearshaft

armed with its head of bronze. She left him there
and overtook lord Hektor — but she seemed
Deiphobos[9] in form and resonant voice,
appearing at his shoulder, saying swiftly:

"Ai! Dear brother, how he runs, Akhilleus,
harrying you around the town of Priam!
Come, we'll stand and take him on."
To this,
great Hektor in his shimmering helm replied:

"Deiphobos, you were the closest to me
in the old days, of all my brothers, sons
of Hekabe and Priam. Now I can say
I honor you still more
because you dared this foray for my sake,
seeing me run. The rest stay under cover."

Again the gray-eyed goddess Athena spoke:

"Dear brother, how your father and gentle mother
begged and begged me to remain! So did
the soldiers round me, all undone by fear.
But in my heart I ached for you.
Now let us fight him, and fight hard.
No holding back. We'll see if this Akhilleus
conquers both, to take our armor seaward,
or if he can be brought down by your spear."

This way, by guile, Athena led him on.
And when at last the two men faced each other,
Hektor was the first to speak. He said:

"I will no longer fear you as before,
son of Peleus, thought I ran from you
round Priam's town three times and could not face you.

Now my soul would have me stand and fight,
whether I kill you or am killed. So come,
we'll summon gods here as our witnesses,
none higher, arbiters of a pact: I swear
that, terrible as you are,
I'll not insult your corpse should Zeus allow me
victory in the end, your life as prize.
Once I have your gear, I'll give your body
back to Akhaians. Grant me, too, this grace."

But swift Akhilleus frowned at him and said:

"Hektor, I'll have no talk of pacts with you,
forever unforgiven as you are.
As between men and lions there are none,
no concord between wolves and sheep, but all
hold one another hateful through and through,
so there can be no courtesy between us,
no sworn truce, till one of us is down
and glutting with his blood the wargod Ares.
Summon up what skills you have. By god,
you'd better be a spearman and a fighter!
Now there is no way out. Pallas Athena
will have the upper hand of you. The weapon
belongs to me. You'll pay the reckoning
in full for all the pain my men have borne,
who met death by your spear.

He twirled and cast
his shaft with its long shadow. Splendid Hektor,
keeping his eye upon the point, eluded it
by ducking at the instant of the cast,
so shaft and bronze shank passed him overhead
and punched into the earth. But unperceived

by Hektor, Pallas Athena plucked it out
and gave it back to Aknilleus, Hektor said:

"A clean miss. Godlike as you are,
you have not yet known doom for me from Zeus.
You thought you had, by heaven. Then you turned
into a word — thrower, hoping to make me lose
my fighting heart and head in fear of you.
You cannot plant your spear between my shoulders
while I am running. If you have the gift,
just put it through my chest as I come forward.
Now it's for you to dodge my own. Would god
you'd give the whole shaft lodging in your body!
War for the Trojans would be eased
if you were blotted out, bane that your are."

With this he twirled his long spearshaft and cast it,
hitting his enemy mid-shield, but off
and away the spear rebounded. Furious
that he had lost it, made this throw for nothing,
Hektor stood bemused. He had no other.
Then he gave a great shout to Deiphobos
to ask for a long spear. But there was no one
hear him, not a soul. Now in his heart
the Trojan realized the truth and said:

"This is the end. The gods are calling deathward.
I had thought
a good soldier, Deiphobos, was with me.
He is inside the walls. Athena tricked me.
Death is near, and black, not at a distance,
not to be evaded. Long ago
this hour must have been to Zeus's liking
and to the liking of his archer son.

They have been well disposed before, but now
the appointed time's upon me. Still, I would not
die without delivering a stroke,
or die ingloriously, but in some action
memorable to men in days to come."

With this he drew the whetted blade that hung
upon his left flank, ponderous and long,
collecting all his might the way an eagle
narrows himself to dive through shady cloud
and strike a lamb or cowering hare: so Hektor
lanced ahead and swung his whetted blade.
Akhilleus with wild fury in his heart
pulled in upon his chest his beautiful shield —
his helmet with four burnished metal ridges
nodding above it, and the golden crest
Hephatistos locked there tossing in the wind.
Conspicuous as the evening star that comes,
amid the first in heaven, at fall of night,
and sunlight the fine-pointed spear
Akhilleus poised in his right hand, with deadly
aim at Hektor, at the skin where most
it lay exposed. But nearly all was covered
by the bronze gear he took from slain Partoklos'
showing only, where his collarbones
divided neck and shoulders, the bare throat
where the destruction of life is quickest.
Here, then, as the Trojan charged, Akhilleus
drove his point straight through the tender neck,
but did not cut the windpipe, leaving Hektor
able to speak and to respond. He fell
aside into the dust. And Prince Akhilleus
now exulted:

"Hektor, had you thought
that you could kill Patroklos and be safe?
Nothing to dread from me; I was not there.
All childishness. Though distant then, Patroklos'
comrade in arms was greater far than he—
and it is I who had been left behind
that day beside the deep-sea ships who now
have made your knees give way. The dogs and kites
will rip your body. He will lie in honor
when the Akhaians give him funeral."

Hektor, barely whispering, replied:

"I beg you by your soul and by your parents,
do not let the dogs feed on me
in your encampment by the ships, Accept
the bronze and gold my father will provide
as gifts, my father and her ladyship
my mother. Let them have my body back,
so that our men and women may accord me
decency of fire when I am dead."

Akhilleus the great runner scowled and said:

"Beg me no beggary by soul or parents,
whining dog! Would god my passion drove me
to slaughter you and eat you raw, you've caused
such agony to me! No man exists
who could defend you from the carrion pack—
not if they spread for me ten times your ransom,
twenty times, and promise more as well;
aye, not if Priam, son of Dardanos,
tells them to buy you for your weight in gold!
You'll have no bed of death, nor will you be
laid out and mourned by her who gave you birth.

Dogs and birds will have you, every scrap. "

Then at the point of death Lord Hektor said:

"I see you now for what you are. No chance
to win you over. Iron in your breast
your heart is. Think a bit, though, this may be
a thing the gods in anger hold against you
on that day when Paris and Apollo
destroy you at the Gates, [10] great as you are. "

Even as he spoke, the end came, and death hid him:
spirit from body fluttered to undergloom,
bewailing fate that made him leave his youth
and manhood in the world. And as he died
Akhilleus spoke again. He said:

"Die, make an end. I shall accept my own
whenever Zeus and the other gods desire. "

At this he pulled his spearhead from the body,
laying it aside, and stripped
the bloodstained shield and cuirass from his shoulders.
Others Akhaians hastened round to see
Hektor's fine body and his comely face,
and no one came who did not stab the body.
Glancing at one another they would say:

"Now Hektor has turned vulnerable, softer
than when he put the torches to the ships!"

Notes

1. Orion's dog: The constellation Canis Major. The star is Sirius, the "dog star. "
2. Lykaon and Polydoros: Both already killed by Akhilleus in the fighting outside the city.

3. Laothoe: Priam, in oriental style, has more than one wife.

4. Altes: Laothoe's father

5. charms: charming talk

6. Ida: The great mountain range near Troy.

7. quarters: Criss-crosses

8. Lord of distances: The literal meaning of this title of Apollo is "who works from far off."

9. Deiphobos: A brother of Hektor

10. the Gates: The Skaian of Troy

OEDIPUS REX
Act 1 Scene 4
by Sophocles
[*Enter OEDIPUS*]

OEDIPUS: My Lords, I have never met him, but could that be the shepherd we have been waiting for? He seems to be of the same age as the stranger from Corinth. And I can see now — those are my servants who are bringing him here. But, perhaps you know — if you have seen him before. Is he the shepherd?

[*Enter SHEPHERD*]

CHORUS: Yes. I recognize him. He was a shepherd in the service of Laius — as loyal as any man could be.

OEDIPUS: Corinthian, I ask you — is this the man you mean?

MESSNGER 1: Yes, my Lord. This is the man.

OEDIPUS: And you, old man, look at me and answer what I ask. Were you in the service of Laius?

SHEPHERD: I was. But not bought. I was reared in his house.

DEPIPUS: What occupation? What way of life?

SHEPHERD: Tending flocks — for most of my life.

DEPIPUS: And where did you tend those flocks?

SHEPHERD: Sometimes Cithaeron, sometimes the neighboring places.

OEDIPUS: Have you ever seen this man before?

SHEPHERD: What man do you mean? Doing what?

OEDIPUS: This man. Have you ever met him before?

MESSENGER 1: No wonder, my Lord. But I shall help him to recall. I am sure that he'll remember the time we spent on Cithaeron — he with his two flocks and I with one. Six months — spring to autumn — every year — for three years. In the winter I would drive my flocks to my fold in Corinth, and he to the fold of Laius, Isn't that right, sir?

SHEPHERD: That is what happened. But it was a long time ago.

MESSENGER 1: Then tell me this. Do you remember a child you gave me to bring up as my own?

SHEPHERD: What are you saying? Why are you asking me this?

MESSENGER 1: This, my friend, this — is that child.

SHEPHERD: Damn you! Will you keep your mouth shut!

OEDIPUS: Save your reproaches, old man. It is you who deserve them — your words deserve them.

SHEPHERD: But master — how have I offended?

OEDIPUS: By refusing to answer his question about the child.

SHEPHERD: He doesn't know what he's saying. He's crazy.

OEDIPUS: If you don't answer of your own accord, we'll make you talk.

SHEPHERD: No! My Lord, please! Don't hurt an old man.

OEDIPUS [to the CHORUS]: One of you — twist his hands behind his back!

SHEPHERD: Why? Why? What do you want to know?

OEDIPUS: Did you or did you not give him that child?

SHEPHERD: I did, I gave it to him — and I wish that I had died that day.

OEDIPPUS: You tell the truth, or you'll have your wish now.

SHEPHERD: If I tell, it will be worse.

OEDIPUS: Still he puts it off!

SHEPHERD: I said that I gave him the child!

OEDIPUS: Where did you get it? Your house? Someone else's? Where?

SHEPHERD: Not mine. Someone else's,

OEDIPUS: Whose? One of the citizens'? Whose house?

SHEPHERD: O God, master! Don't ask me any more.

OEDIPUS: This is the last time that I ask you.

SHEPHERD: It was a child — of the house of Laius.

OEDIPUS: A slave? Or of his own line?

SHEPHERD: Ah slave? Or of his own line?

OEDIPUS: You have to. And I have to hear.

SHEPHERD: They said — it was his child. But the queen could tell you best.

OEDIPUS: Why? Did she give you the child?

SHEPHERD: Yes, my Lord.

OEDIPUS: Why?

SHEPHERD: To — kill!

OEDIPUS: Her own child!

SHEPHERD: Yes. Because she was terrified of some dreadful prophecy.

OEDIPUS: What prophecy?

SHEPHERD: The child would kill his father,

OEDIPUS: Then why did you give him to this man?

SHEPHERD: I felt sorry for him, master. And I thought that he would take him to his own home. But he saved him from his suffering — for worse suffering yet. My Lord, if you are the man he says you are — O God — you were born to suffering!

OEDIPUS: O God! O no! I see it now! All clear! O Light! I will

never look on you again! Sin! Sin in my birth! Sin in my marriage! Sin in blood!

[Exit OEDIPUS]

Considerations

What philosophy does the play intend to communicate? Is the
search for knowledge bound to end in disaster? Is Oedipus — together with others involved — a victim of circumstances trapped
in a tragedy of fate? Or do Oedipus' problems proceed from the
very basis of his character?

POETICS
by Aristotle

... Tragedy, then, is an imitation of an action that is serious,
complete, and of a certain magnitude; in language embellished
with each kind of artistic ornarnent, the several kinds being found
in separate parts of the play; in the from of action, not of narrative; through pity and fear effecting the proper purgation[1] of these
emotions. By 'language embellished', I mean language into which
rhythm, 'harmony', and song enter. By 'the several kinds in separate parts', I mean, that some parts are rendered through the
medium of verse alone, others again with the aid of song.

Now as tragic imitation implies persons' acting, it necessarily
follows, in the first place, that Scenic equipment will be a part of
Tragedy. Next, Song and Diction, for these are the means of imitation. By 'Diction' I mean the mere metrical arrangement of the
words: as for 'Song', it is a term whose full sense is well understood.

Again, Tragedy is the imitation of an action; and an action implies personal agents, who necessarily possess certain qualities of actions themselves; these — thought and character — are the two natural causes from which actions spring: on these causes, again, all success or failure depends. Hence, the plot is the imitation of the action — for by plot I here mean the arrangement of the incidents. By Character I mean that in virtue of which we ascribe certain qualities to agents. By Thought, that whereby a statement is proved, or a general truth expressed. Every Tragedy, therefore, must have six parts, which parts determine its quality — namely, Plot, Character, Diction, Thought, Scenery, Song. Two of the parts constitute the means of imitation, one the manner, and three the objects of imitation. And these complete the list. These elements have been employed, we may say, by almost all poets; in fact, every play contains Scenic accessories as well as Character, Plot, Diction, Song, and Thought.

But most important of all is the structure of the incidents. For Tragedy is an imitation, not of men, but of an action and of life — of happiness and misery; and happiness and misery consist in action, the end of human life being a mode of action, not a quality. Now the characters of men determine their qualities, but it is by their actions that they are happy or the reverse. Dramatic action, therefore, is not with a view to the representation of character, character comes in as subsidiary to the action. Hence the incidents and the plot are the end of a tragedy; and the end[2] is the chief thing of all. Again, without action there cannot be a tragedy; there may be without character . . .

These principles being established, let us now discuss the proper structure of the Plot, since this is the first, and also the most important part of Tragedy.

Now, according to our definition, Tragedy is an imitation of an action, that is complete, and whole, and of a certain magnitude;

西方文学

for there may be a whole that is wanting in magnitude. A whole is that which has beginning, middle, and end. A beginning is that which does not itself follow anything by causal necessity, but after which something naturally is or comes to be. An end, on the contrary, is that which itself naturally follows some other thing, either by necessity, or in the regular course of events, but has nothing following it. A middle is that which follows something as some other thing follows it. A well constructed plot, therefore, must neither begin nor end at haphazard, but conform to the type here described . . .

Unity of plot does not, as some persons think, consist in the unity of the hero. For infinitely various are the incidents in one man's life, which cannot be reduced to unity; and so, too, there are many actions of one man out of which we cannot make one action. Hence the error, as it appears, of all poets who have composed a Heracleid, a Theseid, or other poems of the kind. They imagine that as Heracles was one man, the story of Heracles ought also to be a unity . . .

It is, moreover, evident from what has been said, that it is not the function of the poet to relate what has happened, but what may happen — what is possible according to the law of probability of necessity. The poet and historian differ not by writing in verse or in prose. The work of Herodotus[3] might be put into verse, and it would still be a species of history, with meter no less than without it. The true difference is that one relates what has happened, the other what may happen. Poetry, therefore, is a more philosophical and a higher thing than history: for poetry tends to express the universal, history the particular. The universal tells us how a person of given character will on occasion speak or act, according to the law of probability or necessity; and it is this universality at which Poetry aims in giving expressive names to the characters, The particular is — for example — what Alcibiades did or suffered . . .

Of all plots and actions the episodic are the worst. I call a plot episodic in which the episodes or acts succeed one another without probable or necessary sequence. Bad poets compose such pieces by their own fault, good poets, to please the players; for, as they write for competing rivals, they draw out the plot beyond its capacity, and are often forced to break the natural continuity . . .

Notes

1. purgation: The Greek word is katharsis. This is probably the most disputed passage in European literary criticism. There are two main schools of interpretation; they differ in their understanding of the metaphor implied in the word katharsis. Some critics take the word to mean "purification," implying a metaphor from the religious process of purification from guilt; the passions are "purified" by the tragic performance since the excitement of these passions by the performance weakens them and reduces them to just proportions in the individual. (This theory was supported by the German critic Lessing.) Others take the metaphor to be medical, reading the word as "purging" and interpreting the phrase to mean that the tragic performance excites the emotions only to allay them, thus ridding the spectator of the disquieting emotions from which he suffers in everyday life; tragedy thus has a therapeutic effect.

2. end: purpose.

3. Herodotus: the 5th-century historian of the Persian wars.

Chapter Ⅱ The Middle Ages

1. Historical Introduction

The period of the Middle Ages (467-1500 A D) encompasses a thousand years of European history distinguished by the unique fusion of heroic Age society with Greco-Roman culture and Christian religion. It begins with the collapse of the Roman Empire in Western Europe, a development coincident with and partly occasioned by the settlement of Germanic peoples within the territory of the empire. It ends with the discovery of the Western Hemisphere, the invention of the printing press, the consolidation of strong national states, the break in religions brought about by the protestant reformation and the renewal — after a lapse of nearly a thousand years — of direct contact with Greek art, thought and literature. The medieval centuries created and bequeathed to us such institutional patterns as the Christian church; the monarchical state; the town and village; the traditional European social order — the "lords spiritual," the "lords temporal," with the hierarchy of nobility and gentry ranging from duke to knight and the bourgeois estate; the university; the system and logical method of scholastic philosophy; Romanesque and Gothic architecture; and a rich variety of literary forms.

The literature of the earlier Middle Ages reflects directly the life and civilization of a heroic Age. The dominant figure is the fighting king or chieftain; the favorite pursuit is war; the characteristic goals are power, wealth, and glory; and the primary virtues are valor and loyalty. The literary pattern is based on actuality, of which it presents a kind of idealization. In early Germanic and Celtic society the king ruled a small, essentially tribal nation; he and his companions in battle constituted a formal or informal class controlling the life of the people. The poems of such a society naturally tell chiefly of the fights of great champions. Among literature of such kind are the *Song of Roland* and the Arthurian romances.

In the literature of the 14th century, the warrior plays a smaller role and is assimilated to the more extensive pattern of later medieval civilization in which Christianity ordered the Greco-Roman culture to new ends. Indeed the medieval period was an age of faith. The first half of the period was occupied in winning the new people of Europe to Christianity. When this had been accomplished, the Crusades began (a series of holy wars intended to rescue Palestine from pagan occupation and, in general, to defeat and either destroy or convert the pagans, chiefly Mohammedan), and achieved the religious unity and authority, which resulted in a remarkable unanimity of spiritual, moral, and intellectual attitudes and ideas in medieval Europe. In such a community of European culture, the themes and subjects and techniques of art and literature circulated freely throughout Europe. Christianity itself furnished a common subject matter for artists and writers and the biblical stories and scenes had the same meaning in every country. As a whole, writers of this period engaged in a study in human life judged according to the

Christian order of values, in which the spiritual side of man transcends the material and the contemplative life is superior to any form of the active life. This order is represented clearly in Dante's *Divine Comedy*.

The Middle Ages did not see such great literary critics as Plato, Aristotle, Horace and Longinus of the Ancient world. Among the few works which are concerned with literary theory are St. Augustine's *Confessions* (397 A D) and Dante's *De Vulgar Eloquentia* and *Divina Commedia*.

2. Literary Giants and Works

The Song of Roland is the first great heroic narrative poem in French. It has been said that French literature begins with it. The story was developed from a historical incident in the career of Charlemagne (Charles the Great). As the Emperor was returning from a successful war in northern Spain, the Saracens attacked his baggage train and rear guard partly because of the treason of his man Ganelon. The rear guard perished, including his nephew Roland, the hero of the poem. The first half of the poem deals with the anger of Ganelon at Roland, out of which grows his treachery and the attack of the Saracens; the valor of Roland and the rest in battle; and their heroic death. The second half relates the vengeance taken by Charles against the Saracens and the trial and execution of Ganelon. Imbued with the spirit of the First Crusade, the poem is infused with a warm glow of regional patriotism of the feudal society in the early 12th century.

Beowulf (700-750 A D), a folk legend in alliterative verse, was the national epic of the Anglo-Saxon and English people.

The story is set in Denmark and tells how Beowulf, the hero, defeats the terrible sea monster Grendel and Grendel's mother, but eventually receives his own death in fighting with a fire dragon. Beowulf is a grand hero by his deeds. For the deliverance of his people, he forgets himself in face of death. The poem, though written in the 10th century, was mainly the product of a primitive, tribal society on the Continent.

Sir Gawain and the Green Knight is the best English example of Arthurian romances of the Middle Ages. A romance is a narrative poem presenting, usually, knightly adventures and courtly love. The adventures typically involve the hero in fighting or jousting with other knights, and often also in encounters with giants or monsters. The Gawain story begins at King Arthur's court on New Year's day. Arthur and his knights are having a feast when a gigantic knight in green enters the banquet hall on horseback and challenges the bravest knight present to an exchange of blows; that is, he will expose his neck to a blow of his own big battle-ax if any knight will agree to abide a blow in return on the next New Year's day. Gawain accepts the challenge, takes the battle-ax, and with one blow sends the giant's head rolling through the hall. The Green Knight, who turns out to be a terrible magician, picks up his head and mounts his horse. He holds out his head and with the ghastly lips tells Gawain to find the Green Chapel to receive his return blow the next year. Then the story goes on to deal with Gawain's long journey through many perils to seek for the Green Chapel, his resistance to the temptation of the lady of the Bercilak's castle, his arrival at the Green Chapel and his compromise with the Green Knight, and his final return to Arthur's court with his whole adventurous story.

The Divine Comedy, the greatest poem of the Middle Ages, was written in the early 14th century. Its author, Dante Alighieri, born in Florence in 1265, was exiled from his native city in 1302 for political reasons and died at Ravenna in 1321. The poem is the narrative of the writer's journey down through hell, up the mountain of purgatory, and through the revolving heavens into the presence of God. Through his experiences in three imaginative worlds, Dante summarizes the literature, the philosophy, the science and the religion of the Middle Ages. The poem contains three divisions — Hell (Inferno), Purgatory (Purgatorio), and Paradise (Paradiso). Each of the last two has thirty-three cantos, and the first the Hell has thirty-four with the opening canto as the prologue to the entire poem. In Hell, the lost souls are arranged in three main groups, and occupy nine circles according to the degree of their sinfulness. Purgatory and Paradise are also divided into nine circles each. Purgatory is situated on a lofty mountain. It is divided into the ante-purgatory (at the bottom), the Earthly paradise (at the summit), and the purgatory proper (in the middle). The last division is arranged in seven ledges, each devoted to the purification of souls from particular kinds of sinful disposition — Pride, Envy, Anger, Sloth, Avarice, Gluttony, and Illicit Love. The Paradise takes us through the circles of the seven planets of medieval astronomy — the moon, Mercury, Venus, the sun, Mars, Jupiter, and Saturn; then through the circles of the fixed stars and the outermost circles; and finally to heaven itself, the abode of God, the angels, and the redeemed souls.

Decameron was completed about 1353 by the Italian author Boccaccio. It is a collection of tales, which constitute the created achievement of prose fiction in a vernacular language of southern Europe during the medieval centuries. These tales, about one hundred in number, are supposed to be told by seven young ladies and three young gentlemen who have withdrawn from Florence to the countryside, to escape the Black Death of 1348. In these stories, Boccaccio presents a great variety of people and situations and abundant dialogues of varying liveliness and realism. He attacks the medieval asceticism and the feudal hierarchy; eulogizes love and the equality of men and women; and satirizes and criticizes the hypocrisy and inhumanity of the monks and priests, thus proving himself to be the precursor of humanism advocated in the following period of Renaissance.

The Canterbury Tales is one of the world's masterpieces. It was written by Geoffrey Chaucer in the early 14th century. Like *Decameron*, the poem is a collection of tales and stories strung together according to a simple plan provided by the prologue. But Chaucer's story-tellers are thirty miscellaneous pilgrims travelling to a famous shrine. Through these pilgrims who represent nearly all classes of the English feudal society, the poet gave us a true-to-life picture of typical medieval figures and their lives. In his tales, Chaucer affirms men and women's right to pursue their happiness on earth and opposes the dogma of asceticism preached by the church. As a forerunner of humanism, he praised man's energy, intellect, wit and love of life, and attacked the corruption of the Church.

3. Readings

THE DIVINE COMEDY
HELL (INFERNO)
CANTO V
by Dante

From Limbo Virgil leads his ward down to the threshold of the
Second Circle of Hell where, for the first time, he will see the
damned in Hell being punished for their sins. There, barring their
way, is the hideous figure of Minos, the bestial judge of Dante's
underworld; but after strong words from Vigil, the poets are allowed to pass into the dark space of this circle, where can be
heard the wailing voices of the Lustful, whose punishment consists
of being forever whirled about in a dark, stormy wind. After seeing
a thousand or more famous lovers — including Semiramis, Dido,
Helen, Achilles, and Paris — the Pilgrim asks to speak to two figures he sees together. They are Francesca da Rimini and her lover
Paolo, and the scene in which they appear is probably the most famous episode of the Inferno. At the end of the scene, the Pilgrim,
who has been overcome by pity for the lovers, faints to the
ground.

This way I went, descending form the first
    into the second circle, that holds less space
    but much more pain — stinging the soul to wailing.
There stands Minos¹ grotesquely, and he snarls,
    examining the guilty at the entrance;
    he judges and dispatches, tail in coils.
By this I mean that when the evil soul
    appears before him, it confesses all,

and he who is the expert judge of sins
sees what place in Hell the soul belongs to;
　　the times he wraps his tail around himself
　　tells just how far the sinner must go down.
The damned keep crowding up in front of him:
　　they pass along to judgment one by one;
　　they speak, they hear, and then are hurled below.
"Oh you who come to the place where pain is host,"
　　Minos spoke out when he caught sight of me,
　　putting aside the duties of his office,
"be careful how you enter and whom you trust:
　　it is easy to get in, but don't be fooled!"
　　And my guide to him:"Why do you keep on shouting
Do not attempt to stop his fated journey;
　　it is so willed there where the power is
　　for what is willed; that's all you need to know."
And now the notes of anguish start to play
　　upon my ears; and now I find myself
　　where sounds on sounds of weeping pound at me.
I came to a place where no light shone at all,
　　bellowing like the sea racked by a tempest,
　　when warring winds attack it from both sides.
The infernal storm, eternal in its rage,
　　sweeps and drives the spirits with its blast[2]:
　　it whirls them, lashing them with punishment.
When they are swept back past their place of judgment[3],
　　then come the shrieks, laments and anguished cries
　　there they blaspheme the power of almighty God.
I learned that to this place of punishment
　　all those who sin in lust have been condemned,
　　those who make reason slave to appetite;
and as the wings of starlings in the winter

bear them along in wide-spread, crowded flocks,
    so does that wind propel the evil spirits:
here, then there, and up and down, it sweeps them
    forever, without hope to comfort them
    （hope, not of taking rest, but of suffering less）.
And just like cranes in flight, chanting their lays,
    stretching an endless line in their formation,
    I saw approaching, crying their laments,
spirits carried along by the battling winds,
    And so I asked, "Teacher, tell me, what souls
    are these punished in the sweep of the black wind?"
"The first of those whose story you should know,"
    my master wasted no time answering,
    "was empress over lands of many tongues;
her vicious tastes had so corrupted her,
    she licensed every form of lust with laws
    to cleanse the stain of scandal she had spread;
she is Semiramis[4] who, legend says,
    was Ninus' wife and successor to his throne;
    she governed all the land the Sultan rules,
The next is she who killed herself for love
    and broke faith with the ashes of Sichaeus[5];
    and there is Cleopatra who loved men's lusting.
See Helen[6] there, the root of evil woe
    lasting long years, and see the great Achilles
    who lost his life to love, in final combat[7];
see Paris[8], Tristan" — then, more than a thousand
    he pointed out to me, and named them all,
    those shades whom love cut off from life on earth.
After I heard my teacher call the names
    of all these knights and ladies of ancient times,
    pit confused my senses, and I was dazed.

I began: "Poet, I would like, with all my heart,

to speak to those two there who move together[9]

and seem to be so light upon the winds."

And he: "you'll see for yourself when they are closer;

if you entreat them by that love of theirs

that carries them along, they will come to you."

When the winds bent their course in our direction

I raised my voice to them, "Oh, wearied souls,

come speak with us if it be not forbidden."

As doves[10], called by desire to return

to their sweet nest, with wings outstretched and poised

float downward through the air, guided by their will,

so these two left the flock where Dido is

and came toward us through the malignant air,

such was the tender power of my call.

"O living creature, gracious and so kind,

who make your way here through this dingy air

to visit us who stained the world with blood,

if we could claim as friend, the King of Kings,

we would beseech him that he grant you peace,

you who show pity for our atrocious plight.

Whatever pleases you to hear or speak

we will hear and we will speak about with you

as long as the wind, here where we are, is silent.

The place where I was born[11] lies on the shore

where the river Po with its attendant streams

descends to seek its final resting place.

Love, that kindles quick in the gentle heart,

seized this one for the beauty of my body,

torn from me. (How it happened still offends me!)

Love, that excuses no one loved from loving,

seized me so strongly with delight in him

that, as you see, he never leaves my side.
Love led us straight to sudden death together.
  Caina[12] awaits the one who quenched our lives."
  These were the words that came from them to us[13].
When those offended souls had told their stow,
  I bowed my head and kept it bowed until
  the poet said, "What are you thinking of?"
When finally I spoke, I sighed, "Alas,
  what sweet thoughts, and oh, how much desiring
  brought these two down into this agony."
And then I turned to them and tried to speak;
  I said, "Francesca, the torment that you suffer
  brings painful tears of pity to my eyes,
But tell me, in that time of your sweet sighing
  how, and by what signs, did love allow you
  to recognize your dubious desires?"
And she to me: "There is no greater pain
  than to remember, in our present grief,
  past happiness (as well your teacher knows)!
But if your great desire is to learn
  the very root of such a love as ours,
  I shall tell you but in words of flowing tears,
One day we read, to pass the time away,
  of Lancelot, how he had fallen in love;
  we were alone, innocent of suspicion.
Time and again our eyes were brought together
  by the book we read; our faces flushed and paled.
  To the moment of one line alone we yielded:
it was when we read about those longed-for lips
  now being kissed by such a famous lover,
  that this one (who shall never leave my side)
then kissed my mouth, and trembled as he did.

The book and its author was our galehot!
That day we read no further." And all the while
the one of the two spirits spoke these words,
the other wept, in such a way that pity
blurred my senses; I swooned as though to die,
and fell to Hell's floor as a body, dead, falls.

Notes

1. Minos: the son of Zeus and Europa. As king of Crete he was revered for his wisdom and judicial gifts. For these qualities he became chief magistrate of the underworld in classical literature. Although Dante did not alter Minos's official function, he transformed him into a demonic figure, both in his physical characteristics and in his bestial activities.

2. The punishment suggests that lust (the "infernal storm") is pursued without the light d reason (in the darkness).

3. In Italian this line reads, "Quando giungon davanfi a la ruina," literally, "When they come before the falling place." According to Busnelli (Miscellanea dantesea, Padova, 1922, pp. 51-53) the ruina refers to the tribunal of Minos; that is, to the place where the condemned sinners "fall" before him at the entrance to the second circle to be judged. Therefore ruina can be translated as "their place of judgment"; the entire tercet means that every time the sinners in the windstorm are blown near Minos they shriek, lament, and blaspheme.

4. "Semiramis": The legendary queen of Assytia who, although renowned for her military conquests and civic projects, fell prey to her passions and became dissolute to the extent of legalizing lust. Dante conceived her as the motivating force of the degenerate society that ultimately opposes God's divine order.

5. According to Virgil (*Aeneid* I and IV), Dido, the queen of Carthage, swore faithfulness to the memory of her dead husband, Siehaeus. However, when the Trojan survivors of the war arrived in port, she fell helpless-

ly in love with their leader, Aeneas, and they lived together as man and wife until the gods reminded Aeneas of his higher destiny: the founding of Rome and the Roman Empire. Immediately he set sail for Italy and Dido, deserted, committed suicide.

6. Helen of Troy.

7. Enticed by the beauty of Polyxena, a daughter of the Trojan king, Achilles desired her to be his wife, but Hecuba, Polyxena's mother, arranged a counterplot with Paris so that when Achilles entered the temple for his presumed marriage, he was treacherously slain by Paris.

8. "Paris": the son of Priam, king of Troy, whose abduction of Helen ignited the Trojan War. "Tristan": the central figure of numerous medieval French, German, and Italian romances. Sent as a messenger by his uncle, King Mark of Cornwall, to obtain Isolt for him in marriage, Tristan became enamored of her, and she of him. After Isolt's marriage to Mark, the lovers continued their love affair, and in order to maintain its secrecy they necessarily employed many deceits and ruses. According to one version however, Mark, growing continuously more suspicious of their attachment, finally discovered them together and ended the incestuous relationship by mortally wounding Tristan with a lance.

9. "those two there who move together": Francesca, daughter of Guido Vecchio da Polenta, lord of Ravenna, and Paolo Malatesta, third son of Malatesta da Verrucchio, lord of Rimini. Around 1275 the aristocratic Francesca was married for political reasons to Gianciotto, the physically deformed second son of Malatersta da Verrucchio. In time a love affair developed between Francesca and Gianeiotto's younger brother, Paolo. One day the betrayed husband discovered them in an amorous embrace and slew them both.

10. "As doves": Paolo and Francesca are compared to"doves, called by desire" who "float downward through the air, guided by their will. " The use of the words "desire" and "will" is particularly interesting because it suggests the nature of lust as a sin: the subjugation of the will to desire.

11. "The place where I was born": Ravenna, a city on the Adriatic coast.

12. "Caina": one of the four divisions of Cocytus, the lowest part of Hell, wherein are tormented those souls who treacherously betrayed their kin.

13. "Love ... Love ... Love ... ": These three tercets, each beginning with the word "Love", are particularly important as revealing the deceptive nature of Francesca. In lines 100 and 103, Francesca deliberately employs the style of stilnovisti poets such as Guinizelli and Cavalcanti in order to ensure the Pilgrim's sympathy, but she follows each of those lines with sensual and most unstilnovistic ideas. For in the idealistic world of the dolce still nuovo love would never "seize" a man for the beauty of the woman's body alone, nor would the sensual delight which "seized" Francesca be appropriate to stilnovistic love, which was distant, nonsexual, and ideal.

THE DECAMERON
The 9th Tale of the 5th Day[1]
by Boccaccio

There was once in Florence a young man named Federigo, the son of Messer Filippo Alberighi, renowned above all other men in Tuscany for his prowess in arms and for his courtliness. As often happens to most gentlemen, he fell in love with a lady named Monna Giovanna, in her day considered to be one of the most beautiful and one of the most charming women that ever there was in Florence; and in order to win her love, he participated in jousts and tournaments, organized and gave feasts, and spent his money without restraint; but she, no less virtuous than beautiful, cared little for these things done on her behalf, nor did she care for he who did them. Now, as Federigo was spending far beyond his means and was taking nothing in, as easily happened he lost his wealth and became poor, with nothing but his little farm to his name (from whose revenues he lived very meagerly) and one falcon which was among the best in the world.

More in love than ever, but knowing that he would never be able to live the way he wished to in the city, he went to live at Campi, where his farm was. There he passed his time hawking whenever he could, asked nothing of anyone, and endured his poverty patiently. Now, during the time that Federigo was reduced to dire need, it happened that the husband of Monna Giovanna fell ill, and realizing death was near, he made his last will: he was very rich, and he made his son, who was growing up, his heir, and, since he had loved Monna Giovanna very much, he made her his heir should his son die without a legitimate heir; and then he died.

Monna Giovanna was now a widow, and as is the custom among our women, she went to the country with her son to spend a year on one of her possessions very close by to Federigo's farm, and it happened that this young boy became friends with Federigo and began to enjoy birds and hunting dogs; and after he had seen Federigo's falcon fly many times, it pleased him so much that he very much wished it were his own, but he did not dare to ask for it, for he could see how dear it was to Federigo. And during this time, it happened that the young boy took ill, and his mother was much grieved, for he was her only child and she loved him enormously; she would spend the entire day by his side, never ceasing to comfort him, and often asking him if there was anything he desired, begging him to tell her what it might be, for if it were possible to obtain it, she would certainly do every thing possible to get it. After the young boy had heard her make this offer many times, he said:

"Mother, if you can arrange for me to have Federigo's falcon, I think I would be well very soon."

When the lady heard this, she was taken aback for a moment,

and she began to think what she should do. She knew that Federigo had loved her for a long while, in spite of the fact that he never received a single glance from her, and so, she said to herself: "How can I send or go and ask for this falcon of his which is, as I have heard tell, the best that ever flew, and besides this, his only means of support? And how can I be so insensitive as to wish to take away from this gentleman the only pleasure which is left to him?"

And involved in these thoughts, knowing that she was certain to have the bird if she asked for it, but not knowing what to say to her son, she stood there without answering him. Finally the love she bore her son persuaded her that she should make him happy, and no matter what the consequences might be, she would not send for the bird, but rather go herself for it and bring it back to him; so she answered her son:

"My son, take comfort and think only of getting well, for I promise you that the first thing I shall do tomorrow morning is to go for it and bring it back to you."

The child was so happy that he showed some improvement that very day. The following morning, the lady, accompanied by another woman, as if going for a stroll, went to Federigo's modest house and asked for him. Since it was not the season for it, Federigo had not been hawking for some days and was in his orchard, attending to certain tasks; when he heard that Monna Giovanna was asking for him at the door, he was very surprised and happy to run there; as she saw him coming, she greeted him with feminine charm, and once Federigo had welcomed her courteously, she said:

"Greetings, Federigo!" Then she continued. "I have come to compensate you for the harm you have suffered on my account by loving me more than you needed to; and the compensation is this: I, along with this companion of mine, intend to dine with you — a simple meal — this very day. "

To this Federigo humbly replied: "Madonna[2], I never remember having suffered any harm because of you; on the contrary: so much good have I received from you that if ever I have been worth anything, it has been because of your merit and the love I bore for you; and your generous visit is certainly so dear to me that I would spend all over again that which I spent in the past; but you have come to a poor host. "

And having said this, he received her into his home humbly, and from there he led her into his garden, and since he had no one there to keep her company, he said:

"My lady, since there is no one else, this good woman here, the wife of this workman, will keep you company while I go to set the table. "

Though he was very poor, Federigo, until now, had never before realized to what extent he had wasted his wealth; but this morning, the fact that he found nothing with which he could honor the lady for the love of whom he had once entertained countless men in the past gave him cause to reflect: in great anguish, he cursed himself and his fortune and, like a man beside himself, he started running here and there, but could find neither money nor a pawnable object. The hour was late and his desire to honor the gracious lady was great, but not wishing to turn for help to others (not even to his own workman), he set his eyes upon his good falcon, perched in a small room; and since he had nowhere else to turn, he took the bird, and finding it plump, he decided that it would be a worthy food for such a lady. So, without further thought, he wrung its neck and quickly gave it to his servant girl to pluck, prepare, and place on a spit to be roasted with care; and when he had set the table with the whitest of tablecloths (a few of which he still had left), he returned, with a cheerful face, to the lady in his garden, saying that the meal he was able to prepare for

西方文学

her was ready.

The lady and her companion rose, went to the table together with Federigo, who waited upon them with the greatest devotion, and they ate the good falcon without knowing what it was they were eating. And having left the table and spent some time in pleasant conversation, the lady thought it time now to say what she had come to say, and so she spoke these kind words to Federigo:

"Federigo, if you recall your past life and my virtue, which you perhaps mistook for harshness and cruelty, I do not doubt at all that you will be amazed by my presumption when you hear what my main reason for coming here is; but if you had children, through whom you might have experienced the power of parental love, it seems certain to me that you would, at least in part, forgive me. But, just as you have no child, I do have one, and I cannot escape the common laws of other mothers; the force of such laws compels me to follow them, against my own will and against good manners and duty, and to ask of you a gift which I know is most precious to you; and it is naturally so, since your extreme condition has left you no other delight, no other pleasure, no other consolation; and this gift is your falcon, which my son is so taken by that if I do not bring it to him, I fear his sickness will grow so much worse that I may lose him. And therefore I beg you, not because of the love that you bear for me, which does not oblige you in the least, but because of your own nobleness, which you have shown to be greater than that of all other in practicing courtliness, that you be pleased to give it to me, so that I may say that I have saved the life of my son by means of this gift, and because of it I have placed him in your debt forever."

When he heard what the lady requested and knew that he could not oblige her since he had given her the falcon to eat, Federigo began to weep in her presence, for he could not utter a word in reply. The lady, at first, thought his tears were caused more by

西方文学

the sorrow of having to part with the good falcon than by anything else, and she was on the verge of telling him she no longer wished it, but she held back and waited for Federigo's reply after he stopped weeping. And he said:

"My lady, ever since it pleased God for me to place my love in you, I have felt that Fortune has been hostile to me in many things, and I have complained of her, but all this is nothing compared to what she has just done to me, and I must never be at peace with her again, thinking about how you have come here to my poor home where, while it was rich, you never deigned to come, and you requested a small gift, and fortune worked to make it impossible for me to give it to you; and why this is so I shall tell you briefly. When I heard that you, out of your kindness, wished to dine with me, I considered it fitting and right, taking into account your excellence and your worthiness, that I should honor you, according to my possibilities, with a more precious food than that which I usually serve to other people; therefore, remembering the falcon that you requested and its value, I judged it a food worthy of you, and this very day I had it roasted and served to you as best I could; but seeing now that you desired it in another way, my sorrow in not being able to serve you is so great that I shall never be able to console myself again."

And after he had said this, he laid the feathers, the feet, and the beak of the bird before her as proof. When the lady heard and saw this, she first reproached him for having killed such a falcon to serve as a meal to a woman; but then to herself she commended the greatness of his spirit, which no poverty was able or would be able to diminish; then, having lost all hope of getting the falcon and, perhaps because of this, of improving the health of her son as well, she thanked Federigo both for the honor paid to her and for his good will, and she left in grief, and returned to her son. To his mother's extreme sorrow, either because of his disappointment that he could not have the falcon, or because his illness must have necessarily led to it, the boy passed from this life only a few days later.

After the period of her mourning and bitterness had passed, the lady was repeatedly urged by her brothers to remarry, since she was very rich and was still young; and although she did not wish to do so, they became so insistent that she remembered the merits of Federigo and his last act of generosity — that is, to have killed such a falcon to do her honor — and she said to her brothers:

"I would prefer to remain a widow, if that would please you; but if you wish me to take a husband, you may rest assured that I shall take no man but Federigo degli Alberighi."

In answer to this, making fun of her, her brothers replied:

"You foolish woman, what are you saying? How can you want him; he hasn't a penny to his name?"

To this she replied: "My brothers, I am well aware of what you say, but I would rather have a man who needs money than money that needs a man."

Her brothers, seeing that she was determined and knowing Federigo to be of noble birth, no matter how poor he was, accepted her wishes and gave her in marriage to him with all her riches; when he found himself the husband of such a great lady, whom he had loved so much and who was so wealthy besides, he managed his financial affairs with more prudence than in the past and lived with her happily the rest of his days.

Notes

1. Told by Dioneo. On the 5th day, in Fiammetta's reign, the friends were to tell love stories which end happily after a period of misfortune.
2. My lady.

THE CANTERBURY TALES[1]
General Prologue
by Chaucer

As soon as April pierces to the root
The drought of March, and bathes each bud and shoot
Through every vein of sap with gentle showers
From whose engendering liquor spring the flowers;
When zephyrs[2] have breathed softly all about
Inspiring every wood and field to sprout,
And in the zodiac the youthful sun
His journey halfway through the Ram[3] has run;
When little birds are busy with their song
Who sleep with open eyes the whole night long
Life stirs their hearts and tingles in them so,
Then off as pilgrims people long to go,
And palmers[4] to sot out for distant strands
And foreign shrines renowned in many lands.
And specially in England people ride
To Canterbury from every countryside
To visit there the blessed martyred saint[5]
Who gave them strength when they were sick and faint.

   In Southward at the Tabard[6] one spring day
It happened, as I stopped there on my way,
Myself a pilgrim with a heart devout
Ready for Canterbury to set out,
At night came all of twenty-nine assorted
Travelers, and to that same inn resorted,
Who by a turn of fortune chanced to fall
In fellowship together, and they were all

Pilgrims who had it in their minds to ride
Toward Canterbury. The stables' doors were wide,
The rooms were large, and we enjoyed the best,
And Shortly, when the sun had gone to rest,
I had so talked with each that presently
I was a member of their company
And promised to rise early the next day
To start, as I shall show, upon our way.

But none the less, while I have time and space,
Before this tale has gone a further pace,
I should in reason tell you the condition
Of each of them, his rank and his position,
And also what array they all were in;
And so then, with a knight I will begin.

A knight was with us, and an excellent man,
Who from the earliest moment he began
To follow his career loved chivalry,
Truth, openhandedness, and courtesy.
He was a stout man in the king's campaigns
And in that cause had gripped his horse's reins
In Christian lands and pagan through the earth,
None farther, and always honored for his worth.
He was on hand at Alexandria's fall[7].
He had often sat in precedence to all
The nations at the banquet board in Prussia.
He had fought in Lithuania and in Russia,
No Christian knight more often, he had been
In Moorish Africa at Benmarin,
At the siege of Algeciras in Granada,
In the Mediterranean, and fought as well
At Ayas and Attalia when they fell
In Armenia and on Asia Minor's coast.

Of fifteen deadly battles he could boast,
And in Algeria, at Trernesson,
Fought for the faith and killed three separate men
In single combat. He had done good work
Joining against another pagan Turk
With the king of Palathia. And he was wise,
Despite his prowess, honored in men's eyes,
Meek as a girl and gentle in his ways.
He had never spoken ignobly all his days
To any man by even a rude inflection.
He was knight in all things to perfection.
He rode a good horse, but his gear was plain,
For he had lately served on a campaign.
His tunic was still spattered by the rust
Left by his coat of mail, for he had just
Returned and set out on his pilgrimage.

      His son was with him, a young Squire, in age
Some twenty years as near as I could guess,
His hair curled as if taken from a press.
He was a lover and would become a knight.
In stature he was of a moderate height
But powerful and wonderfully quick.
He had been in Flankers, riding in the thick
Of forays in Artois and Picardy,
And bore up well for one so young as he,
Still hoping by his exploits in such places
To stand the better in his lady's graces.
He wore embroidered flowers, red and white,
And blazed like a spring meadow to the sight,
He sang or played his flute the livelong day.
He was as lusty as the month of May.
His coat was short, its sleeves were long and wide.

He sat his horse well, and knew how to ride,
And how to make a song and use his lance,
And he could write and draw well, too, and dance.
So hot his love that when the moon rose pale
He got no more sleep than a nightingale.
He was modest, and helped whomever he was able,
And carved as his father's squire at the table.

But one more servant had the Knight beside,
Choosing thus simply for the time to ride:
A Yeoman, in a coat and hood of green.
His peacock-feathered arrows, bright and keen,
He carried under his pelt in tidy fashion.
For well-kept gear he had a yeoman's passion,
No draggled feather might his arrows show,
And in his hand he held a might bow.
He kept his hair close-cropped, his face was brown.
He knew the lore of woodcraft up and down.
His arm was guarded from the bowstring's whip
By a bracer, gaily trimmed. He had at hip
A sword and buckler, and at his other side
A dagger whose fine mounting was his pride,
Sharp-pointed as a spear. His horn he bore
In a sling of green, and on his chest he wore
A silver image of St. Christoper.
His patron, since he was a forester.

There was also a Nun, A Prioress,
Whose smile was gentle and full of guilelessness.
"By St. Loy!"[8] was the worst oath she would say.
She sang mass well, in a becoming way,
Intoning through her nose the words divine,
And she was known as Madame Eglantine.
She spoke good French, as taught at Stratford-Bow[9]

For the Parisian French she did not know.
She was schooled to eat so primly and so well
That from her lips no morsel ever fell.
She wet her fingers lightly in the dish
Of sauce, for courtesy was her first wish.
With every bite she did her skillful best
To see that no drop fell upon her breast.
She always wiped her upper lip so clean
That in her cup was never to be seen
A hint of grease when she had drunk her share,
She reached out for her meat with comely air.
She was a great delight, and always tried
To imitate court ways, and had her pride,
Both amiable and gracious in her dealings.
As for her charity and tender feelings,
She melted at whatever was piteous.
She would weep if she but came upon a mouse
Caught in a trap, if it were dead of bleeding.
Some little dogs that she took pleasure feeding
On roasted meat or milk or good wheat bread
She had, but how she wept to find one dead
Or yelping from a blow that made it smart,
And all was sympathy and loving heart.
Neat was her wimple in its every plait,
Her nose well formed, her eyes as gray as slate.
Her mouth was very small and soft and red.
She had so wide a brow I think her head
Was nearly a span broad, for certainly
She was not undergrown, as all could see.
She wore her cloak with dignity and charm,
And had her rosary about her arm,
The small beads coral and the larger green,

And from them hung a brooch of golden sheen,
On it a large A and a crown above;
Beneath, "All things are subject onto love. "
. . .

Notes

1. In the modern English-translation by Theodore Morrison, Chaucer's original metrical form, the heroic couplet, is used.
2. Zephyrs: the west wind.
3. Ram: sign of the zodiac (Aries); The sun is in the Ram from March 12 to April 11.
4. palmers: pilgrims, who, originally, brought back palm leaves from the Holy Land.
5. saint: St. Thomas Becket, slain in Canterbury cathedral in 1170.
6. Tabard: an inn at Southwark, across the river Thames from London.
7. Alexandria's fall: in Egypt, captured in 1365 by king Peter of Cyprus.
8. "By St. Loy!": perhaps St. Eligius, apparently a popular saint at that time.
9. Stratford-Bow: in Middlesex, near London, where there was a nunnery.

西方文学

Chapter Ⅲ The Renaissance

1. Historical Introduction

Renaissance is commonly applied to the movement of the revival of art, learning, and literature in Europe extending over a period of 300 years from about 1350 to 1650 and marking the transition from the medieval to the modern world. The peak of it occurred at different times in different countries, the movement having had its inception in Italy, where its impact was at first most visible in the fine arts, while in England, for instance, it developed later and its main achievements were in literature, particularly in Drama. It resulted from many new facts and forces arising within the older order of the Medieval period, such as: the Hellenistic spirit which taught people that human beings, far from being groveling worms, were glorious creatures capable of individual development in the direction of perfection; the Protestant Reformation, which, itself in part an aspect of the Renaissance in Germany, fused Christian with classical traditions; the introduction of printing, which led to a commercial market for literature; the great economic and political changes leading to the rise of democracy, the spirit of nationalism, an ambitious commercialism, and opportunities for individuals to rise above their birth economically and politically; the revitalized university life; the courtly encouragement of the growing new science, which made human beings and nature the results of natural and demonstrable law rather than a mysterious group of entities subject to occult powers.

In literature, the period of Renaissance was notable for a revival of interest in a rediscovery of classic works of Greek and Roman origins and the doctrine of humanism. Indeed, the new humanistic learning that resulted from the rediscovery of classical literature is frequently taken as the beginning of Renaissance on its conscious, intellectual side, since it was to the treasures of classical culture and to the authority of classical writers that the people of the Renaissance turned for inspiration. Here the radical departure from medievalism was inescapable. In the medieval society of theology, people's interests as individuals were subordinated to their function as elements in a social unit and their relations to the world around them were largely reduced to a problem of adapting or avoiding the circumstances of earthly life in an effort to prepare their souls for a future life. But the Renaissance humanists caught from their glimpses of classical culture a vision of human life quite at odds with the medieval attitudes. They believed that man was the center of the universe and that he was capable of living a life of reason, dignity, morality, and even happiness. Advocates of humanism in literary history range from Petrarch, Thomas More, Erasmus, and Sir Philip Sidney to Shakespeare and Milton.

2. Literary Giants and Works

Francis Petrarch (1304-1374), Italian scholar and poet, was a prominent figure of his time. In his life he travelled widely, as a humanist searching for ancient texts, as a man of letters, and as a diplomat. His attitude toward classical antiquity makes him the first writer of the Renaissance. As a writer he modeled his work on classical examples and self-consciously attended to the creation of his own image, defining, ordering, and polishing with exquisite care his poems, thus helping to establish a new poetic form, the Italian sonnet, which is also called Petrarchan sonnet for his contribution. The style introduced by the poet in his sonnets is called petrarchism, which is notable for its formal perfection, grammatical complexity, and elaborate figurative language.

Desiderius Erasmus (1466-1536), Dutch humanist, stands as the supreme type of cultivated common sense applied to human affairs. He rescued theology from the pedantries of the Schoolmen, exposed the abuses of the Church, and did more than any other single person to advance the Revival of Learning. Erasmus's editions of Greek and Latin classics and of the Fathers of the Church (especially of Jerome and Athanasius) were his chief occupation for years. His Latin edition of the *New Testament* was based on the original Greek text. Erasmus combined vast learning with a fine style, a keen and sometimes sharp humor, moderation, and tolerance. His *The Praise of Folly* is the best known work of the greatest of the renaissance humanists. It is a fantasy which starts off as a learned frivolity but turns into a full-scale ironic encomium after the manner of the Greek satirist Lucian, the first and in its way the finest example of a new form of renaissance satire. It ends with a straightforward and touching statement of the Christian ideals which Erasmus shared notably with his English friends, John Colet and Thomas More.

Baldesar Castiglione (1478-1529) was an Italian Renaissance writer and courtier best known for *Libro Del Cortegiano*, or *The Book of the Courtier*, which was first published in 1528 and hasn't been out of print since. That work is the best explication of the Renaissance ideal of the universal man — the courtier, or "professional amateur", as Sydney Angelo put it. In it, Castiglione outlines in the form of a dialog amongst nobles at the court of the duke of Urbino how the perfect courtier should look, act, and think, and pursue his interests of literature, art, love, music, sport, rhetoric, and arms.

Niccolò Machiavelli (1469-1527) was born on May 3, 1469, in Florence, Italy. He began his career as an active politician in the independent city-state of Florence, engaging in diplomatic missions through France and Germany as well as Italy. After more than a decade of public service, he was driven from his post when the republic collapsed. Repeated efforts to win the confidence and approval of the new regime were unsuccessful, and Machiavelli was forced into retirement and a life of detached scholarship about the political process instead of direct participation in it. The books for which he is remembered were published only after his death. Machiavelli originally wrote *Principe* (*The Prince*) (1513) in hopes of securing the favor of the ruling Medici family, and he deliberately made its claims provocative. *The Prince* is an intensely practical guide to the exercise of raw political power over a Renaissance principality. Allowing for the unpredictable influence of fortune, Machiavelli argued that it is primarily the character or vitality or skill of the individual leader that determines the success of any state. The book surveys various bold means of acquiring and maintaining the principality and evaluates each of them solely by reference to its likelihood of augmenting the glory of the prince while serving the public interest. It is this focus on practical success by any means, even at the expense of traditional moral values, that earned Machiavelli's scheme a reputation for ruthlessness, deception, and cruelty.

Francois Rabelais (1494-1553) was the French monk, physician, humanist scholar and writer who sought to free medieval life of the pretence and superstition. His influential and much-imitated satiric masterpiece, *Gargantua and Pantagruel* (five books, 1532-1552) is in the mock-quest tradition. It attacked clerical education and monastic orders and expressed an appreciation for secular learning and a confidence in human nature. Like other humanists, Rabelais criticized medieval philosophy for its concern with obscure, confused, and irrelevant questions. Expressing his aversion to medieval asceticism, he attacked monasticism as life-denying and regarded worldly pleasure as a legitimate need and aim of human nature.

Michel de Montaigne (1533-1592) is a great French Renaissance thinker who took himself as the great object of study in his *Essays*. In studying himself Montaigne is studying mankind. He attempted to weigh or 'assay' his nature, habits, his own opinions and those of others. He is searching for truth by reflecting on his readings, his travels as well as his experiences both public and private. Montaigne's writing style is light and untechnical. He was also a striking representative of Renaissance skepticism and fideism. Essentially fideism is a strategy which uses skepticism in order to clear the ground for the entrance of Catholicism.

Montaigne's skepticism is largely confined to *An Apology for Raymond Sebond* which was originally the (very long) 12th chapter of Book Ⅱ of the *Essays* but is often published separately. Montaigne seeks to humble man's pride: " ... there is a plague on Man, the opinion that he knows something." This skepticism is connected with the doctrine of Christian "folly" which says that God's wisdom is to be found in the lowly and the meek, and that the belief that one has knowledge prevents one from accepting the truths of religion. Montaigne is famous for arguing that man is not in any way superior to the beasts, in fact, quite the contrary.

Miguel de Cervantes (1547-1616) was the great Spanish writer during the Renaissance. In his literary career, he wrote more than twenty plays with little success. In 1605, he published *Don Quixote*, which was very popular with the audience. *Don Quixote* is a work of considerable novelty about the adventures of Don Quixote and his servant Sancho Panza. Don Quixote is originally an impoverished country gentleman. He takes interest in reading the romances of chivalry and are insanely infatuated with them. He sets out to live according to the chivalrous patterns of action and belief. Departing from reality and obsessed in his illusion, he behaves himself fantastically, for instance, seeing windmills as giants, country inns as castles, and flocks of sheep as armies. His insane actions not only turn himself into a laughing stock of the modern world, but make himself suffer a lot. Yet he has not realized his folly until he is dying. The initial and overt purpose of the story was to satirize the very popular type of literature, the romances of chivalry. Yet it is not merely a parody. It is also

西方文学

a tragedy of a modern man who decides to live by the standards of a remote and imaginary world in a modern and realistic context.

William Shakespeare (1564-1616), the greatest English playwright and poet, embodies nearly all of the currents in the Renaissance Reformation period. Like Leonard and Luther, he was a giant in an age of geniuses — one who discovered and mastered new worlds of thoughts and expression. His characters demonstrate a range of feeling from the early humanists' confidence in humanity's abilities and powers to late Renaissance skepticism and relativism and the Reformation's doubt that human beings can accomplish much of anything on their own. His Hamlet is a new man of the Renaissance. He is a humanist, who is free from medieval prejudices and superstitions. He has an unbounded love for the world rather for Heaven, and cherishes a profound reverence for man and a firm belief in man's power over destiny. Yet the murder of his father and his uncle's usurpation bring him to the understanding that "The time is out of joint," and awaken him to the realization of a great responsibility, the reformation of the world as a whole. But to realise his ideal in his own time was beyond him. This is the cause of his profound melancholy, which expresses, in a way, the crisis of humanism at the end of the 16th and the beginning of the 17th centuries.

John Milton (1608-1674) is the greatest English epic poet. The quality of his literary achievements places him within the long tradition of Renaissance Christian humanism. On the one hand, the Renaissance is responsible for the rich and complex texture of his style, the multiplicity of its classical references, its wealth of ornament and decoration. *Paradise Lost*, being an epic, not only challenges comparison with Homer and Vigil, but undertakes to encompass the whole life of mankind — war, love, religion, Hell, Heaven, the cosmos. It is a poem vastly capacious of worldly experience. On the other hand, the Reformation speaks with equal authority in Milton's earnest and individually minded Christianity. The great epic, which, resounds with the grandeur and multiplicity of the world, is also a poem whose central actions take place inwardly, at the core of man's conscience. Adam's fate culminates in an act of passive suffering, not of active heroism. He picks up the burden of worldly existence, and triumphs over his guilt by admitting it and repenting of it. So the subject of the epic is not merely the Christian fallen man, but the transgressor's discovery and acceptance of their new mortal status, implying moral awareness and hope along with corruptibility and guilt.

Sir Philip Sidney (1554-1586) was the great Renaissance English poet and critic. As a poet, he went to classical writers for his model and wrote a collection of sonnets under the title of *Astrophel and Stella*. As a critic, his fame chiefly rests on his critical prose "An Apology for Poetry", the only major work of literary criticism produced in the English Renaissance. This long essay was written to answer an attack on poetry and drama as "the school of abuse". In it, Sidney defends poetry by exalting the role of the poet and the moral value of poetry. For Sidney, poetry is the best agent for leading men to act virtuously; it is a better teacher than oral philosophy or history, since poetry combines the precepts of one with the examples of the other, and in addition uses all the pleasurable devices of art to make instruction palatable.

Thomas More（1478-1535）was the quintessential Renaissance man — a writer, scholar, statesman, diplomat, political theorist and patron of the arts. He was the foremost English Humanist of his day. More's most important work was his *Utopia*, published in 1516. The name, which is Greek, means No-Place, and the book is one of the most famous of that series of attempts to outline an imaginary ideal condition of society. The book, broadly considered, deals primarily with the question of the relation of the State and the individual. It consists of two parts. In the first there is a vivid picture of the terrible evils which England was suffering through war, lawlessness, the wholesale and foolish application of the death penalty, the misery of the peasants, the absorption of the land by the rich, and the other distressing corruptions in Church and State. In the second part, in contrast to all this, a certain imaginary Raphael Hythlodaye describes the customs of Utopia, a remote island in the New World, to which chance has carried him. The controlling purpose in the life of the Utopians is to secure both the welfare of the State and the full development of the individual. The State is democratic, socialistic, and communistic, and the will of the individual is subordinated to the advantage of all, but the real interests of each and all are recognized as identical.

Edmund Spenser（1552-1999）was the great British poet of the Renaissance, known to his contemporaries as 'the prince of poets', as great in English as Virgil in Latin. He left behind him masterful essays in every genre of poetry, from pastoral and elegy to epithalamium and epic. Generations of readers, students,

西方文学

81

and scholars have admired him for his subtle use of language, his unbounded imagination, his immense classical and religious learning, his keen understanding of moral and political philosophy, and his unerring ability to synthesize and, ultimately, to delight.

Spenser is the inventor of one of the most individual and romantic styles in literature, the chief marks of which are the meter and the vocabulary. The Spenserian stanza of nine lines, intricately rhymed and ending with an Alexandrine, was revived by Thomson and others in the eighteen century, and has since been imitated by many great poets. Spenser, more than any other writer, is the founder of English diction. His practice of preserving old words has been of great service to the English poets. He also enjoys the rare distinction of having added words of his own coining to the English language. Spenser's masterpiece is *The Faerie Queene*, which was intended to look back to a golden age of pastoral harmony but also to celebrate the court of Elizabeth, through drawing a parallel with King Arthur's legendary court. The poem absorbs and reflects a vast range of myth, legend, superstition and magic, and explores both history and contemporary politics.

Francis Bacon (1561-1626) was the great British writer of Renaissance and one of the pioneers of modern scientific thought. Bacon's writings fall into three categories: philosophical, purely literary, and professional. His essays are scarcely less notable for style than for ideas. With characteristic intellectual independence Bacon strikes out for himself an extremely terse and clear manner of expression, doubtless influenced by such Latin authors

as Tacitus, which stands in marked contrast to the formless dif-
fuseness or artificial elaborateness of most Elizabethan and Jacobean prose. His unit of structure is always a short clause. The
sentences are sometimes short, sometimes consist of a number of
connected clauses; but they are always essentially loose rather
than periodic; so that the thought is perfectly simple and its
movement clear and systematic. But Bacon's most important
work was not in the field of pure literature but in the general advancement of knowledge, particularly knowledge of natural science. *The Advancement of Learning* attempted to draw a distinction between two kinds of Truth, a theological Truth "drawn
from the word and oracles of God" and determined by faith, and
a scientific Truth based on the light of nature and the distastes of
reason. Both, he freely conceded, possessed an equal intellectual
validity. Throughout his work, Bacon is a great classifier, a
forthright proponent of the innovative power of human reason, a
firm believer in a "perpetual renovation" of knowledge. The theories of *The Advancement of Learning*, were later reworked and
expanded in its Latin version, *De Augmentic Scientiarum* of
1623, but both works should properly be seen as preliminaries to
the larger overarching argument of "true directions concerning
the interpretation of nature" contained in *Norum Organum* (the
"New Instrument" by which human understanding would be advanced). The *Novum Organum* argues in Latin for a new method
of scientific thinking, free of the prejudices of the past and the
received affectations of the present. It marks a decisive rejection
of the old ways of syllogistic deduction and a defense of the inductive investigation of nature.

Christopher Marlowe (1564-1593) the first great dramatist of the Renaissance period, was born in 1564, the same year as Shakespeare. Marlowe's plays explore the boundaries of the new world and the risks that mankind will run in the quest for power, for knowledge, and for love. His plays are full of spectacular action, bloodshed, and passion, to match his language of calculated exaggeration coupled with a great control of metrical pace and inventive poetic effect. All these help to determine the often startling and disconcerting quality of Marlowe's dramatic verse, verse that brought English iambic pentameter to its first maturity. Marlowe's first great theatrical success is *Tamburlaine the Great* (1587), a dramatization of the stupendous career of the bloodthirsty Mongol fourteenth-century conqueror. *Doctor Faustus* (1592), Marlowe's most famous play, tells the story of a man who sold his soul to the Devil for twenty-four years of power, knowledge and pleasure. At the start of the play Faustus, tired of traditional learning and science, turns to magic, calls up the devil Mephistopheles and makes a compact with him. In return for his soul, Faustus will be given whatever he desires. The central section of the play shows Faustus enjoying his power, but not gaining the kind of knowledge of heaven and hell that he thirsts for. As time runs out — the bargain is for no more than twenty-four years — and his eternal damnation approaches, Faustus hovers between despair and belief. The play consequently seems to teach a moral lesson in the fashion of the earlier morality plays, but also questions the limits placed on human knowledge by an apparently vengeful God.

西方文学

3. Readings

DON QUIXOTE
Chapter 8
by Miguel de Cervantes

Of the good fortune which the valorous Don Quixote had in the terrifying and never-before-imagined adventure of the windmills, along with other events that deserve to be suitably recorded.

At this point they caught sight of thirty or forty windmills which were standing on the plain there, and no sooner had Don Quixote laid eyes upon them than he turned to his squire and said, "Fortune is guiding our affairs better than we could have wished; for you see there before you, friend Sancho Panza, some thirty or more lawless giants with whom I mean to do battle. I shall deprive them of their lives, and with the spoils from this encounter we shall begin to enrich ourselves; for this is righteous warfare, and it is a great service to God to remove so accursed a breed from the face of the earth."

"What giants?"said Sancho Panza.

"Those that you see there," replied his master, "those with the long arms some of which are as much as two leagues in length. "

"But look, our Grace, those are not giants but windmills, and what appear to be arms are their wings which, when whirled in the breeze, cause the millstone to go. "

"It is plain to be seen," said Don Quixote, "that you have had little experience in this matter of adventures. If you are afraid, go off to one side and say your prayers while I am engaging them in fierce, unequal combat. "

Saying this, he gave spurs to his steed Rocinante, without paying any heed to Sancho's warning that these were truly windmills and not giants that he was riding forth to attack. Nor even when he was close upon them did he perceive what they really were, but shouted at the top of his lungs, "Do not seek to flee, cowards and vile creatures that you are, for it is but a single knight with whom you have to deal!"

At that moment a little wind came up and the big wings began tuming.

"Though you flourish as many arms as did the giant Briareus,"[1] said Don Quixote when he perceived this, "you still shall have to answer to me. "

He thereupon commended himself with all his heart to his lady Dulcinea, beseeching her to succor him in this peril; and, being well covered with his shield and with his lance at rest, he bore down upon them at a full gallop and fell upon the first mill that stood in his way, giving a thrust at the wing, which was whirling at such a speed that his lance was broken into bits and both horse and horseman went rolling over the plain, very much battered indeed. Sancho upon his donkey came hurrying to his master's assistance as fast as he could, but when he reached the spot, the knight was unable to move, so great was the shock with which he and Rocinante had hit the ground.

"God help us!" exclaimed Sancho, "did I not tell your Grace to look well, that those were nothing but windmills, a fact which no one could fail to see unless he had other mills of the same sort in his head?"

"Be quiet, friend Sancho," said Don Quixote. "Such are the fortunes of war, which more than any other are subject to constant change. What is more, when I come to think of it, I am sure that this must be the work of that magician Freestone, the one who

robbed me of my study and my books,[2] and who has thus changed
the giants into windmills in order to deprive me of the glory of over-
coming them, so great is the enmity that he bears me; but in the
end his evil arts shall not prevail against this trusty sword of mine. "

"May God's will be done," was Sancho Panza's response.
And with the aid of his squire the knight was once more mounted on
Rocinante, who stood there with one shoulder half out of joint. And
so, speaking of the adventure that had just befallen them, they
continued along the Puerto Lapice highway; for there, Don Quixote
said, they could not fail to find many and varied adventures, this
being a much traveled thoroughfare.

Notes

1. mythological giant with a hundred arms.
2. Don Quixote had promptly attributed the ruin of his library, performed by
   the curate and the barber, to magical intervention.

HAMLET
Act Ⅲ
Scene Ⅰ (Excerpt)
by William Shakespeare

HAMLET: To be, or not to be, that is the question:
　　　　Whether'tis nobler in the mind to suffer
　　　　The slings and arrows of outrageous fortune,
　　　　Or to take arms against a sea of troubles,
　　　　And by opposing, end them. To die: to sleep;
　　　　No more; and by a sleep to say we end
　　　　The heart-ache, and the thousand natural shocks
　　　　That flesh is heir to; 'tis a consummation[1]
　　　　Devoutly to be wished. To die, to sleep;

To sleep: perchance to dream: aye, there's the rub;[2]
For in that sleep of death what dreams may come,
When we have shuffled off this mortal coil,[3]
Must give us pause: there's the respect[4]
That makes calamity of so long life;[5]
For who would bear the whips and scorns of time,
The oppressor's wrong, the proud man's contumely[6]
The pangs of despised love, the law's delay,
The insolence of office, and the spurns
That patient merit of the unworthy takes,
When he himself might his quietus[7] make
With a bare bodkin?[8] who would fardels[9] bear,
To grunt and sweat under a weary life,
But that the dread of something after death,
The undiscovered country from whose bourn[10]
No traveler returns, puzzles the will,
And makes us rather bear those ills we have
Than fly to others that we know not of?
Thus conscience does make cowards of us all,
And thus the native hue of resolution
Is sicklied o'er with the pale cast of thought,
And enterprises of great pitch[11] and moment
With this regard their currents turn awry
And lose the name of action. Soft you now!
The fair Ophelia! Nymph, in thy orisons[12]
Be all my sins remembered.

Notes

1. consummation: final settlement.
2. the rub: the impediment (a bowling term).
3. have shuffled off this mortal coil: have rid ourseves of the turmoil of mortal life.

4. respect: consideration.

5. of so long life: so long-lived

6. contumely: scorn.

7. quietus: settlement of accounts.

8. bodkin: poniard, dagger.

9. fardels: burdens.

10. bourn: boundary.

11. pitch: height.

12. orisons: prayers.

Considerations

From this soliloquy, what can we learn about the character Hamlet?

西方文学

89

PARADISE LOST
BOOK IV (Excerpt)
by John Milton

Two of far nobler shape erect and tall,
Godlike erect, with native honor clad,[1]
In native majesty, seemed lords of all,
And worthy seemed: for in their looks divine
The image of their glorious Maker[2] shone,
Truth, wisdom, sanctity severe and pure,
Severe, but in true filial freedom placed,[3]
Whence true authority in men: though both[4]
Not equal, as their sex not equal seemed;
For contemplation he and valour formed,
For softness she and sweet attractive grace;
He for God only, she for God in him.

His fair large front[5] and eye sublime declared
Absolute rule; and hyacinthine locks[6]
Round from his parted forelock manly hung.
Clustering, but not beneath his shoulders broad;
She as a veil down to the slender waist
Her unadorned golden tresses wore
Disheveled, but in wanton ringlets waved
As the vine curls her tendrils, which implied
Subjection, but required with gentle sway[7],
And by her yielded, by him best received,
Yielded with coy submission, modest pride,
And sweet reluctant amorous delay.
Nor those mysterious parts[8] were then concealed;
Then was[9] not guilty shame; dishonest shame
Of nature's works,[10] honor dishonorable,
Sin-bred,[11] how have ye troubled all mankind
With shows instead, mere shows of seeming pure,
And banished from man's life his happiest life,
Simplicity and spotless innocence!
So passed they naked on, nor shunned the sight
Of God or Angel, for they thought no ill;
So hand in hand they passed, the loveliest pair
That ever since in love's embraces met;
Adam the goodliest[12] man of men since born
His sons, the fairest or her daughters Eve.

. . .

One fatal Tree there stands of Knowledge called
Forbidden them to taste: knowledge forbidden?
Suspicious, reasonless. Why should their Lord
Envy them that? Can it be sin to know?
Can it be death? And to they only stand

西方文学

By ignorance? Is that their happy state,
The proof of their obedience and their faith?
O fair foundation laid whereon to build
Their ruin! Hence I will excite their minds
With more desire to know, and to reject
Envious commands, invented with design
To keep them low, whom knowledge might exalt
Equal with Gods; aspiring to be such,
They taste and die: what likelier can ensue?

Notes

1. with native honour clad: dressed in only the flesh they had been born in, which had a natural honorableness.
2. the image of their glorious Maker: Man was made in the image of God, according to *Genesis*, the first book of the *Bible*.
3. in true filial freedom placed: they were free, and at the same time they were God's filial children, that is, still they must obey God's wishes.
4. both: the two of them.
5. front: forehead.
6. hyacinthine locks: beautifully curly and perhaps reddish brown in colour.
7. which implied Subjection, but required with gentle sway: Subjection means obedience on Eve's part, but that obedience was required by Adam with gentle influence over her.
8. mysterious parts: private parts or genitals.
9. Then was: Then there was.
10. nature's works: human bodies. To feel ashamed of the naked bodies is dishonest, because they're works of nature.
11. honour dishonorable, / Sin-bred: When man has covered up his naked body he thinks it is honorable, but in fact it is dishonorable, because this is fake honour, bred in sin.
12. goodliest: most handsome.

Chapter Ⅳ   Classicism

1. The Rise of Classicism

Classicism (neo-classicism) began in France in the 17th century and had its force in other European countries in the 18th century, mainly as a result of the establisbment of the Monarchy. In the 17th century, France had just emerged as a national state with the King as its head. The King, to weaken the power of the feudal nobility and strengthen his own power, made some concessions to the bourgeoise, who were new and weak and in need of the help of the Monarch. The King and the bourgeoisie worked in combination and wiped out the feudal rules of separation. Thus the political power was centered in the hand of the King. The unity of the nation in politics demanded an authoritative literature corresponding with it. To meet this demand arose the French Classicism, which set a series of rules to overcome the anarchic literary state of the time and to direct the literary creation.

2. The Features of Classicism

Classicism had three striking features: 1) The early Classicism supported and defended the power of King. It held that literary works should serve the Monarchy, and that writers should make it their duty to sing of the King and safeguard the interests of the Monarchy. Thus Classicism had apparent court tendency and ignored the artistic demand of the working class. 2) Classicism advocated rationalism, which was fathered by the French philosopher, Descartes, who upheld that reason should be placed above everything else, for truth and beauty could be obtained only through reason. Classicists believed in the power of reason and thought. For them, logical thought was the dominant element in literary creation, and emotion and imagination advocated by Romanticism should be restricted. The rationalistic attitude of classicism called for elegant form, precise idea, true-to-life description and standardized language. 3) Classicists modeled themselves after the Greek and Latin authors, and tried to guide literary creation by some fixed laws and rules drawn from Greek and Latin works. According to classicists, poetry, following the ancient divisions, should be epic, didactic, satiric or dramatic, and each class should be guided by its own principles; prose should be precise, direct, smooth and flexible; drama should be characterized by such qualities as rhymed couplet instead of blank verse; the three unities of time, place, and action; regularity in construction; and the presentation of types rather than individuals. Among these rules prescribed by classicists, the three unities was the most influential. It required that a play should have one plot which was to be carried out at one place in no more than twenty-four hours.

3. The Representatives of Classicism

The greatest achievement of classicism lay in drama. Its best representatives were the French dramatists — Pierre Gorneille, Jean Racine, and Molière. Gorneille and Racine were the greatest tragedians of the French neoclassical theatre, while Molière was the greatest comedian. In England classicism arose later than in France, and reached its zenith in the 18th-century writings of John Dryden, Alexander Pope, Ben Jonson, and Samel Johnson. In Germany, Goethe and Schiller were major figures in the German classical literary movement. They claimed themselves as classicists. However, their works were romantic in spirit. In America, the greatest representative of classicism was Benjamin Franklin, who was the man that opened the story of American literature. In the early 20th century, T. S. Eliot and proponents of the "new criticism" were sometimes considered classicists because of their emphasis on form and discipline.

Jean-Baptiste Poquelin Molière (1622-1673) was the great French comedian of the 17th century. He wrote both broad farces and comedies of character, in which he caricatured some vice or folly by embodying it in a single figure. His target in his masterpiece, *Tartuffe* or *The Imposter*, is the religious hypocrite. *Tartuffe* is the story of a young man, who pretends to be profoundly pious in church; attracts the attention of a rich merchant who blocks the love of his daughter with another young man and disinherits his son in favor of the imposter; and at last is exposed and sent to prison. The play ends happily in the classical restoration of order, in which good triumphs and rationality renews itself despite the temporary deviations of the foolish and the vicious.

Jean Racine (1638-1699) was the greatest French classic tragedian. His fame rests on his capacity to communicate the full intensity of passion in tragedies marked by their formal decorum and their elevated tone. Racine's material was mainly adapted from classic texts, to which he added an immediacy of psychological insight. His masterpiece. *Phaedra* (1677) adapts the action of Euripides' *Hippolytus* with new emphasis, making the guilty woman rather than the relatively passive man the protagonist and using the highly charged sexual situation between the two to generate intense psychological drama. The story goes like this: Phaedra falls in love with Hippolytus, her husband's son with his ex-wife. At the news of her husband's death, she makes her love known to Hippolytus and is rejected. News comes again that her husband has not died. Being afraid of Hippolytus' exposure of her guilt, Phaedra has her nurse tell her husband that his son has attempted to seduce her. Her husband believes the bare assertion, banishes his son, and invokes Neptune's power to destroy him. Then Arica's hints lead him to suspect his wife, who confesses her own emotional sin while already on the verge of self-inflicted death. In this play, passion triumphs over all principles of control, and brings death to the two central characters and misery to their survivors.

Pierre Gorneille (1606-1684) was the first great French classical dramatist. His masterpiece was *Le Cid*, a tragicomedy. The play took its story from a Spanish legend. Rodrigo and Ximena, children of two conflicting noble families, fall in love with each other. As a filial son, Rodrigo has to avenge his father for a public insult from Ximena's father. In a duel, he kills Ximena's father and Ximena decides to seek justice from the King. At that moment, their country is attacked by the Moors and Rodrigo is sent to fight the Moors. He returned as hero and is given the title "Le Cid", a Moorish name meaning the lord. This event, together with the King's later arrangement, makes Rodrigo and Ximena make it up in the end. The story itself is romantic, while the writer's stress on the repression of emotion in favor of reason and his observation of "the three unities" are classic indeed.

Jean de Fontaine (1621-1695) was a French poet, whose *Fables* rank among the masterpieces of world literature. In his own time, La Fontaine was considered a vagabond, dreamer, and lover of pleasure. A rustic character, he never was a real courtier and drifted happily from one patron to another. Because of the universal nature of his fables, La Fontaine's poems about industrious ants, brave lions, and carefree grasshoppers are still widely read. His *Fables Choisies Mises en Vers*, usually called *La Fontaine Fables*, were published over the last 25 years of his life. The first volume appeared when the author was 47. The book includes some 240 poems and timeless stories of countryfolk, heroes from Greek mythology, and familiar beasts from the fables of Aesop, from which La Fontaine unhesitatingly borrowed his material. The last of his tales were published posthumously. Each tale has a moral — an instruction how to behave correctly or how life should be lived. In the second volume La Fontaine based his tales on stories from Asia and other places. La Fontaine's fables were marked by his love of rural life and belief in ethical hedonism. They were widely translated and imitated during the 17th and 18th centuries all over Europe, and beyond.

Denis Diderot (1713-1784) was the brightest light of the French Enlightenment — a man of intelligence, passion and genius. He yearned for knowledge as he sought the answer to the ultimate enigma of all our Universe. He studied history and developed a great fear that knowledge would continue to be destroyed by the Christians, who had a one-thousand year's history of destroying libraries, burning books, ripping paintings, smashing marbles, and torturing anyone who voiced an unorthodox thought. To prevent it from happening in the future he produced the *Encyclopedia*, a history of what was known, and then distributed it world-wide. He wrote almost a thousand of its articles, over a 20-year period. The rest were submitted by the scholars of the world including Ben Franklin, Thomas Jefferson, and Benjamin Rush. It took 35 volumes and a lot of commotion to get it all together.

Benjamin Franklin (1706-1790) was one of the most extraordinary human beings the world has ever known. Born into the family of a Boston candle maker, Benjamin Franklin became the most famous American of his time. He helped found a new nation and defined the American character. He was Jack of all trades — writer, inventor, diplomat, businessman, musician, scientist, humorist. *The Autobiography of Benjamin Franklin* is the traditional name for the unfinished record of his own life written by Benjamin Franklin from 1771 to 1790; however, Franklin himself appears to have called the work his *Memoirs*. Although it had a tortuous publication history after Franklin's death, this work has become one of the most famous and influential examples of autobiography ever written.

Voltaire (1694-1778) was born as Jean Francois Arouset. He was the foremost representative of the French Enlightenment, directing his campaigns against intolerance and injustice. Voltaire's first serious work was *Oedipus*, a tragedy on Greek lines. His masterpiece was *Candide*, a satire of the romance, the adventure story, and the pedagogical novel. It is the story of a naive and innocent young man who becomes gradually disillusioned. Young Candide is brought up in the castle of a baron with the baron's son and daughter. The family teacher is always telling them that the world they are living in is the best of all possible worlds. But when he falls in love with the baron's daughter, Candide is turned out of the castle. Through misfortunes and hardships in this world, Candide becomes disillusioned.

Samuel Johnson (1709-1784) was a British lexicographer, critic and poet. His principal poems are "London" and "The Vanity of Human Wishes", two satires in heroic couplets. Among his more important literary works are the "Preface and Comments of the Plays of Shakespeare" and "Lives of Poets", which pass judgement on a century of English poetry. These essays of literary criticism were written in line with the classic rules. Nowadays Johnson is mainly remembered as the editor of *A Dictionary of the English Language*, the first great English dictionary that marked an epoc in the study and development of the English language.

Joseph Addison (1672-1719) and **Richard Steele** (1672-1729) were two famous essayists in the 18th-century England. Their periodical essays were included in their papers *The Tatler* and *The Spectator*, which dealt with almost all the aspects and types of character in the attempt to shape a new code of social morality for the rising bourgeoisie. Addison and Steele contributed a lot to the English literature. It was in their hands, the English essay had completely established itself as a literary genre. By using it as a form of character sketching and story-telling, they ushered in the dawn of the modern novel.

John Dryden (1631-1700) was the most distinguished literary figure of the Restoration period of England. He was a poet, playwright, and critic. As the forerunner of the English classical

西方文学

school, he followed the standards of classicism and established the heroic couplet as one of the principal English verse forms. He also clarified English prose, making it concise and direct, and raised English literary criticism to a new level. He wrote prefaces and essays, the best known being "An Essay of Dramatic Poesy" (1668). This essay, which is a dramatization of debate in dialogue form, presents critical perspectives on every major issue of the late 17th century: the value of the unities, the ancients vs. the moderns, the neoclassical French vs. black verse, and so forth. Despite the varied arguments, the essay comes to a development of principles that are intended to apply to all poetic drama.

Alexander Pope (1688-1744) was not merely the leading poet of his generation but also its most significant critic with his prefaces to translation of Homer, his edition of Shakespeare, and his *Essay on Criticism* (1711) — one of the best pieces of verse criticism in the language, which was regarded as the manifesto of English Neoclassicism. Here Pope set forth the neoclassic principles of following nature (the ancients), outlined the causes of bad criticism, described the good critic, and concluded with a short history of criticism.

4. The Rise of the English Realistic Novel

The classical time in Western literature was a period of rapid growth of capitalism in politics in England. Novelists like Defoe, Swift, and Fielding rose up to depict and expose the brutal world of conquering capitalism. Thus began the modern English realistic novel.

Daniel Defoe (1661-1731) was one of the forerunners of the

English realistic novelists. His masterpiece, *Robinson Crusoe*, tells of how Robinson Crusoe, a mariner, having shipwrecked on an island, managed to survive with his hard labor, rescued a black man, whom he named Friday, from the cannibals, and finally sailed home. Robinson Crusoe was typical of the English bourgeoisie at the earlier stages of its development. He was most practical and exact, always religious and at the same time mindful of his own profit. His voyage is connected with some commercial enterprise.

Jonathan Swift (1667-1745) was the most powerful satirist of his age. His immortal work *Gulliver's Travels* gave an unparalleled satirical depiction of the vices of his age by creating the images of man like creatures, the Yahoos. In many of his other famous works such as *A Tale of a Tub*, *The Battle of the Books*, and his pamphlets on Ireland, among which are the famous *The Drapier's Letters* and *A Modest Proposal*, Swift addressed himself to the common people and drew ruthless pictures of the depraved aristocracy with bitter irony.

Henry Fielding (1707-1754) was the founder of the English realistic novel. He set up the theory of realism in literary creation. The basis of his work was "nature herself". By nature he meant the close and constant study of men and women in real life. He drew his characters from the living human nature which he observed in the people around him. The result was an assemblage of living characters in his novels. Fielding's major novels are *The History of Tom Jones, a Foundling*; *Josoph Andrews*, and *Jonathan Wild*.

5. Readings

TARTUFFE
Act Ⅳ
Scene 4. Elmire, Orgon[1]
by Moliere

ELMIRE: Pull up this table, and get under it.
ORGON: What?
ELMIRF: It's essential that you be well-hidden.
ORGON: Why there?
ELMIRE: Oh, Heavens! Just do as you are bidden.
    I have my plans, we'll soon see how they fare.
    Under the table, now; and once you're there.
    Take care that you are neither seen nor heard.
ORGON: Well, I'll indulge you, since I gave my word.
    To see you through this infantile charade.
ELMIRE: Once it is over, you'll be glad we played.
[*To her husband, who is now under the table*]
    I'm going to act quite strangely, now, and you
    Must not be shocked at anything I do.
    Whatever I may say, you must excuse
    As part of that deceit I'm forced to use.
    I shall employ sweet speeches in the task
    Of making that impostor drop his mask;
    I'll give encouragement to his bold desires,
    And furnish fuel to his amorous fires,
    Since it's for your sake, and for his destruction,
    That I shall seem to yield to his seduction,
    I'll gladly stop whenever you decide.

That all your doubts are fully satisfied.
I'll count on you, as soon as you have seen
What sort of man he is, to intervene,
And not expose me to his odious lust
One moment longer than you feel you must.
Remember: you're to save me from my plight
Whenever ... He's coming! Hush! Keep out of sight!

Scene 5. Tartuffe, Elmire, Orgon

TARTUFFE: You wish to have a word with me, I'm told.
ELMIRE: Yes, I've a little secret to unfold.
Before I speak, however, it would be wise
To close that door, and look about for spies.
[TARTUFFE *goes to the door, closes it, and returns.*]
The very last thing that must happen now
is a repetition of this moming's row[2]
I've never been so badly caught off guard.
Oh, how I feared for you! You saw how hard
I tried to make that troublesome Damis[3]
Control his dreadful temper, and hold his peace.
In my confusion, I didn't have the sense
Simply to contradict his evidence;
But as it happened, that was for the best.
And all has worked out in our interest.
This storm has only bettered your position;
My husband doesn't have the least suspicion,
And now, in mockery of those who do.
He bids me be continually with you.
And that is why, quite fearless of reproof,

I now can be alone with my Tartuffe,
And why my heart — perhaps too quick to yield —
Feels free to let its passion be revealed.

TARTUFFE: Madam, your words confuse me. Not long ago.
You spoke in quite a different style, you know.

ELMIRE: Ah, Sir, if that refusal made you smart,
It's little that you know of woman's heart,
Or what that heart is trying to convey
When it resists in such a feeble way!
Always, at first, our modesty prevents
The frank avowal of tender sentiments;
However high the passion which inflames us,
Still, to confess its power somehow shames us.
Thus we reluct, at first, yet in a tone
Which tells you that our heart is overthrown.
That what our lips deny, our pulse confesses,
And that, in time, all noes will turn to yeses,
I fear my words are all too frank and free.
And a poor proof of woman's modesty;
But since I'm started, tell me, if you will —
Would I have tried to make Damis be still
Would I have listened, calm and unoffended,
Until your lengthy offer of love was ended,
And been so very mild in my reaction,
Had your sweet words not given me satisfaction?
And when I tried to force you to undo
The marriage-plans[4] my husband has in view,
What did my urgent pleading signify
If not that I admired you, and that!
Deplored the thought that someone else might own
Part of a heart I wished for mine alone?

TARTUFFE: Madam, no happiness is so complete

As when, from lips we love, come words so sweet;
Then near floods my every sense, and drains
In honeyed rivulets through all my vein.
To please you is my joy, my only goal;
Your love is the restorer of my soul;
And yet I must beg leave, now, to confess
Some lingering doubts as to my happiness.
Might this not be a trick? Might not the catch
Be that you wish me to break off the match
With Mariane, and so have feigned to love me?
I shan't quite trust your fond opinion of me
Until the feelings you've expressed so sweetly,
Are demonstrated somewhat more concretely,
And you have shown, by certain kind concessions,
That I may put my faith in your professions

ELMIRE: [*She coughs, to warn her husband.*] Why be in such a
hurry?
Must my heart
Exhaust its bounty at the very start?
To make that sweet admission cost me dear,
But you'll not be content, it would appear,
Unless my store of favors is disbursed
To the last farthing, and at the very first.

TARTUFFE: The less we merit, the less we dare to hope,
And with our doubts, mere words can never cope.
We trust no promised bliss till we receive it;
Not till a joy is ours can we believe it.
I, who so little merit your esteem,
Can't credit this fulfillment of my dream,
And shan't believe it, Madam, until I savor
Some palpable assurance of your favor.

ELMIRE: My, how tyrannical your love can be,

And how it flusters and perplexes me!
How furiously you take one's heart in hand,
And make your every wish a fierce command!
Come, must you hound and harry me to death?
Will you not give me time to catch my breath?
Can it be right to press me with such force,
Give me no quarter, show me no remorse,
And take advantage, by your stern insistence,
Of the fond feelings which weaken my resistance?

TARTUFFE: Well, if you look with favor upon my love,
Why then, begrudge my some clear proof thereof?

ELMIRE: But how can I consent without offense
To Heaven, toward which you feel such reverence?

TARTUFFE: If Heaven is all that holds you back, don't worry.
I can remove that hindrance in a hurry.
Nothing of that short need obstruct our path.

ELMIRE: Must one not be afraid of Heaven's wrath?

TARTUFFE: Madam, forget such fears, and be my pupil,
And I shall teach you how to conquer scruple.
Some joys, it's true, are wrong in Heaven's eyes;
Yet Heaven is not averse to compromise;
There is a science, lately formulated,
Whereby one's conscience may be liberated,
And any wrongful act you care to mention
May be redeemed by purity of intention.
I'll teach you, Madam, the secrets of that science;
Meanwhile, just place on me your full reliance.
Assuage my keen desires, and feel no dread;
The sin, if any, shall be on my head.

[ELMIRE *coughs, this time more loudly.*]
You've a bad cough.

ELMIRE: Yes, yes, It's bad indeed.

TARTUFFE: [*Producing a little paper bag*]

    A bit of licorice may be what you need.

ELMIRE: No, I've stubbom cold, it seems. I'm sure it

    Will take much more than licorice to cure it.

TARTUFFE: How aggravating.

ELMIRE: Oh, more that I can say.

TARTUFFE: If you're still troubled, think of things this way:

    No one shall know our joys, save us alone,

    And there's no evil till the act is known;

    It's scandal, Madam, which makes it an offense,

    And it's no sin in confidence.

ELMIRE: [*Having coughed once more*]

    Well, clearly I must do as you require,

    And yield to your importunate desire,

    It is apparent, now, that nothing less

    Will satisfy you, and so I acquiesce.

    To go so far is much against my will;

    I'm vexed that it should come to this; but still,

    Since you are so determined on it, since you

    Will not allow mere language to convince you,

    And since you ask for concrete evidence, I

    See nothing for it, now, but to comply.

    If this is sinful, if I'm wrong to do it,

    So much the worse for him who drove me to it.

    The fault can surely not be charged to me.

TARTUFFE: Madam, the fault is mine, if fault there be,

    And ...

ELMIRE: Open the door a little, and peek out;

    I wouldn't want my husband poking about.

TARTUFFE: Why worry about the man? Each day he grows

    More gullible; one can lead him by the nose.

    To find us here would fill him with delight,

And if he saw the worst, he'd doubt his sight.

ELMIRE: Nevertheless, do step out for a minute

Into the hall, and see that no one's in it.

Scene 6. Orgon, Elmire

ORGON: [*Coming out from under the table*]

That man's a perfect monster, I must admit!

I'm simply stunned. I can't get over it.

ELMIRE: What, coming out so soon? How premature!

Get back in hiding, and wait until you're sure.

Stay till the end, and be convinced completely;

We mustn't stop till things are proved concretely.

ORGON: Hell never harbored anything so vicious!

ELMIRE: Tut, don't be hasty. Try to be judicious.

Wait, and be certain that there's no mistake.

No jumping to conclusions, for Heaven's sake!

[*She places ORGON behind her, as TARTUFFE re-enters.*]

Scene 7. Tartuffe, Elmire, Orgon

TARTUFFE: [*Not seeing* ORGON]

Madam, all things have worked out to perfection;

I've given the neighboring rooms a full inspection;

No one's about; and now I may at last . . .

ORGON: [*Intercepting him*] Hold on, my passionate fellow, not so fast!

I should advise a little more restraint.

Well, so you thought you'd fool me, my dear saint!

How soon you wearied of the saintly life —
Wedding my daughter, and coveting my wife!
I've long suspected you, and had a feeling
That soon I'd catch you at your double-dealing,
Just now, you've given me evidence galore;
It's quite enough; I have no wish for more.
ELMIRE: [TO TARTUFFE] I'm sorry to have treated you so slyly,
But circumstances forced me to be wily.
TARTUFFE: Brother, you can't think . . .
ORGON: No more talk from you;
Just leave this household, without more ado.
TARTUFFE: What I intended . . .
ORGON: That seems fairly clear.
Spare me your falsehoods and get out of here.
TARTUFFE: No, I'm the master, and you're the one to go!
This house belongs to me, I'll have you know,
And I shall show you that you can't hurt me
By this contemptible conspiracy.
That those who cross me know not what they do,
And that I've means to expose and punish you,
Avenge offended Heaven, and make you grieve
That ever you dared order me to leave.

Notes

1. Elmire and Orgon are husband and wife. In this scene and the following,
   Elmire is trying to lead her husband to the truth that Tarufffe, the imposter, has indeed paid court to her, as Orgon's son, Damis, reports. She has
   Tarufffe come into her room and pretends to be in love with him within the
   sight of her husband, who is hidden under the table. Tartuffe is carried a-
   way by Elmire's sweet words and his real vicious nature is exposed to Orgon.

2. this morning's row: refers to Damis' report to his father that Tartuffe has-wooed his stepmother. Orgon, cheated by Tartuffe's superficial sincerity, does not believe Damis. In fury, he disinherits his son and endows all his property to Tartuffe.

3. the marriage-plans: Orgon's plan to marry his daughter Marine to Tartuffe.

VOLPONE[1]
Act I Scene I
Volpone, Mosca
by Ben Johnson

Vol: Good moming to the day; and, next, my gold:
    Open the shrine,[2] that I may see my saint.
    Hail the world's soul, and mine. More glad than is
    The teeming earth[3] to see the longed-for sun
    Peep through the horns of the celestial ram,
    Am I, to view thy splendor, darkening his.

Act I. Scene IV.

. . .

Mosca, Corbaccio, Volpone.
(Another knocks)
Vol: Who's that, there, now? a third?
MOS: Close,[4] to your couch again. I hear his voice.
    It is Corvine, our spruce[5] Merchant.
Vol: Dead.[6]
Mos: Another bout, sir, with your eyes.[7] Who's there?

. . .

Act I. Scene V.

Mosca, Corvino, Volpone.

MOS : Signior Corvino! Come most wish for! O, How happy were
    you, if you knew it, new!

CORV: Why? What? Wherein?

MOS: The tardy hour is come, sir.

CORV: He is not dead?

MOS: Not dead, sir, but as good;

    He knows no man.

CORV: How shall I do, then?

MOS: Why, sir?

CORV: I have brought him, here, a pearl.

MOS: Perhaps, he has

    So much remembrance left, as to know you, sir;

    He still calls on you, nothing but your name
    Is in his mouth: is your pearl orient,[8] sir?

CORV: Venice was never owner of the like.

VOLP: Signior Corvino.

MOS: Hark.[9]

VOLP: Signior Corvino.

MOS: He calls you, step and give it him. He's here, sir, And he
    has brought you a rich pearl.

CORV: How do you, sir?

    Tell him, it doubles the twelve carats.[10]

MOS: Sir,

    He cannot understand, his hearing's gone;
    And yet it comforts him, to see you —

CORV: Say,

    I have a diamond for him, too.

MOS: Best shew't, sir,

    Put it into his hand; 'tis only there

    He apprehends: he has his feeling, yet.

    See, how he grasps it!

CORV: "Lass, good gentleman!

    How pitiful the sight is!

MOS: Tut, forget, sir.

    The weeping of an heir should still be laughter,

    Uneer a visor, [11]

CORV: Why? Am I his heir?

MOS: Sir, I am sworn, I may not shew the will,

    Till he be dead: but, here has been Corbaccio,

    Here has been Voltore, here were others too,

    I cannot number 'em, they were so many,

    All gaping here for legacies; but I,

    Taking the vantage of his naming you,

    (Signior Corvino, Signior Corvino) take

    Paper, and pen, and ink, and there I asked him,

    Whom he would have his heir? Corvino. Who

    Should be executor? Corvino, And,

    To any question, he was silent too,

    I still interpreted the nods, he made

    (through weakness) for consent: and sent home the others,

    Nothing bequeathed them, but to cry, and curse.

                               (*They embrace*)

CORV: O, my dear Mosca. Do's he not perceive us?

MOS: No more than a blind harper. He knows no men,

    No face of friend, nor name of any servant,

    Who't was that fed him last, or gave him drink:

    Not those, he hath begotten or brought up

Can he remember.

CORV: Has he children?

MOS: Bastards,

　Some dozen, or more, that he begot on beggars,

　Gipseys, and Jews, and black-moors, when he was drunk.

　Knew you not that, sir? 'Tis the common fable, [12]

　The Dwarf, the Fool, the Eunuch are all his;

　He is the true father of his family,

　In all, save me. but he has given "them" nothing.

CORV: That's well, that's well. Art sure he does not hear us?

MOS: Sure, sir? Why, look you, credit your own sense. [13]

　The pox approach, and add to your diseases,

　If it would send you hence the sooner, sir.

　For, your incontinence, it hath deserved it

　Thoroughly, and thoroughly, and the plague to boot. [14]

　(You may come near, sir) would you once close

　Those filthy eyes of yours, that flow with slime, [15]

　Like two frog-pits; and those same hanging cheeks,

　Covered with hide, instead of skin: (nay, help, sir) [16]

　That look like frozen dish-clouts, set on end. [17]

CORV: Or, like an old smoked wall, on which the rain ran down in

　streaks.

MOS: Excellent, sir, speak out;

　You may be louder yet; a culvering, [18]

　Discharged in his ear, would hardly bore it. [19]

CORV: His nose is like a common sewer, still running.

MOS: "Tis good!" And what his mouth?

CORV: A very draught.

Mos: O, stop it up-

CORV: By no means.

MOS: Pray you let me.

　Faith, I could stifle him, rarely, with a pillow,

As well as any women, that should keep[20] him.

CORV: Do as you will, but I'll be gone.

MOS: Be so;

It is your presence makes him last so long.

CORV: I pray you, use no violence.

MOS: No, sir? Why?

Why should you be thus scrupulous? Pray you, sir.

CORV: Nay, at your discretion.

MOS: Well, good sir, be gone.

CORV: I will not trouble him now, to take my pearl?

MOS: Pub, nor your diamond. What a needless care

Is this afflicts you? Is not all, here, yours?

Am not I here whom you have made your creature

That owe my being to you?

CORV: Grateful Mosca!

Thou art my friend, my fellow, my companion,

My partner, and shalt share in all my fortunes.

MOS: Excepting one.

CORV: What's that?

MOS: Your gallant[21] wife, sir.

Now is he gone: we had no other means,

To shoot him hence, but this.

VOLP: My divine Mosea!

Thou hast today outgone thyself.

(*Another knocks*)

Who's there

I will be troubled with no more. Prepare

Me music, dances, banquets, all delights;

The Turk[22] is not more sensual, in his pleasures,

Than will Volpone. Let me see, a pearl?

A diamond? Plate? Cecchines? Good morning's purchase;[23]

Why, this is better than rob churches, yet.

Or fat, by eating (once a month) a man.

Notes

1. One of the best known comedies of Ben Johnson, the most renowned British playwright after Shakespeare. Written in the rule of the three unifies, the play is a satire on the avarice of the bourgeoisie. Volpone is a miser, greedy of money for its own sake. To increase his wealth, he plays upon the avarice of men. He pretends to be at the point of death. This attracts a number of men who try to be his heirs by giving him rich presents, as he has no children. But to the disappointment of all, Volpone draws up a will in which he bequeaths all his property to his servant Mosca. Mosca, also a cunning fellow, makes advantages of the will and proclaims his master dead. As a heir, he claims possession of Volpone's property. At last, both are revealed and sent to prison.

2. cabinet for keeping his gold.

3. full of living things.

4. Keep still.

5. well-dressed

6. Tell him I'm dead.

7. It is the religious ritual to apply grease to the dying person's eyelids.

8. pure and bright.

9. listen.

10. weight unit of diamond.

11. cover.

12. talk.

13. Believe your own eyes.

14. Besides, may plague fall upon him.

15. sticky substance.

16. Join me in cursing.

17. dish-cloth standing upright down.

18. Culverin.

19. He could hardly hear the report of a culverin.
20. be in love with.
21. excellent.
22. kind of people who like enjoying themselves.
23. business.

AN ESSAY ON CRITICISM[1]

II

by Alexander Pope

. . .

A little learning is a dangerous thing;
Drink deep, or taste not the Pierian spring[2]:
There shallow draughts[3] intoxicate the brain,
And drinking largely sobers us again.
Fired at first sight with what the Muse imparts,
In fearless youth we tempt the heights of Arts,
While from the bounded level of our mind
Short views we take, nor see the lengths behind;
But more advanced behold with strange surprise
New distant scenes of endless science rise!
So pleased at first the towering Alps we try
Mount over the vales, and seem to tread the sky,
The eternal snows appear already past,
And the first clouds and mountains seem the last;
But, those attained, we tremble to survey
The growing labours of the lengthened way,
The increasing prospect tires our wandering, eyes.
Hills peep over hills, and Alps on Alps Arise.

Notes

1. Written in the classical heroic couplet, the poem contains three parts. Part One praises the ancients and lists out the rules of the ancients for literary guidance. Part Two explains the dangers that may beset the critics and lead them to faulty criticism. Part Three provides the rules that are to be adopted by critics.
2. On Mount Helicon. In Greek Mythology, people who drink the water in it can get inspiration.
3. amount of water drunk.

Considerations

What problems of literary criticism does Pope point out here? How can these problems be avoided?

Chapter V   Romanticism

1. The Rise of Romanticism

Romanticism was a literary movement which developed in the late 18th and early 19th century. Its emergence was closely connected with the French Revolution, the European national liberation movement, and the Industrial Revolution.

In the late 18th and early 19th century, the political and economic situations went through great changes. In 1789 broke out the French Revolution which made a stir in the Western countries. It destroyed the absolute rule of feudalism and established the bourgeois democracy with its slogans of liberty, equality and fraternity. Individualism prevailed. Writers sought to express man's inner feelings freely. Inspired by the French Revolution, the national liberation movement swept over Europe and called for the national literature in their wake.

With the development of the national liberation movement, some advanced bourgeois countries such as England underwent the Industrial Revolution, which brought unforeseen changes to each individual and society as a whole. Man's thinking was fundamentally affected. New economic ideas were put forward by Adam Smith (1723-1790) in his book *The Wealth and Nations* (1776), which laid the theoretical ground work for capitalism. Capitalist industrialization, however, brought sufferings and poverty instead of wealth to the working class. As a protest against the Industrial Revolution, writers looked to the Middle Ages and to direct contact with nature, wanting to return to the simpler life of the past and to consolation in nature.

Besides the social forces, the German classical philosophy and the Utopian socialism played a part in the rise of Romanticism. The German classical philosophy was romantic in nature. Its representatives — Immauuel Kand (1724-1804) and Friedrich Hegel (1770-1831) — were idealists. They stressed the subjective, the personal, and even the supernatural aspects of human endeavor, putting individualism above everything else, and thus exerted great influence on Romanticism. The Utopian socialists like Robert Owen (1771-1858) in England, Saint Simen (1760-1825) and Charles Fourier (1772-1837) in France had also influenced Romanticism in that they criticized capitalism, dreamed of its destruction, and indulged in fancies of a better social order in the future.

Romanticism spread in America at the beginning of the 19th century, and developed into Transcendentalism in the 1830s.

2. The Features of Romanticism

Romanticism was pluralistic. It had varied manifestations with different cultures and intellects. However, as a movement rising against the same social background and based on the same ideas and philosophy, it had certain general characteristics.

1) Romanticists were discontented with and opposed to the development of capitalism. They tried to idealize the life of a non-capitalist society and thus laid emphasis on subjective idealism

and emotional expression. They held that emotion and imagination were superior to formal rules and reason, and advocated freedom and individualism in literary creation. But because of their difference in political attitudes Romanticists split into two trends, the passive and the active, which differed from each other in expressing their emotions and finding their ideals. The passive romantic writers reflected the thinking of the classes ruined by the bourgeoisie, and by way of protest against capitalist development returned to the past as their ideal. The active romantic writers expressed the democratic aspirations of the middle and petty bourgeois classes having emerged in the national liberation struggle, and dreamed of an ideal society in the future, free from oppression and exploitation.

2) Romanticists had a persistent interest in the medieval literature, such as epics, ballads, and other forms of folk literature, which were not restricted by various kinds of classical rules, and were characterized by rich imagination, strong emotion, free expression, and common language.

3) Romanticists showed a profound admiration and love for nature. To them, man's societies were a source of corruption while the world of nature was a source of goodness. In their works, the beauty and perfection of nature were in sharp contrast with the corrupt and polluted urban civilization.

4) Romanticists were full of moral enthusiasm, believing ideality and elevation was a reality that was more lofty and realistic than the evidence of the substantial thing.

5) Romanticists took interest in the strange, the mysterious, and the supernatural as opposed to common sense.

3. The Representatives of Romanticism

Literature took the full force of Romanticism, which brought forth a full flowering of literary talents. The leading romantic figures were Blake, Wordsworth, Coleridge, Scott, Byron, Shelly, and Keats in England; Hugo and Sand in France; Geothe, Schiller, and Heine in Germany; Irving, Cooper, Poe, Whitman, Dickinson, Emerson, Thoreau, Hawthorne, and Melville in America.

Jean-Jacques Rousseau (1712-1778), born on June 28, 1712 in Geneva, Switzerland, was one of the most influential thinkers during the Enlightenment in the 18th century Europe. His first major philosophical work, *A Discourse on the Sciences and Arts*, was the winning response to an essay contest conducted by the Academy of Dijon in 1750. In this work, Rousseau argues that the progression of the sciences and arts has caused the corruption of virtue and morality. This discourse won Rousseau fame and recognition, and it laid much of the philosophical groundwork for a second, longer work, *The Discourse on the Origin of Inequality*. The second discourse did not win the Academy's prize, but like the first, it was widely read and further solidified Rousseau's place as a significant intellectual figure. The central claim of the work is that human beings are basically good by nature, but were corrupted by the complex historical events that resulted in present day civil society. Rousseau's praise of nature is a theme that continues throughout his later works as well, the most significant of which include his comprehensive work on the philosophy of education, the *Emile*, and his major work on political philosophy, *The Social Contract*: both published in 1762. These works caused great controversy in France and were immediately banned by Paris authorities. Rousseau fled France and settled in Switzerland, but he continued to find difficulties with authorities and quarrel with friends. The end of Rousseau's life was marked in large part by his growing paranoia and his continued attempts to justify his life and his work. This is especially evident in his later books, *The Confessions*, *The Reveries of the Solitary Walker*, and *Rousseau: Judge of Jean-Jacques*.

George Sand (1804-1876), pseudonym of Amandine-Aurore-Lucile Dupin, was French Romantic writer. In her novels Sand questioned the sexual identity and gender destinies in fiction. Sand herself was accused of lesbianism and nymphomania. In her mid-life autobiography, *Histoire de mavie* (1854-1855, *Story of My Life*), Sand displaces conventional distinctions separating male from female, fact from fiction, and public from private life. "Life in common among people who love each other is the ideal of happiness. " Among Sand's best works are her countryside novels *La Mare au diable* (1846), in which Germain, a young widower, must choose between a rich woman and a poor girl, *Franois le champi* (1847-1848, *Francis the Waif*), *La Petite Fadette* (1849, *Fanchon the Cricket*), and *Les Matres sonneurs* (1853, *the master bell-ringers*). She also wrote memoirs, short stories, essays and fairy tales. All Sand's books are distinguished by a romantic love of nature as well as an extravagant moral idealism.

Wolfgang von Goethe (1749-1832) was the greatest of all German poets. Yet he was a versatile writer. In addition to poetry, he wrote novels and plays. His masterpieces are his novel *The*

Sorrows of Young Werther and his tragedy in verse *Faust*. The former played an enormous role in the spread of Romantic sentiment among the young people, with its suicidal end of the youth Werther, who aspired for love, freedom, and equality in a corrupt society full of inequality and prejudice. The later portrayed the tragedy of Doctor Faust, who sacrificed his life to the devil to satisfy his insatiable thirst for knowledge.

Friedrich von Schiller (1759-1805) was one of the greatest German dramatists and poets. His best play *Cabal and Love* is about a young aristocrat's love with a girl of humble background conveying the theme of the revolt of humble feeling against the social convention of feudalism.

Heinrich Heine (1797-1856) was the German democratic poet. He was most famous as a lyric poet. Many of his lyrics adopt simple diction and metrical patterns taken from traditional ballads. They do not announce grandly important themes, and they work largely by the power of suggestion. Frequently they reiterate the characteristic Romantic desire for an unattainable and convey the high importance of the emotional life. Heine also wrote drama, narrative poetry, political commentary, and literary criticism. His best-known narrative poem is "Germany — a Winter's Tale", in which the poet compares the corrupt feudal system of Germany to winter, approaching its doom.

Victor Hugo (1802-1885) was an ardent Romantic. He wrote in the preface of his play *Cromwell* a veritable manifesto of romantic drama. Hugo is best known for his novels *Notre Dame de Paris* and *Les Miserables*. *Les Miserables* is about the life story of a man named Jean Valiean. Jean stole a loaf of bread to feed his starving sister and was sentenced to 19 years' imprisonment for the minor theft. Finally released, he tried to live a decent life. Under the disguise of a false name, he became a well-to-do businessman, and then was elected Mayor. His past revealed, he was sent to prison again. He managed to escape from prison, helped a helpless poor girl of a prostitute out of a knave, and ran to Paris. Later, he was constantly chased by the police. Through the description of the miserable life of Jean, Hugo exposed the evils of the bourgeoisie world which was characterized by the extremes of poverty and wealth.

William Blake (1757-1827) was an engraver by trade. He wrote the most original kind of poetry in the simplest language in his two early collections: *Songs of Innocence* and *Songs of Experience*. The two collections marked a progress in the poet's outlook on life. In *Songs of Innocence*, Blake depicted the happy condition of a child before he knows anything about the pains of existence. In *Songs of Experience*, the poet drew pictures of poverty and distress, and showed the sufferings of the miserable. For the poet, the first glimpse of the world was a picture of light, harmony, peace, and love, while experience of the later years brought a fuller sense of the evil, the great misery of the common people.

William Wordsworth (1770-1850) and **Samuel Coleridge** (1772-1834) were the English "lake poets", both of whom began as radicals and ended up as conservatives. In 1789, they jointly published a volume of poetry under the title *Lyrical Ballads*, which marked the break with classicism and the beginning of the Romantic revival in England. In the preface of the book, Wordsworh set forth the principle of poetry — "poetry is the spontaneous overflow of powerful feelings … recollected in tranquility" Coleridge's contribution to the collection was his masterpiece *The Rime of the Ancient Mariner*, which tells the story of the experience of an old sailor on the sea, introducing the reader to a supernatural realm. Coleridge represented the mysterious and exotic side of Romanticism. Coleridge was also a critic, in fact, the first critic of the Romantic school.

George Gorden Byron (1788-1824) was a staunch champion of the people's cause. His poetry expressed an ardent love of liberty and a fierce hatred of tyranny. His masterpiece is *Don Juan*, a long satirical epic. The hero, Don Juan, is a Spanish youth of noble birth. Through the vicissitudes of his life and his adventures in many countries, the poet presented a broad panorama of his contemporary life. His another famous poem is *Childe Harold Pilgrimage*, in which emerged the Byronic hero, a proud, solitary, stubborn, but brilliant rebel against his high society.

Percy Bysshe Shelley (1792-1827) was the greatest revolutionary and lyrical British poet. His revolutionary romantic masterpiece is *Prometheus Unbound*, a lyrical drama. The story was borrowed from Greek myth. Prometheus stole fire from heaven and taught man how to use it. For this he was punished by Zeus, the supreme god, who chained him to a rock on Mt. Caucasus, where during the daytime a vulture fed on his liver, which was restored each succeeding night. Despite the great pains he had to suffer each day, Prometheus, the symbol of those noble-hearted revolutionaries, refused to yield to Zeus, the symbol of the reactionary tyrant. Finally, Zeus, overthrown by the huge spirit Demogorgon, the symbol of change and revolution, toppled from his throne and sank into the eternal abyss with cowardly wails. Prometheus was set free by Hercules, the most valiant hero in Geek Mythology. Prometheus' triumph symbolized the victory of mankind over tyranny and oppression, and the regeneration of humanity. Shelley's other poems include *Queen Mab*, *The Revolt of Islam* and his well-known lyric "Ode to the West Wind".

John Keats (1795-1821) died young, when he was only 26. He wrote some of the most beautiful odes in the English language, such as *Ode on Melancholy*, *Ode to A Nightingale*, *Ode on a Grecian Urn*, *Ode to Autumn*. All of these odes were intended to create a beautiful world of imagination as opposed to the sordid reality of his day. Keats was also famous for his sonnets, which, like his odes, had the eulogy of beauty as their themes, for Keats' leading principle is "Beauty is truth, truth beauty. "

Washington Irving (1783-1859) was the first American writer to gain international fame. His best known work is *The Sketch Book*, a collection of short stories, which initiated the short story as a genre in American literature and marked the beginning of American romanticism with such romantic subjects as the Gothic, the supernatural, and the longing for the good old days. Today Irving was mainly remembered as the author of *Rip Van Winkle* and *The Legend of Sleepy Hollow*. The former is a fantasy tale about a man who somehow stepped outside the main stream of life, and the latter is about an unsuccessful love affair. Both stories shared legendary elements, which revealed, to some extent, the conservative attitude of the author toward the American Rev-

西方文学

125

olution and his nostalgia for the life before the Revolution.

James Fenimore Cooper (1789-1851) was the first distinguished American novel writer. His fame rests on his frontier stories, especially the *Leather Stocking Tales*, which was made up of five novels — *The Deerslayer*, *The Last of the Mohicans*, *The Pathfinder*, *The Pioneers* and *The Prairie*. The five novels depicted the frontier life of American early settlers and created a myth about the formative period of the Americanization.

Walt Whitman (1819-1892) held a unique position in the history of American literature. He was a great innovator who has had great influence on modern American writers like Eliot, Pound, and Sandburg. His collections of poems under the title of *Leaves of Grass* broke free of the conventional iambic pentametre and exhibited a freedom in form unknown before — the free verse. In content, it extoled the ideals of equality and democracy and celebrated the dignity, the self-reliant spirit and the joy of the common man.

Emily Dickinson (1830-1886) was a chief American poet, as great as Whitman in the late 19th century. This recluse woman poet was wholly original. She took stuffs of his poetry merely from her personal experience and wrote poems of death, love, and nature, which are characterized by abundant use of dashes, irregular punctuation and capitalization, clear-cut imagery, precise diction, and fragmentary and enigmatic metrical pattern.

Edgar Allan Poe (1809-1849) was a great poet, a great writer of fiction, and the first important American literary critic. Poe's most noted critical works include "Philosophy of Composition" and "The Poetic Principle", in which he formulated his theories for the short story and poetry. In Poe's opinion, the short story should be short, direct, precise, giving the reader an impression of totality and finality; poetry should be the rhythmical creation of beauty; the highest development of beauty should be melancholy which could be best achieved by the death of a beautiful woman. These theories were best exemplified in his best-known short story *The Fall of the House of Usher*. The poem is about the melancholy experience of a bereaved lover, and the story deals with the disintegration of the soul in a world of nothingness, Poe's frequent theme.

Ralph Waldo Emerson (1803-1883) and **Henry David Thoreau** (1817-1862) were the greatest prose writers of New England Transcendentalism. They were also great poets. Emerson's *Nature* and Thoreau's *Walden* are representative works of Transcendentalism, exemplifying the Transcendentalist doctrines: the omnipresent and omnipotent Oversoul, the importance of the individual, and the symbolic significance of nature.

Nathanial Hawthorne (1804-1864) and **Herman Melville** (1819-1891) were two great American novelists of the mid-19th century. They were good friends and represented the position of tragic humanism of their time. They both took a negative attitude towards the world. To Hawthorne, evil existed in everyone. He mainly concerned his works with evil and sin, and their moral and psychological effect on human soul. His masterpiece *The Scarlet Letter* was about the sin of adultery and its effect on different people involved. To Melville, the world was godless and purposeless, where man lived a meaningless and futile life. His works were mainly concerned with man's alienation and man's quest for the meaning of life. His greatest work *Moby Dick gave a detailed account of the operations of whaling industry* and expressed the tragedy of man fighting against overwhelming odds in an indifferent and even hostile universe.

4. Readings

ODE TO THE WEST WIND[1]
by Percy Bysshe Shelley

I

O wild West Wind, thou breath of Autumn's being,
Thou, from whose unseen presence the leaves dead
Are driven, like ghosts from an enchanter fleeing,

Yellow, and black, and pale, and hectic red,[2]
Pestilence stricken multitudes[3] O thou,
Who chariotest to their dark wintry bed

The winged seeds[4], where they lie cold and low,
Each like a corpse within its grave, until
Thine azure sister of the Spring[5] shall blow

Her clarion[6] o'er the dreaming earth, and fill
(Driving sweet buds like flocks to feed in air)
With living hues and odours plain and hill:

Wild Spirit, which are moving everywhere;
Destroyer and preserver, hear, oh, hear!

II

Thou on whose stream, mid the steep sky's commotion,

Loose clouds like earth's decaying leaves are shed,
Shook from the tangled boughs of Heaven and Ocean,[7]

Angels of rain and lightning: there are spread
On the blue surface of thine aery surge,
Like the bright hair uplifted from the head

Of some fierce Maenad,[8] even from the dim verge
Of the horizon to the zenith's height,
The locks[9] of the approaching storm. Thou dirge
That's such a jig; as if I would go feel it,

Of the dying year, to which this closing night
Will be the dome of a vast sepulchre,
Vaulted with all thy congregated night

Of vapours, from whose solid atmosphere
Black rain, and fire, and hail will burst: oh, hear!

III

Thou who didst waken from his summer dreams
The blue Mediterranean, where he lay,
Lulled by the coil of his crystalline streams,[10]

Beside a pumice isle in Baiae's bay,[11]
And saw in sleep old palaces and towers
Quivering within the wave's intenser day,[12]

All overgrown with azure moss and flowers
So sweet, the sense faints picturing them! Thou
For whose path the Atlantic's level powers

Cleave themselves into chasms, while far below
The sea-blooms and the oozy woods which wear
The sapless foliage of the ocean, know

Thy voice, and suddenly grow grey with fear,
And tremble and despoil themselves: oh, hear!

IV

if I were a dead leaf thou mightiest bear,
If I were a swift cloud to fly with thee;
A wave to paint beneath thy power, and share

The impulse of thy strength, only less free
Than thou, O uncontrollable If even
I were as in my boyhood, and could be

The comrade of thy wandering over Heaven,
As then, when to outstrip thy skiey speed
Scarce seemed a vision; I would ne'er have striven

As thus with thee in prayer in my sore need.
Oh, lift me as a wave, a leaf, a cloud!
I fall upon the thorns of life! I bleed!

A heavy weight of hours has chained and bowed
One too like thee: tameless, and swift, and proud.

V

Make me thy lyre even as the forest is:
What if my leaves are falling like its own!
The tumult of thy mighty harmonies

Will take from both a deep, autumnal tone,
Sweet though in sadness. Be thou, Spirit fierce,
My spirit! Be thou me, impetuous one!

Drive my dead thoughts over the universe

Like withered leaves to quicken a new birth!
And, by the incantation of this verse,

Scatter, as from an unextinguished hearth
Ashes and sparks, my words among mankind!
Be through my lips to unawakened earth
The trumpet of a prophecy![13] O, Wind.
If Winter comes, can Spring be far behind?

Notes

1. Shelly's best Lyric on nature. Here the west wind is a symbol of spirit, which on earth, sky, and sea destroys in the autumn in order to revive in the Spring. Around this central image, the poet expressed his love of, and aspiration for union with, nature, which suggests the poet's eager longing for some thing free from the squalor of real life.

2. The kind of fever which occurs in tuberculosis.

3. A Large number of dead leaves stricken by plague

4. Seeds seem to have wings because of the blowing of the wind.

5. The west wind that will blow in the spring.

6. A high, shrill trumpet.

7. The fragmentary clouds are torn by the wind from the larger and higher clouds, which are formed by a union of air with vapor drawn up by the sun from the ocean.

8. The Greek god of wine and vegetation, who was fabled to die in the fall and to be resurrected in the spring.

9. The fragmentary clouds.

10. The sounds of the currents that flow in the Mediterranean sea.

11. It is west of Naples, the locale of imposing villas erected by Roman emperors.

12. Sun reflected in waves is intense than the sun in the day.

13. A reference to the "clarion" of line 10.

Considerations

What words and patterns are repeated in the different stanzas? How do the rhymes and repeated stanza patterns contribute to the tone and the meaning of the poem? In what sense is the poem revolutionary or cyclical?

THE MINISTER'S BLACK VEIL
by Nathanial Howthorne

The sexton stood in the porch of Milford meeting-house, pulling lustily at bellrope. The old people of the village came stooping along the street. Children, with bright faces, tript merrily beside their parents, or mimicked a graver gait, in the conscious dignity of their Sunday clothes. Spruce bachelors looked sidelong at pretty maidens and fancied that the Sabbath sunshine made them prettier than on week-days. When the throng had mostly streamed into the porch, the sexton began to toll the bell, keeping his eyes on the Reverend Mr. Hooper's door. The first glimpse of the clergyman's figure was the signal for the bell to cease its summons.

"But what has good Parson Hooper got upon his face" cried the sexton in astonishment.

All within hearing immediately turned about, and beheld the semblance of Mr. Hooper, pacing slowly his meditative way towards the meeting-house. With one accord they started expressing more wonder than if some strange minister were coming to dust the cushions of Mr. Hooper's pulpit.

"Are you sure it is our parson?" inquired Goodman Gray[1] of the sexton.

"Of a certainty it is good Mr. Hooper", replied the sexton. "He was to have exchanged pulpits with Parson Shuts of Westbury;

but Parson Shute sent to excuse himself yesterday, being to preach a funeral sermon."

The cause of so much amazement may appear sufficiently slight. Mr. Hooper, a gentlemanly person of about thirty, though still a bachelor, was dressed with due clerical neatness, as if a careful wife had starched his band[2], and brushed the weekly dust from his Sunday's garb. There was but one thing remarkable in his appearance. Swathed about his forehead, and hanging down over his face, so low as to be shaken by his breath, Mr. Hooper had on a black veil. On a nearer view, it seemed to consist of two folds of crape, which entirely concealed his features, except the mouth and chin, but probably did not intercept his sight farther than to give a darkened aspect to all living and inanimate things, With this gloomy shade before him, good Mr. Hooper walked onward, at a slow and quiet pace, stooping somewhat and looking on the ground, as is customary with abstracted men, yet nodding kindly to those of his parishioners who still waited on the meeting-house steps, But so wonder struck were they, that his greeting hardly met with a return.

"I can't really feel as if good Mr. Hooper's face was behind that piece of crape," said the sexton.

"I don't like it", muttered an old woman, as she hobbled into the meeting-house. "He has changed himself into something awful, only by hiding his face. "

"Our parson has gone mad!" cried Goodman Gray, following him across the threshold.

A rumor of some unaccountable phenomenon had preceded Mr. Hooper into the meeting-house, and set all the congregation a-stir. Few could refrain from twisting their heads towards the door; many stood upright, and turned directly about; while several little boys clambered upon the seats, and came down again with a terrible racket. There was a general bustle, a rustling of the women's

gowns and shuffling of the men's feet, greatly at variance with that
hushed repose which should attend the entrance of the minister.
But Mr. Hooper appeared not to notice the perturbation of his people. He entered with an almost noiseless step, bent his head mildly
to the pews on each side, and bowed as he passed his oldest parishioner, a white-haired great-grandsire, who occupied an arm-
chair in the center of the aisle. It was strange to observe, how
slowly this venerable man became conscious of something singular
in the appearance of his pastor. He seemed not fully to partake of
the prevailing wonder, till Mr. Hooper had ascended the stairs,
and showed himself in the pulpit, face to face with his congregation, except for the black veil. That mysterious emblem was never
once withdrawn. It shook with his measured breath as he gave out
the psalm; it threw its obscurity between him and the holy page,
as he read the Scriptures,[3] and while he prayed, the veil lay heavily on his uplifted countenance. Did he seek to hide it from the
dread Being[4] whom he was addressing?

Such was the effect of this simple piece of crape, that more
than one woman of delicate nerves was forced to leave the meeting-house. Yet perhaps the pale-faced congregation was almost as
fearful a sight to the minister, as his black veil to them.

Mr. Hooper had the reputation of a good preacher, but not an
energetic one: he strove to win his people heavenward, by mild
persuasive influences, rather than to drive them thither, by the
thunders of the word.[5] The sermon which he now delivered was
marked by the same characteristics of style and manner as the
general series of his pulpit oratory. But there was something, either in the sentiment of the discourse itself, or in the imagination of
the auditors, which made it greatly the most powerful effort that
they had ever heard from their pastor's lips. It was tinged, rather
more darkly than usual, with the gentle gloom of Mr. Hooper's
temperament. The subject had reference to secret sin, and those

sad mysteries which we hide from our nearest and dearest, and would fain conceal from our own consciousness, even forgetting that the omniscient⁶ can detect them. A subtle power was breathed into his words. Each member of the congregation, the most innocent girl, and the man of hardened breast, felt as if the preacher had crept upon them, behind his awful veil, and discovered their hoarded iniquity of deed or thought. Many spread their clasped hands on their bosoms. There was nothing terrible in what Mr. Hooper said; at least, no violence; and yet, with every tremor of his melancholy voice, the hearers quaked. An unsought pathos came hand in hand with awe. So sensible were the audience of some unwonted attribute in their minister, that they longed for a breath of wind to blow aside the veil, almost believing that a stranger's visage would be discovered, though the form, gesture, and voice were those of Mr. Hooper.

At the close of the services, the people hurried out with indecorous confusion, eager to communicate their pent-up amazement, and conscious of lighter spirits, the moment they lost sight of the black veil. Some gathered in little circles, huddled closely together, with their mouths all whispering in the center; some went homeward alone, wrapt in silent meditation; some talked loudly, and profaned the Sabbath-day with ostentatious laughter. A few shook their sagacious heads, intimating that they could penetrate the mystery; while one or two affirmed that there was no mystery at all, but only that Mr. Hooper's eyes were so weakened by the midnight lamp, as to require a shade. After a brief interval, forth came good Mr. Hooper also, in the rear of his flock. Turning his veiled face from one group to another, he paid due reverence to the hoary heads, saluted the middle-aged with kind dignity, as their friend and spiritual guide, greeted the young with mingled authority and love, and laid his hands on the little children's heads to bless them. Such was always his custom on the Sabbath-day.

西方文学

Strange and bewildered looks repaid him for his courtesy. None,
as on former occasions, aspired to the honor of walking by their
pastor's side. Old Squire Saunders, doubtless by an accidental
lapse of memory, neglected to invite Mr. Hooper to his tale,
where the good clergyman had been wont to bless the food, almost
every Sunday since his settlement.[7] He returned, therefore, to the
parsonage, and, at the moment of closing the door, was observed
to look back upon the people, all of whom had their eyes fixed upon the minister. A sad smile gleamed faintly from beneath the
black veil, and flickered about this mouth, glimmering as he disappeared.

"How strange,"said a lady, "that a simple black veil, such as
any woman might wear on her bonnet, should become such a terrible thing on Mr. Hooper's face!"

"Something must surely be amiss with Mr. Hooper's intellects," observed her husband, the physician of the village. "But
the strangest part of the affair is the effect of this vagary,even on a
sober-minded man like myself. The black veil, though it covers only our pastor's face, throws its influence over his whole person,
and makes him ghost-like from head to foot. Do you not feel it so?"

"Truly do I", replied the lady. "and I would not be alone with
him for the world.[8] I wonder he is not afraid to be alone with himself!"

'Men sometimes are so,' said her husband.

The afternoon service was attended with similar circumstances. At its conclusion, the bell tolled for the funeral of a young
lady. The relatives and friends were assembled in the house, and
the more distant acquaintances stood about the door, speaking of
the good qualities of the deceased, when their talk was interrupted
by the appearance of Mr. Hooper, still covered with his black
veil. it was now an appropriate emblem. The clergyman stepped
into the room where the corpse was laid, and bent over the coffin,

to take a last farewell of his deceased parishioner. As he stooped,
the veil hung straight down from his forehead, so that, if her eyelids had not been closed for ever, the dead maiden might have
seen his face. Could Mr. Hooper be fearful of her glance, that he
so hastily caught back the black veil? A person, who watched the
interview between the dead and living, scrupled not to affirm,
that, at the instant when the clergyman's features were disclosed,
the corpse had slightly shuddered, rustling the shroud and muslin-
cap, though the countenance retained the composure of death. A
superstitious old woman was the only witness of this prodigy. From
the coffin, Mr. Hooper passed into the chambers of the mourners,
and thence to the head of the staircase, to make the funeral prayer. It was a tender and heart-dissolving prayer, full of sorrow, yet
so imbued with celestial hopes, that the music of a heavenly harp,
swept by the fingers of the dead, seemed faintly to be heard a-
mong the saddest accents of the minister. The people trembled,
though they but darkly understood him, when he prayed that they,
and himself, and all of mortal race, might be ready, as he trusted
this young maiden had been, for the dreadful hour that should
snatch the veil from their faces. The bearers went heavily forth,
and the mourners followed, saddening all the street, with the dead
before them, and Mr. Hooper in his black veil behind.

'Why do you look back?' said one in the procession to his
partner.

'And so had I, at the same moment,' said the other.

That night, the handsomest couple in Milford Village were to
be joined in wedlock. Though reckoned a melancholy man, Mr.
Hooper had a placid cheerfulness for such occasions, which often
excited a sympathetic smile, where livelier merriment would have
been thrown away[9]. There was no quality of his disposition which
made him more beloved than this. The company at the wedding a-
waited his arrival with impatience, trusting that the strange awe,

which had gathered over him throughout the day, would now be dispelled. But such was not the result. When Mr. Hooper came, the first thing that their eyes rested on was the same horrible black veil, which had added deeper gloom to the funeral, and could portend nothing but evil to the wedding. Such was its immediate effect on the guests, that a cloud seemed to have rolled duskily from beneath the black crape, and dimmed the light of the candles. The bridal pair stood up before the minister. But the bride's cold fingers quivered in the tremulous hand of the bridegroom, and her deathlike paleness caused a whisper, that the maiden who had been buried a few hours before, was come from her grave to be married. If ever another wedding were so dismal, it was that famous one, where they tolled the wedding-kneel,[10] After performing the ceremony, Mr. Hooper raised, a glass of wine to his lips, wishing happiness to the new-married couple, in a strain of mild pleasantry that ought to have brightened the features of the guests, like a cheerful gleam from the hearth. At that instant, catching a glimpse of his figure in the looking-glass, the black veil involved his own spirit in the horror with which it overwhelmed all others. His frame shuddered — his lips grew white — he spilt the untested wine upon the carpet and rushed forth into the darkness. For the Earth, too, had on her Black Veil.

"The next day, the whole village of Milford talked of little else than Parson Hooper's black veil. That, and the mystery concealed behind it, supplied a topic for discussion between acquaintances meeting in the street, and good women gossiping at their open windows. It was the first-item of news that the taverm-keeper told to his guests. The children babbled of it on their way to school. One imitative little imp covered his face with an old black handkerchief, thereby so affrighting his playmates, that the panic seized himself, and he well nigh lost his wits by his own waggery.[11]

It was remarkable, that, of all the busy-bodies and impertinent people in the parish, not one ventured to put the plain question to Mr. Hooper, wherefore he did this thing. Hitherto, whenever there appeared the slightest call for such interference, he had never lacked advisers, or shown himself averse to be guided by their judgment. If he erred at all, it was by so painful a degree of self-distrust, that even the mildest censure would lead him to consider an indifferent[12] action as a crime. Yet, though so well acquainted with this amiable weakness, no individual among his parishioners chose to make the black veil a subject of friendly remonstrance. There was a feeling of dread, neither plainly confessed nor carefully concealed, which caused each to shift the responsibility upon another, till at length it was found expedient to send a deputation of the church, in order to deal with Mr. Hooper about the mystery, before it should grow into a scandal. Never did an embassy so ill discharge its duties. The minister received them with friendly courtesy, but became silent, after they were seated, leaving to his visitors the whole burden of introducing their important business. The topic, it might be supposed, was obvious enough. There was the black veil, swathed round Mr. Hooper's forehead, and concealing every feature above his placid mouth, on which, at times, they could perceive the glimmering of a melancholy smile. But that piece of crape, to their imagination, seemed to hang down before his heart, the symbol of a fearful secret between him and them. Were the veil but cast aside, they might speak freely of it, but not till then. Thus they sat a considerable time, speechless, confused, and shrinking uneasily from Mr. Hooper's eyes, which they felt to be fixed upon them with an invisible glance. Finally, the deputies returned abashed to their constituents, pronouncing the matter too weighty to be handled, except by a council of the churches if, indeed, it might not require a general synod. [13]

But there was one person in the village, unappalled by the awe with which the black veil had impressed all beside herself.

When the deputies returned without an explanation, or even venturing to demand one, she, with the calm energy of her character, determined to chase away the strange cloud that appeared to be settling round Mr. Hooper, every moment more darkly than before. As his plighted wife,[14] it should be her privilege to know what the black veil concealed. At the minister's first visit, therefore, she entered upon the subject, with a direct simplicity, which made the task easier both for him and her. After he had seated himself, she fixed her eyes steadfastly upon the veil, but could discern nothing of the dreadful gloom that had so overawed the multitude: it was but a double fold of crape, hanging down from his forehead to his mouth, and slightly stirring with his breath.

'No,' said she aloud, and smiling, 'there is nothing terrible in this piece of crape, except that it hides a face which I am always glad to look upon. Come, good sir, let the sun shine from behind the cloud. First lay aside your black veil, then tell me why you put it on.'

Mr. Hooper's smile glimmered faintly.

'There is an hour to come,' said he, 'when all of us shall cast aside our veils. Take it not amiss,[15] beloved friend, if I wear this piece of crape till then.'

'Your words are a mystery too,' returned the young lady. 'Take away the veil from them, at least.'

'Elizabeth, I will,' said he, 'so far as my vow may suffer me. Know, then, this veil is a type and a symbol,[16] and I am bound to wear it ever, both in light and darkness, in solitude and before the gaze of multitudes, and as with strangers, so with my familiar friends. No mortal eye will see it withdrawn. This dismal shade must separate me from the world: even you, Elizabeth, can never come behind it!'

"What grievous affliction hath befallen you," she earnestly inquired, "that you should thus darken your eyes for ever?"

"If it be a sign of mourning," replied Mr. Hooper, "I, perhaps, like most other mortals, have sorrows dark enough to be typified by a black veil."

"But what if the world will not believe that it is the type of an innocent sorrow?" urged Elizabeth. "Beloved and respected as you are, there may be whispers, that you hide your face under the consciousness of secret sin. For the sake of your holy office, do away this scandal!"

The color rose into her cheeks, as she intimated the nature of the rumors that were already abroad in the village. But Mr. Hooper's mildness did not forsake him. He even smiled again that same sad smile, which always appeared like a faint glimmering of light, proceeding from the obscurity beneath the veil.

"If I hide my face for sorrow, there is cause enough," he merely replied; "and if I cover it for secret sin, what mortal might not do the same?"

And with this gentle, but unconquerable obstinacy, did he resist all her entreaties. At length Elizabeth sat silent. For a few moments she appeared lost in thought, considering, probably, what new methods might be tried, to withdraw her lover from so dark a fantasy, which, if it had no other meaning, was perhaps a symptom of mental disease. Though of a firmer character than his own, the tears rolled down her cheeks. But, in an instant, as it were, a new feeling took the place of sorrow: her eyes were fixed insensibly[17] on the black veil, when, like a sudden twilight in the air, its terrors fell around her. She arose, and stood trembling before him.

"And do you feel it then at last?" said he mournfully.

She made no reply, but covered her eyes with her hand, and turned to leave the room. He rushed forward and caught her arm.

"Have patience with me, Elizabeth!" cried he passionately. "Do not desert me, though this veil must be between us here on earth, Be mine, and hereafter there shall be no veil over my face, no darkness between our souls! It is but a mortal veil — it is not for eternity! Oh, you know not how lonely I am and how frightened to be lone behind my black veil. Do not leave me in this miserable obscurity for ever!"

"Lift the veil but once, and look me in the face," said she.

"Never! It cannot be!" replied Mr. Hooper.

"Then, farewell!" said Elizabeth.

She withdrew her arm from his grasp, and slowly departed, pausing at the door, to give one long, shuddering gaze, that seemed almost to penetrate the mystery of the black veil. But, even amid his grief, Mr. Hooper smiled to think that only a material emblem had separated him from happiness, though the horrors which it shadowed forth must be drawn darkly between the fondest of lovers.

From that time no attempts were made to remove Mr. Hooper's black veil, or, by a direct appeal, to discover the secret which it was supposed to hide. By persons who claimed a superiority to popular prejudice, it was reckoned merely an eccentric whim, such as often mingles with the sober actions of men otherwise rational, and tinges them all with its own semblance of insanity. But with the multitude, good Mr. Hooper was irreparably a bugbear. [18] He could not walk the street with any peace of mind, so conscious was he that the gentle and timid would turn aside to avoid him, and that others would make it a point of hardihood to throw themselves in his way. The impertinence of the latter class compelled him to give up his customary walk, at sunset, to the burial ground; for when he leaned pensively over the gate, there would always be faces behind the grave-stones, peeping at his black veil. A fable went the rounds[19] that the stare of the dead people drove him thence. It grieved him, to the very depth of his kind heart, to observe how the children fled from his approach, break-

ing up their merriest sports, while his melancholy figure was yet a-
far off. Their instinctive dread caused him to feel, mere strongly
than aught else, that a preternatural horror was interwoven with
the threads of the black crape. In truth, his own antipathy to the
veil was known to be so great, that he never willingly passed before a mirror, nor stooped to drink at a still fountain, lest, in its
peaceful bosom, he should be affrighted by himself. This was what
gave plausibility to the whispers, that Mr. Hooper's conscience
tortured him for some great crime, too horrible to be entirely concealed, or otherwise than so obscurely intimated. [20] Thus, from beneath the black veil, there rolled a cloud into the sunshine, an ambiguity of sin or sorrow, which enveloped the poor minister, so
that love or sympathy could never reach him. It was said, that
ghost and fiend consorted with him there. With self-shudderings
and outward terrors, he walked continually in its shadow, groping
darkly within his own soul, or gazing through a medium that sad-
dened the whole world. Even the lawless wind, it was believed,
respected his dreadful secret, and never blew aside the veil. But
still good Mr. Hooper sadly smiled at the pale visages of the
worldly throng as he passed by.

Among all its bad influences, the black veil had the one desir-
able effect, of making its wearer a very efficient clergyman. By
the aid of his mysterious emblem — for there was no other apparent cause — he became a man of awful power, over souls that
were in agony for sin. His converts always regarded him with a
dread peculiar to themselves, affirming, though but figuratively,
that, before he brought them to celestial light, they had been with
him behind the black veil. Its gloom, indeed, enabled him to sympathize with all dark affections. Dying sinners cried aloud for Mr.
Hooper, and would not yield their breath till he appeared; though
ever, as he stooped to whisper consolation, they shuddered at the
veiled face so near their own. Such were the terrors of the black

veil, even when death had bared his visage! Strangers came long distances to attend service at his church, with the mere idle purpose of gazing at his figure, because it was forbidden them to behold his face. But many were made to quake ere they departed! Once during Governor Belcher's[21] administration, Mr. Hooper was appointed to preach the election sermon. Covered with his black veil, he stood before the chief magistrate, the council, and the representatives, and wrought so deep an impression, that the legislative measures of that year were characterized by all the gloom and piety of our earliest ancestral sway.

In this manner Mr. Hooper spent a long life, irreproachable in outward act, yet shrouded in dismal suspicions; kind and loving, though unloved, and dimly feared; a man apart from men, shunned in their health and joy, but ever summoned to their aid in mortal anguish. As years wore on, shedding their snows above his sable veil, he acquired a name throughout the New England churches, and they called him Father Hooper. Nearly all his parishioners, who were of mature age when he was settled, had been borne away by many a funeral; he had one congregation in the church, and a more crowded one in the church-yard; and having wrought so late into the evening, and done his work so well, it was now good FatherHooper's turn to rest.

Several persons were visible by the shaded candlelight, in the death-chamber of the old clergyman. Natural connections[22] he had none. But there was the decorously grave, though unmoved physician, seeking only to mitigate the last pangs of the patient whom he could not save. There were the deacons, and other eminently pious members of his church. There, also, was the Reverend Mr. Clark, of Westbury, a young and zealous divine, who had ridden in haste to pray by the bed-side of the expiring minister. There was the nurse, no hired handmaiden of death, but one whose calm affection had endured thus long, in secrecy, in solitude, amid the chill of age, and would not perish, even at the dying hour. Who, but Elizabeth! And there lay the hoary head of good Father Hooper upon the deathpillow, with the black veil still swathed about his brow and reaching down over his face, so that each more difficult gasp of his faint breath caused it to stir. All through life that piece of crape had hung between him and the world; it had separated him from cheerful brotherhood and woman's love, and kept him in that saddest of all prisons, his own heart; and still it lay upon his face, as if to deepen the gloom of his darksome chamber, and shade him from the sunshine of eternity.

For some time previous, his mind had been confused, wavering doubtfully between the past and the present, and hovering forward, as it were, at intervals, into the indistinctness of the world to come. There had been feverish turns,[23] which tossed him from side to side, and wore away what little strength he had. But in his most convulsive struggles, and in the wildest vagaries of his intellect, when no other thought retained its sober influence, he still showed an awful solicitude lest the black veil should slip aside. Even if his bewildered soul could have forgotten, there was a faithful woman at his pillow, who, with averted eyes, would have covered that aged face, which she had last beheld in the comeliness of manhood. At length the death-stricken old man lay quietly in the torpor of mental and bodily exhaustion, with an imperceptible pulse, end breath that grew fainter end fainter, except when a long, deep, and irregular inspiration seemed to prelude the flight of his spirit.

The minister of Westbury approached the bedside.

"Venerable Father Hooper," said he, "the moment of your release[24] is at hand. Are you ready for the lifting of the veil, that shuts in time from eternity?"

Father Hooper at first replied merely by a feeble motion of his head; then, apprehensive, perhaps, that his meaning might be doubtful, he exerted himself to speak.

"Yea," said he, in faint accents, "my soul hath a patient weariness until that veil be lifted."

"And is it fitting," resumed the Reverend Mr. Clark, "that a man so given to prayer, of such a blameless example, holy in deed and thought, so far as mortal judgment may pronounce; is it fitting that a father in the church should leave a shadow on his memory, that may seem to blacken a life so pure? I pray you, my venerable brother, let not this thing be! Suffer us to[25] be gladdened by your triumphant aspect[26], as you go to your reward. Before the veil of eternity be lifted, let me cast aside this black veil from your face!"

And thus speaking, the Reverend Mr. Clark bent forward to reveal the mystery of so many years, But exerting a sudden energy, that made all the beholders stand aghast, Father Hooper snatched both his hands from beneath the bed-clothes, and pressed them strongly on the black veil, resolute to struggle, if the minister of Westbury would contend with a dying man.

"Never!" cried the veiled clergyman. "On earth, never!"

"Dark old man!" exclaimed the affrighted minister, "with what horrible crime upon your soul are you now passing to the judgment[27]"

Father Hooper's breath heaved; it rattled in his throat; but, with a mighty effort, grasping forward with his hands, he caught hold of life, and held it back till he should speak. He even raised himself in bed; and there he sat, shivering with the arms of death around him, while the black veil hung down, awful, at that last moment, in the gathered terrors of a life-time. And yet the faint, sad smile, so often there, now seemed to glimmer from its obscurity, and linger on Father Hooper's lips.

"Why do you tremble at me alone?" cried he, turning his veiled face round the circle of pale spectators. "Tremble also at each other! Have men avoided me, and women shown no pity, and children screamed and fled, only for my black veil? What, but the mystery which it obscurely typifies, has made this piece of crape so awful? When the friend shows his inmost heart to his friend; the lover to his best-beloved; when man does not vainly shrink from the eye of his Creator,[28] loathsomely treasuring up the secret of his sin; then deem me a monster, for the symbol beneath which I have lived, and die! I look around me, and lo! On every visage a black veil!"

While his auditors shrank from one another, in mutual affright, Father Hooper fell back upon his pillow, a veiled corpse, with a faint smile lingering on the lips. Still veiled, they laid him in his coffin, and a veiled corpse they bore him to the grave. The grass of many years has sprung up and withered on that grave, the burialstone is mossgrown, and good Mr. Hooper's face is dust; but awful is still the thought, that it moldered beneath the black veil!

Notes

1. Goodman Gray: Mr. Gray. "Goodman" is a title of address similar to "Mr. ".
2. band: neckband, collar.
3. the Scriptures: the Bible.
4. the dread Being: the dreadful Being, i. e. God.
5. the Word: the Word of God; Jesus Christ as mediator or manifestation of God to man.
6. the Omniscient: God, in his all-knowing aspect.
7. since his settlement: since his installation as a minister.
8. not ... for the world: certainly not.
9. which often exalted a sympathetic smile, where liveller merriment would have been thrown away: Note that "which" refers to "cheerfulness", "where" refers to "smile"(= in which situation), and "would" indicates some past habitual happening.

10. the wedding-knell: a reference to Hawthorne's *The Wedding Knell*, which appeared in the same magazine along with this story.

11. waggery: mischievousness.

12. indifferent: here, not very good.

13. synod: a meeting of church officers to discuss and decide important questions.

14. his plighted wife: his fiancée; "plighted" here means "engaged".

15. Take it not amiss: Don't take offence at it.

16. a type and a symbol: a symbol (the phrase "a type and a symbol" is redundant).

17. insensibly: without feeling or emototion; callously.

18. bagbear: object of dread.

19. A fable went the rounds: A tale was passed on from mouth to mouth among the villager

20. some great crime, too horrible to be entirely concealed, or otherwise than so obscurely intimated: Note that "otherwise than (= in another way than) so obscurely intimated" is governed by "too horrible to be".

21. Governor Belcher: Jonathan Belcher was Govenor(1730-1741) of Massachusetts and New Hampshire. An election sermon was preached at the installing of each new Governor, and it was a great honor for a minister to be chosen to preach this sermon.

22. natural connections: relatives.

23. turns: attacks of illness.

24. release: here, euphemistically, death.

25. suffer us to ... : Allow us to ...

26. aspect: here, appearance, facial expression.

27. the judgment: here, the final judgment of men by God.

28. Greator: God.

Considerations

A symbol is a person, place, thing, event, or pattern in a literary work that designates itself and at the same time figuratively represents or stands for something else. Why does Mr. Hooper wear a black veil? What does the black veil represent?

FAUST
FAUST'S STUDY
by Wolfgang von Goethe

FAUST: Who's knocking? Come in! *Now* who wants to annoy me?
MEPHISTOPHELES: [*Outside door*] It's I.
FAUST: Come in!
MEPHISTOPHELES: [*Outside door*]
    You must say "Come in" three times.
FAUST: Come in then!
MEPHISTOPHELES: [*Entering*] Thank you; you overjoy me.
    We two, I hope, we shall be good friends;
    To chase those megrims of yours away
    I am here like a fine young squire[2] today,
    In a suit of scarlet trimmed with gold
    And a little cape of stiff brocade,
    With a cock's feather in my hat
    And at my side a long sharp blade,
    And the most succinct advice I can give
    Is that you dress up just like me,
    So that uninhibited and free
    You may find out what it means to live.
FAUST: The pain of earth's constricted life, I fancy,
    Will pierce me still, whatever my attire;
    I am too old for mere amusement,
    Too young to be without desire.
    How can the world dispel my doubt?

You must do without, you must do without
That is the everlasting song
Which rings in every ear, which rings,
And which to us our whole life long
Every hour hoarsely sing.
I wake in the morning only to feel appalled,
My eyes with bitter tears could run
To see the day which in its course
Will not fulfil a wish for me, not one;
The day which whittles away with obstinate carping
All pleasure — even those of anticipation,
Which makes a thousand grimaces to obstruct
My heart when it is stirring in creation,
And again, when night comes down, in anguish
I must stretch out upon my bed
And again no rest is granted me,
For wild dreams fill my mind with dread.
The God who dwells within my bosom
Can make my inmost soul react;
The God who sways my every power
Is powerless with external fact.
And so existence weights upon my breast
And I long for death and life — life I detest.

MEPHISTOPHELES: Yet death is never a wholly welcome guest.

FAUST: O happy is he whom death in the dazzle of victory
Crowns with the bloody laurel in the battling swirl!
Or he whom after the mad and breakneck dance
He comes upon in the arms of a girl!
O to have sunk away, delighted, deleted,
Before the Spirit of the Earth, before his might!

MEPHISTOPHELES: Yet I know someone who failed to drink
A brown juice on a certain night.

FAUST: Your hobby is espionage — is it not?

MEPHISTOPHELES: Oh I'm not omniscient — but know a lot.

FAUST: Whereas that tumult in my soul
    Was, stilled by sweet familiar chimes
    Which cozened the child that yet was in me
    With echoes of more happy times,
    I now curse all things that encompass
    The soul with lures and jugglery
    And bind it in this dungeon of grief
    With trickery and flattery.
    Cursed in advance be the high opinion
    That serves our spirit for a cloak!
    Cursed be the dazzle of appearance
    Which bows our senses to its yoke!
    Cursed be the lying dreams of glory,
    The illusion that our name survives!
    Cursed be the flattering things we own,
    Servants and ploughs, children and wives!
    Cursed be Mammo[3] when with his treasures
    He makes us play the adventurous man
    Or when for our luxurious pleasures
    He duly spreads the soft divan!
    A curse on the balsam of the grape!
    A curse on the love that rides for a fall!
    A curse on hope! A ourse on faith!
    And a curse on patience most of all!

[*The invisible* SPIRITS *sing again*]

SPIRITS: Woe! Woe!
    You have destroyed it,
    The beautiful world;
    By your violent had

'Tis downward hurled!
A half-god has dashed it asunder!
From under
We bear off the rubble to nowhere
And ponder
Sadly the beauty departed.
Magnipotent
One among men,
Magnificent
Build it again,
Build it again in your breast!
Let a new course of life
Begin
With vision abounding
And new songs resounding
To welcome it in!
MEPHISTOFHELES: These are the juniors
Of my faction.
Hear how precociously they counsel
Pleasure and action.
Out and away
From your lonely day
Which dries your senses and your juices
Their melody seduces.

Stop playing with your grief which battens
Like a vulture on your life, your mind!
The worst of company would make you feel
That you are a man among mankind.
Not that it's really my proposition
To shove you among the common men.
Though I'm not one of the Upper Ten

If you would like a coalition

With me for your career through life,

I am quite ready to fit in,

I'm yours before you can say knife.

I am your comrade;

If you so crave

I am your servant, I am your slave.

FAUST: And what have I to undertake in return?

MEPHISTIOPHELES: Oh it's early days to discuss what that is.

FAUST: No, no, the devil is an egoist

　　And ready to do nothing gratis

　　Which is to benefit a stranger.

　　Tell me your terms and don't prevaricate!

　　A servant like you in the house is a danger.

MEPHISTIOPHELES: I will bind myself to your service in this

　　world.

　　To be at your beck and never rest nor slack;

　　When we meet again on the other side,

　　In the same coin you shall pay me back.

FAUST: The other side gives me little trouble;

　　First batter this present world to rubble,

　　Then the other may rise — if that's the plan.

　　This earth is where my springs of joy have started,

　　And this sun shines on me when broken-hearted;

　　If I can first from them be parted,

　　Then let happen what will and can!

　　I wish to hear no more about it —

　　Whether there too men hate and love

　　Or whether in those spheres too, in the future,

　　There is a Below or an Above.

MEPHISTIOPHELES: With such an outlook you can risk it.

　　Sign on the line! In these next days you will get

Ravishing samples of my arts;
I am giving you what never man saw yet.
FAUST: Poor devil, can you give anything ever?
Was a human spirit in its high endeavor
Even once understood by one of your breed?
Have you got food which fails to feed?
Or a gold which one never wins?
Like mercury runs away through the hand?
A game at which one never wins?
A girl who, even when on my breast,
Pledges herself to my neighbor with her eyes?
The divine and lovely delight of honour
Which falls like a falling star and dies?
Show me the fruits which, before they are plucked, decay
And the trees which day after day renew their green!
MEPHISTIOPHELES: Such a commission doesn't alarm me,
I have such treasures to purvey.
But, my good friend, the time draws on when we
Should be glad to feast at our ease on something good.
FAUST: If ever I stretch myself on a bed of ease,
Then I am finished! Is that understood?
If ever your flatteries can coax me
To be pleased with myself, if ever you cast
A spell of pleasure that can hoax me
Then let *that* day be my last!
That's my wager!
MEPHISTIOPHELES: Done!
FAUST: Let's shake!
If even I say to the passing moment
"Linger a while! Thou art so fair!"
Then you may cast me into fetters
I will gladly perish then and there!

西方文学

Then you may set the death-bell tolling,
Then from my service you are free,
The clock may stop, its hand may fall,
And that be the end of time for me!
MEPHISTIOPHELES: Think what you're saying, we shall not forget
it.
FAUST: And you are fully within your rights;
I have made no mad or outrageous claim.
If I stay as I am a slave —
Whether yours or another's, it's all the same.
MEPHISTIOPHELES: I shall this very day at the College Banque[4]
Enter your service with no more ado,
But just one point — As a life-and-death insurance
I must trouble you for a line or two.
FAUST: So you, you pedant, you too like things in writing?
Have you never known a man? Or a man's word? Never?
Is it not enough that my word of mouth
Puts all my days in bond for ever?
Does not the world rage on in all its streams
And shall a promise hamper *me*?
Yet this illusion reigns within our hearts
And from it who would be gladly free?
Happy the man who can inwardly keep his word;
But a parchment, duly inscribed and sealed,
Is a bogey from which all wince away.
The word dies on the tip of the pen
And wax and leather lord it then.
What do you, evil spirit, require?
Bronze, marble, parchment, paper?
Quill or chisel or pencil of slate?
You may choose whichever you desire.
MEPHISTIOPHELES: How can you so exaggerate

With such a hectic rhetoric?
Any little snippet is quite good —
Any you sign it with one little drop of blood.[5]
FAUST: If that is enough and is some use,
One may as well pander to your fad.
MEPHISTIOPHELES: Blood is a very special juice.
FAUST: Only do not fear that I shall break this contract.
What I promise is nothing more
Than what all my powers are striving for.
I have puffed myself up too much, it is only
Your sort that really fits my case.
The great Earth Spirit has despised me
And Nature shuts the door in my face.
The thread of thoughts is snapped asunder,
I have long loathed knowledge in all its fashions,
In the depths of sensuality
Let us now quench our glowing passions!
And at once make ready every wonder
Of unpenetrated sorcery!
Let us cast ourselves into the torrent of time,
Into the whirl of eventfulness,
Pleasure and pain may chop and change
As chop and change they will and can;
It is restless action makes the man.
MEPHISTIOPHELES: No limit is fixed for you, no bound;
If you'd like to nibble at everything
Or to seize upon something flying round —
Well, may you have a run for your money!
But seize your chance and don't be funny!
FAUST: I've told you, it is no question of happiness.
The most painful joy, enamoured hate, enlivening
Disgust — I devote myself to all excess.

My breast, now cured of its appetite for knowledge,
From now is open to all and every smart,
And what is allotted to the whole of mankind
That will I sample in my inmost heart,
Grasping the highest and lowest with my spirit,
Piling men's weal and woe upon my neck,
To extend myself to embrace all human selves
And to founder in the end, like them, a wreck.
MEPHISTIOPHELES: O believe *me*, who have been chewing
These iron rations many a thousand year,
No human being can digest
This stuff, from the cradle to the bier.
This universe — believe a devil —
Was made for no one but a god!
He exists in eternal light
But *us* he has brought into the darkness
While *your* sole portion is day and night.
FAUST: I will all the same!
MEPHISTIOPHELES: That's very nice.
There's only one thing I find wrong;
Time is short, art is long.
You could do with a little artistic advice.
Confederate with one of the poets
And let him flog his imagination
To heap all virtues on your head,
A head with such a reputation:
Lion's bravery,
Stag's velocity,
Fire of Italy,
Northem tenacity.
Let *him* find out the secret art
Of combining craft with a noble heart

And of being in love like a young man,
Hotly, but working to a plan.
Such a person — *I'd* like to meet him;
"Mr. Microcosm"[6] is how I'd greet him.

FAUST: What am I then if fate must bar
My efforts to reach that crown of humanity
After which all my senses strive?

MEPHISTIOPHELES: You are in the end ... what you are.
You can put on full-bottomed wigs with a million locks,
You can put on stilts instead of your socks,
You remain for ever what you are.

FAUST: I feel my endeavors have, not been worth a pin
When I raked together the treasures of the human mind,
If at the end I but sit down to find
No new force welling up within.
I have not a hair's breadth more of height,
I am no nearer the Infinite.

MEPHISTIOPHELES: My very good sir, you look at things
Just in the way that people do;
We must be cleverer than that
Or the joys of life will escape from you.
Hell! You have surely hands and feet,
Also a head and you-know-what;
The pleasures I gather on the wing,
Are they less mine? Of course they're not!
Suppose I can afford six stallions,

I can add that horse-power to my score
And dash along and be a proper man
As if my legs were twenty-four.
So good-bye to thinking! On your toes!
The world's before us. Quick! Here goes!
I tell you, a chap who's intellectual

Is like a beast on a blasted heath
Driven in circles by a demon
While a fine green meadow lies round beneath.
FAUST: How do we start?
MEPHISTIOPHELES: We just say go and skip.
But please get ready for this pleasure trip.
[*Exit* FAUST.]
Only look down on knowledge and reason,
highest gifts that men can prize,
Only allow the spirit of lies
To confirm you in magic and illusion,
And then I have you body and soul.
Fate has given this man a spirit
Which is always pressing onwards, beyond control,
And joys of the earth between pole and pole.
Him shall I drag through the wilds of life
And through the flats of meaninglessness,
I shall make him flounder and gape and stick
And to tease his insatiableness
Hang meat and drink in the air before his watering lips;
In vain he will pray to slake his inner thirst,
And even had he not sold himself to the devil
He would be equally accursed.
[*Re-enter* FAUST.]
FAUST: And now, where are we going?
MEPHISTIOPHELES: Wherever you please.
The small world, then the great for us.
With what pleasure and what profit
You will roister through the syllabus!
FAUST: But I, with this long beard of mine,
I lack the easy social touch,
I know the experiment is doomed;

西方文学

159

Out in the world I never could fit in much.

I feel so small in company

I'll be embarrassed constantly.

MEPHISTIOPHELES: My friend, it will solve itself, any such mis-

giving;

Just trust yourself and you'll learn the art of living.

FAUST: Well, then, how do we leave home?

Where are your grooms? Your coach and horses?

MEPHISTIOPHELES: We merely spread this mantle wide,

It will bear us off on airy courses.

But do not on this noble voyage

Cumber yourself with heavy baggage.

A little inflammable gas[7] which I'll prepare

Will lift us quickly into the air.

If we travel light we shall cleave the sky like a knife.

Congratulations on your new course of life!

Notes

1. The play repeated the theme of Christopher Marlowe's *Doctor Faustus*. The story is based on the German legend of the Renaissance scholar, Dr. Faustus, who quested after universal knowledge by means of white magic (orthodox science) and the more terrible instrument of black magic. In this excerpt, Faustus signs a bond with the devil Mephistiopheles, according to which the Devil will work as the Doctor's servant helping to meet the Doctor's needs and desires, but the moment the Doctor is satisfied and pleased with himself, the Devil will take away his life. After the contract, Faustus is going to begin his tour in the universe, in which he will do things as he wishes, such as his marriage with Helen, his military career to save a shaky kingdom from falling, and so forth.

2. a five young squire: In the popular plays based on the Faust legend, the devil often appeared as a monk when the play catered to a Protestant audi-

ence, and as a cavalier when the audience was predominantly Catholic.

3. Mammon: the Aramaic word for "riches," used in the *New Testament*; medieval writers interpreted the word as a proper noun, the name of the devil, as representing covetousness or avarice.

4. College Banquet: actually the Doctorschmaus, or dinner given by a successful candidate for a Ph. D.

5. blood: This method of confirming an agreement with the devil is older than the Faust legend — in which it always appears — and is partly a parody of the role of blood in the Christian Sacrament.

6. Mr. Microcosm: i. e. , man viewed as the epitome of the universe.

7. gas: indicative of Goethe's scientific interests. The first hydrogen balloon was sent aloft in Paris in 1783, and several letters by Goethe refer to this new experiment.

THE PHIILOSOPHY OF COMPOSITION[1]
（Excerpt）
by Edgar Ellan Poe

The initial consideration was that of extent. If any literary work is too long to be read at one sitting, we must be content to dispense with the immensely important effect derivable from unity of impression — for, if two sittings be required, the affairs of the world interfere, and every thing like totality is at once destroyed. But since, ceteris paribus,[2] no poet can afford to dispense with any thing that may advance his design, it but remains to be seen whether there is, in extent, any advantage to counterbalance the loss of unity which attends it. Here I say no, at once. What we term a long poem is, in fact, merely a succession of brief ones — that is to say, of brief poetical effects. It is needless to demonstrate that a poem is such, only inasmuch as it intensely excites, by elevating, the soul and all intense excitements are, through a psychal[3] necessity, brief. For this reason, at least one half of the "Paradise Lost" is essentially prose — a succession of poetical excitements interspersed, inevitably, with corresponding depressions — the whole being deprived, through the extremeness of its length, of the vastly important artistic element, totality, or unity, of effect.

It appears evident, then, that there is a distinct limit, as regards length, to all works of literary art — the limit of a single sitting — and that, although in certain classes of prose composition, such as "Robinson Crusoe,"(demanding no unity) this limit may be advantageously overpassed, it can never properly be overpassed in a poem. Within this limit, the extent of a poem may be made to bear mathematical relation to its merit — in other words, to the excitement or elevation — again in other words, to the degree of the true poetical effect which it is capable of inducing; for it is clear that the brevity must be in direct ratio of the intensity of the intended effect: — this, with one proviso — that a certain degree of duration is absolutely requisite for the production of any effect at all.

Holding in view these considerations, as well as that degree of excitement which I deemmed not above the popular, while not below the critical taste. I reached at once what I conceived the proper length for my intended poem — a length of about one hundred lines. it is, in fact, a hundred and eight.

My next thought concerned the choice of an impression, or effect, to be conveyed: and here I may as well observe that, throughout the construction, I kept steadily in view the design of rendering the work universally appreciable. I should be carried too far out of my immediate topic were I to demonstrate a point upon which I have repeatedly insisted, and which, with the poetical, stands not in the slightest need of demonstration — the point, I mean, that Beauty is the sole legitimate province of the poem. A few words, however, in elucidation of my real rneaning, which some of my friends have evinced a disposition to misrepresent. That pleasure which is at once the most intense, the most elevating, and the most pure, is, I believe, found in the contemplation of the beautiful. When, indeed, men speak of Beauty, they mean, precisely, not a quality, as is supposed, but an effect — they refer, in short, just to that intense and pure elevation of soul — not of intellect, or of heart — upon which I have commented, and which is experienced in consequence of contemplating "the beautiful." Now I designate Beauty as the province of the poem, merely because it is an obvious rule of Art that effects should be made to spring from direct causes — that objects should be attained through means best adapted for their attainment — no one as yet having been weak enough to deny that the peculiar elevation alluded to is most readily attained in the poem. Now the object, Truth, or the satisfaction of the intellect, and the object Passion, or the excitement of the heart, are, although attainable, to a certain extent, in poetry, far more readily attainable in prose. Truth, in fact, demands a precision, and Passion a homeliness (the truly passionate will comprehend me) which are absolutely antagonistic to that Beauty which, I maintain, is the excitement, or pleasurable elevation, of the soul. It by no means follows from any thing here said, that passion, or even truth, may not be introduced, and even profitably introduced, into a poem — for they may serve in elucidation, or aid the general effect, as do discords in music, by contrast — but the true artist will always contrive, first, to tone them into proper subservience to the predominant aim, and, secondly, to unveil them, as far as possible, in that Beauty which is the atmosphere and the essence of the poem.

Regarding, then, Beauty as my province, my next question referred to the tone of its highest manifestation — and all experience has shown that this tone is one of sadness. Beauty of whatever kind, in its supreme development, invariably excites the sensitive soul to tears. Melancholy is thus the most legitimate of all the poetical tones.

The length, the province, and the tone, being thus determined, I betook myself to ordinary induction, with the view of obtaining some artistic piquancy which might serve me as a key-note in the construction of the poem — some pivot upon which the whole structure might turn. In carefully thinking over all the usual artistic effects — or more properly points, in the theatrical sense — I did not fail to perceive immediately that no one had been so universally employed as that of the refrain. The universality of its employment sufficed to assure me of its intrinsic value, and spared me the necessity of submitting it to analysis. I soon saw it to be in a primitive condition. As commonly used, the refrain, or burden not only is limited to lyric verse, but depends for its impression upon the force of monotone — both in sound and thought. The pleasure is deduced solely from the sense of identity — of repetition. I resolved to diversify, and so heighten, the effect, by adhering, in general, to the monotone of sound, while I continually varied that of thought. that is to say, I determined to produce continuously novel effects, by the variation of the application of the refrain — the refrain itself remaining, for the most part, unvaried.

These points being settled, I next bethought me of the mature of my refrain. Since its application was to be repeatedly varied, it was clear that the refrain itself must be brief, for there would have been an insurmountable difficulty in frequent variations of application in any sentence of length. In proportion to the brevity of the sentence, would, of course, be the facility of the variation. This led me at once to a single word as the best refrain.

The question now arose as to the character of the word. Having made up my mind to a refrain, the division of the poem into stanzas was, of course, a corollary; the refrain forming the close of each stanza. That such a close, to have force, must be sonorous and susceptible of protracted emphasis, admitted no doubt, and these considerations inevitably led me to the long "o" as the most sonorous vowel, in connection "r" with as the most producible consonant.

The sound of the refrain being thus determined, it became necessary to select a word embodying this sound, and at the same time in the fullest possible keeping with that melancholy which I had predetermined as the tone of the poem. In such a search it would have been absolutely impossible to overlook the word "Nevermore." In fact, it was the very first which presented itself.

The next desideratum was a pretext for the continuous use of the one word "nevermore." In observing the difficulty which I at once found in inventing a sufficiently plausible reason for its continuous repetition, I did not fail to perceive that this difficulty arose solely from the pre-assumption that the word was to be so continuously or monotonously spoken by a human being — I did not fail to perceive, in short, that the difficulty lay in the reconciliation of this monotony with the exercise of reason on the part of the creature repeating the word. Here, then, immediately arose the idea of a non-reasoning creature capable of speech; and, very naturally, a parrot, in the first instance, suggested itself, but was superseded forth with by a Raven, as equally capable of speech, and infinitely more in keeping with the intended tone.

I had now gone so far as the conception of a Raven — the bird of ill omen — monotonously repeating the one word, "Nevermore," at the conclusion of each stanza, in a poem of melancholy tone, and in length about one hundred lines. Now, never losing sight of the object supremeness, or perfection, at all points, I asked myself — "Of all melancholy topics, what, according to the universal understanding of mankind, is the most melancholy?" Death — was the obvious reply. "And when," I said, "is this most

melancholy of topics most poetical?" From what I have already ex-
plained at some length, the answer, here also, is obvious —
"When it most closely allies itself to Beauty: the death, then, of a
beautiful woman is, unquestionably, the most poetical topic in the
world and equally is it beyond doubt that the lips best suited for
such topic are those of bereaved lover. "

Notes

1. Whether Poe actually composed *The Raven* in the manner described here is
   literary mystery that has long been debated and still remains unsolved.
   Poe's intention in "The Philosophy of Composition" was to show the importance of conscious effort, rather than intuitive inspiration, in the creation of a work of art.
2. Latin: other things being equal.
3. Spiritual or psychological.

Chapter VI   Realism and Naturalism

1. The Rise of Realism

In literature, the term Realism is used to identify a literary movement in Europe and the United States in the last half of the 19th century and the early years of the 20th century. But the practice of realism, like that of romanticism, has a long history and can be traced back to ancient times. There are realistic scenes in the *Odyssey*, and there is plenty of realism in ancient comedies and satires, in medieval stories like some of Chaucer's and Boccaccio's, in many Elizabeth plays, in the English century novel beginning with Defoe, and so on almost ad infinitum.

Realism, as a literary movement, is usually called critical realism, because it rose as a reaction against the social reality. Round about the 1830s, the capitalist system was established successively in the Western countries after the bourgeois revolution. With the development of capitalism, the class contradictions, especially that between the workers and the capitalists, were becoming increasingly intense. The capitalists' ruthless exploitation and suppression left the working class in extreme poverty. The great misery of the workers resulted in a series of proletarian revolutions against capitalism, which started in France in 1848 and swept over the other European countries. But they all failed. The failure brought about a time of disillusionment and loss of hope, which were reflected in a literary revulsion against the false imagination and sentimentality of Romanticism. The literary men felt the need for a return to what was plain and real. Therefore, the name Realism was given to the new movement in literature.

2. The Features of Critical Realism

1) Critical realism succeeded the literary method of traditional realism, which was characterized by the verisimilitude of details and objective description of the representative character in a typical circumstance. Critical realists depicted familiar, ordinary characters with flesh and blood in the various environments of capitalism. Charles Dickens in *Oliver Twist* created a typical poor orphan against the background of the inhuman city life under capitalism.

2) By depicting the representative character in typical circumstances, critical realists provided a vivid picture of the capitalist world, exposed the social contradictions, and criticized the corruption and ugliness of the bourgeois world.

3) The language employed by critical realism was usually simple, clear, and direct, and their tone was often satiric.

4) Critical realists had their own limitations. They showed profound sympathy for the common people, but could not find them a right way out. They criticized the capitalist society from a democratic and humanistic viewpoint. They regarded the evils of capitalism just as the ugly practice against human nature. Their works pointed toward moral evolution and reform rather than revolution.

3. The Representatives of Critical Realism

Realism centered in the novel. Its representatives include Stendhal, Balzac, Flaubert, Maupassant in France; Dickens, Thackeray, Hardy, Galsworthy, Austen, and the Bronte sisters in England; Mark Twain, Henry James, and Howells in America. Critical Realism also prevailed in Russia, bringing forth such famous writers as Dostoevsky, Gogol, Turgenev, Tolstoy, and Chekhov. The outstanding realistic dramatists are Shaw in England and Ibsen in Norway. These great figures of critical realism not only left us a large number of creative masterpieces, but also wrote great works of literary criticism and theory. Stendhal, Tolstoy, Balzac, Henry James, and Howells were the prominent critics of this time, whose critical works developed and expressed their view on critical realism. Matthew Arnold was another great critic of this period, who stood out alone, in defending the predominance of humane studies in general education.

Stendhal (1783-1842) began his career as a critic, then he went on to write novels. As a critic, he defined the novel as "a mirror walking along the road." As a novelist, he wrote the masterpiece, *The Red and the Black*, which described the tragedy of a petty-bourgeois youth of humble birth who aspired to make his way into the upper world but ended up in pillory.

Honore de Balzac (1799-1850) was a great novelist and critic of the 19th century. His novels drew a large number of characters from many walks of life, who represent widely human passions and weaknesses. Today Balzac is particularly celebrated for his monumental work, *The Human Comedy*, the title given by

Balzac to the whole collection of his novels. His project, as he pointed out in his *The Preface to the Human Comedy*, was to present, in a series of books, a comprehensive picture of contemporary French society. Among the best-known individual novels of the series are *Eugenie Grandet* , and *Le Pere Goriot*. The former is about the old man Grandet, a typical bourgeoisie, whose single aim in life was to make money and save money. The latter is about the tragedy of Goriot, a retired flour business man, who was cheated of his money by his two daughters, and then was deserted and died in loneliness and misery.

Gustave Flaubert (1821-1880) was one of the great literary artists of the 19th century. He has been often regarded as the first French realist and the model not only to French writers such as Maupassant and Zola, but to Americans and Russians as well, notably Henry James and Turgenev. His masterpiece *Madame Bovary* is about the fate of Emma Bovary, a typical bourgeoisie woman, who, dissatisfies with her simple country husband and her common everyday life, tries to pursue a strong emotional life, but is deserted by her lovers and finally commits suicide in debts. The novel marked the beginning of a new era in literature with its artistic perfection and its unrelenting objectivity and detachment.

Guy de Maupassant (1850-1893) learned the art of story-telling from Flaubert. Most of his productions are short stories. He chose the subjects for his stories chiefly from actual experience of everyday life. Stories like *The Necklace*, *The Piece of String* and *The Umbrella* were built around simple episodes from the humble life of every day.

Alexander Dumas, père (1802-1870) was one of the most prolific and most popular French authors of the 19th century. Without ever attaining indisputable literary merit, Dumas succeeded in gaining a great reputation first as a dramatist and then as a historical novelist, especially for such works as *The Count of Monte Cristo* and *The Three Musketeers* (a romance about four swashbuckling heroes in the age of Cardinal Richelieu). Dumas' plays, when judged from a modern viewpoint, are crude, brash and melodramatic, but they were received with rapture in the late 1820s and early 1830s. Dumas was the father of the dramatist and novelist Alexander Dumas, called Dumas fils (son). Dumas' main interest was the creation of an exciting story set against a colourful background of history, usually the 16th or 17th century.

Alexander Dumas, fils (1824-1895), French playwright and novelist, one of the founders of the "problem play" — that is, of the middle-class realistic drama treating some contemporary ill and offering suggestions for its remedy. Dumas fils, the illegitimate son of Alexander Dumas père, possessed a good measure of his father's literary fecundity, but the work of the two men could scarcely be more different. His first success was a novel, *La Dame aux Camilias* (1848), but he found his vocation when he adapted the story into a play, known in English as *Camille* or *The Lady of the Camellias*. Although his father had written colorful historical plays and novels, Dumas fils specialized in drama set in the present. The unhappy witness of ruin brought on his father by illicit love affairs, Dumas fils devoted his plays to sermons on the sanctity of the family and of marriage. *Le Demi-*

Monde, for example, dealt with the threat to the institution of marriage posed by prostitutes. Modern audiences usually find Dumas drama verbose and sententious, but in the late 19th century eminent critics praised his plays for their moral seriousness, Among his most interesting plays are *Le Fils Naturel* (*The Natural Son*) and *Un Pète Prodigue*, a dramatization of Dumas' interpretation of his father's character.

Nikolai Gogol (1809-1852) was the first master of fiction in Russia to leave romantic conventions and to go to life for its subjects. Almost alone among Russian writers, he was a humorist. His *Dead Souls* depicts in a series of adventures many aspects of Russian society. It is full of humorous sympathy with plain people and satirical contempt for sham and hypocrisy. Chickikov, the chief character of the novel, moves about the country buying serfs who have died since the last census but who must be carried on the two rolls until the next census. The owners are willing to part with the useless tax burdens for virtually nothing, while Chickikov's motive is to raise money by mortgaging his holdings of dead serfs as living property. At last he is found out. This novel is a picture of the worst aspects of Russian life — the inhumanity of the owners of serfs, and the vanity and immorality of the upper class. Gogol's famous play is the *Inspector General*. The story is about a good-for-nothing, who is forced to stop in a small village, and is mistaken for an examiner sent by the government to inspect the work of the village officials. The imposter is showered with favours and gifts by the local civil servants so that he would not look into their corruption and dishonesty. Gogol's purpose in writing this comedy is to "gather in one heap all that was bad in Russia".

Fyodor Dostoevsky (1821-1881) has become a central figure in the formation of the modern sensibility. He formulated in fictions some of the main predicament of the modern time: the choices between God and atheism, good and evil, freedom and tyranny; the recognition of the limits and even of the fall of man against the belief in progress, revolution, and utopia. Most important, he captured unforgettably the enormous contradictions of which our common human nature is capable and by which it is torn. His novels, such as *The Idiot* and *The Possessed*, are constructed in large, vivid scenes, ending with a scandal or a crime or some act of violence, filled with unforgettable figures torn by great passions and swayed by great ideas. In his *Crime and Punishment*, Raskolnikov, a poor young intellectual, is struggling between his philosophical divisions of man into "the common" and "the uncommon", which drive him first to murder and then to confession.

Ivan Sergeyevih Turgenev (1818-1883) was the first Russian author to gain recognition in the West. His first important work is *A Hunter's Sketches*, which described the miserable life of the peasants and contributed much to the abolition of serfdom in Russia. Turgenev's another important work is *Fathers and Sons*, which, through the tragedy of a young intellectual, reflected the conflict between the revolutionary democrats and the aristocratic liberals during the serf reformation.

Count Leo Tolstoy (1828-1910) was the greatest of Russian realistic novelists and critics. He made the Russian realistic novel a literary genre ranking in importance with classical Greek tragedy and Elizabethan drama. His three important novels are *War and Peace*, *Anna Karenina*, and *Resurrection*. *War and Peace*, against the background of the Napoleonic invasion of Russia, revealed the lives of all classes in the early 19th century of Russia. *Anna Karenina* depicted the tragedy of Anna, who loves freedom, pursues an ideal love, and finally commits suicide. *Resurrection* exposed the corruption, of the law, court, prison, and other state organs by portraying the sufferings of the low class woman Maslova.

Anto Pavlovich Chekhov (1860-1904) was the last Russian realist. He mainly wrote short stories and plays. His novel, *The Man in the Shell*, described a middle school teacher who was a defender of the old things and an opposer of the new. He kept everything in shells, not only the material things but his ideas. Chekhov's famous play is *Chameleon*, which is about a case involving a dog that bit a man's finger. Through the trial of it, the novel exposed the snobbishness and corruption of the court.

Henrik Ibsen (1828-1906) was a famous Norwegian playwright. His works are problem plays critical of the hypocrisy and seamy politics of Norwegian provincial life. His best-known play is *A Doll's House*, which is a plea for the emancipation of women. Nora, the heroine, is a young, beautiful, and naive girl. Since she was born, her parents have loved her as a doll. After her marriage, her husband seems to love her very much and often addresses her as "little bird". Then he begins to curse her because of a small incident. Having realized the nasty soul of her husband, she leaves the doll's house.

Alfred Tennyson (1809-1892), English poet, is often regarded as the chief representative of the Victorian age in poetry. Tennyson succeeded Wordsworth as Poet Laureate in 1850. Tennyson published *Poems, Chiefly Lyrical*, in 1830, which included the popular "Mariana". His next book, *Poems* (1833), received unfavorable reviews, and Tennyson ceased to publish for nearly ten years. In 1833, his friend, Hallam, died suddenly in the same year in Vienna. It was a heavy blow to Tennyson. He began to write "In Memoriam", an elegy for his lost friend — the work took seventeen years. "The Lady of Shalott", "The Lotuseaters" "Morte d'Arthur" and "Ulysses" appeared in 1842 in the two-volume *Poems* and established his reputation as a writer. Tennyson's other major poetic achievements include the patriotic poem "Charge of the Light Brigade", published in *Maud* (1855), *Enoch Arden* (1864), based on a true story of a sailor thought drowned at sea who returned home after several years to find that his wife had remarried, and *Idylls of the King* (1859-1885) dealing with the Arthurian theme. In the 1870s Tennyson wrote several plays, among which are the poetic dramas *Queen Mary* (1875) and *Harold* (1876). In 1884 he was created a baron. Tennyson died at Aldwort on October 6, 1892 and was buried in the Poets' Corner in Westminster Abbey.

Robert Browning (1812-1889), English poet, was noted for his mastery of dramatic monologue. Most of the poet's education came at home. He was an extremely bright child and a voracious reader and learned Latin, Greek, French and Italian by the time he was fourteen. He attended the University of London in 1828, the first year it opened, but left in discontent to pursue his own reading at his own pace. This somewhat idiosyncratic but extensive education has led to difficulties for his readers. In 1845 he saw Elizabeth Barrett's *Poems* and contrived to meet her. Although she was an invalid and very much under the control of a domineering father, the two married in September 1846 and a few days later eloped to Italy, where they lived until her death in 1861. The years in Florence were among the happiest for both of them. Her love for him was demonstrated in the *Sonnets from the Portugese*, and to her he dedicated *Men and Women*, which contains his best poetry. Public sympathy for him after her death (she was a much more popular poet during their lifetimes) surely helped the critical reception of his *Collected Poems* (1862) and *Dramatis Personae* (1863). *The Ring and the Book* (1868-1869), which told of a Roman murder and trial, finally won him considerable popularity. He and Tennyson were now mentioned together as the foremost poets of the age. Although he lived and wrote actively for another twenty years, the late '60s were the peak of his career. His influence continued to grow, however, and finally lead to the founding of the Browning Society in 1881. He died in 1889, on the same day that his final volume of verse, *Asolando*, was published. He is buried in Poets' Corner of Westminster Abbey.

Charles Dickens (1812-1870) was the greatest of English realists. The first book that made him known is *Pickwick Papers*, which was followed up with a quick succession of outstanding novels, in which he masterly depicted the everyday life of the ordinary people of contemporary British society. These novels include *Oliver Twist*, the story of an orphan boy whose adventures provide material for a description of the lower depths of London;

The Old Curiosity Shop, the story of the sufferings and hardships of an old man and his granddaughter; *Dombey and Son*, which attacked the wealth pride of the upper strata of the British bourgeoisie; *Bleak House*, exposing the abuses of the English courts; *Hard Times*, about the failure of the education and ethics of bourgeois utilitarianism; *A Tale of Two Cities*, which took the French Revolution as its background and criticized the bourgeois order of society. Dicken's best work is *David Copperfield*. It is most autobiographical of all his works. It depicted the adventures and sufferings of David as a young man and his final success as an author.

William Makepeace Thackeray (1811-1863), like Dickens, was a great representative of critical realism in the 19th century England. His best known work is *Vanity Fair* with the subtitle, *A Novel Without a Hero*, which suggested that the writer's intention was not to portray individuals, but the bourgeois and aristocratic society as a whole. The novel is a classical example of social satire, comparing the British society to a Vanity fair, where money-grubbing is the main motive for all members of the ruling classes, who have no scruples whatever in employing all possible means to attain that end. Becky Sharp, the heroine, is a classic example of this money-grubbing instinct. Her only aspiration in life is to gain wealth and position by any means, fair or foul. Thackeray did not regard her as exceptional. Everyone wishes to gain something in *Vanity Fair* and acts almost in the same manner as Becky.

George Eliot (1819-1880) was the pseudonym of Mary Ann Evans. She wrote three remarkable novels — *Adam Bede*, *The*

Mill on the Floss, and *Silas Marner*. In these novels, Eliot drew faithful picture of the life of the rural common people such as artisans, farmers, the country clergy, and other native people. But compared with works of Dickens and Thackeray, the novels in Eliot's hands have less social significance. She went deep into the moral searching of the mind, thereby weakening the social importance of the novels.

Thomas Hardy (1840-1928) was one of the English critical realists at the turn of the 19th century. His principal works are the Wessex novels, that is, novels describing the characters and environment of his native countryside. They are *Far from the Madding Crowd*, *The Return of the Native*, *The Mayor of Casterbridge*, *Tess of the D'urbervilles*, and *Jude the Obscure*. These novels have as their setting the agricultural region of the southern countries of England, and depict the impoverishment and decay of small farmers who are mercilessly exploited by the rich landowner. Hardy's novels tend to be tragic because of his pessimistic philosophy. To Hardy, mankind seems to be subjected to the rule of some hostile and mysterious fate. No matter how man may struggle, no matter what noble aspirations he may have, he will ultimately be overcome. This fatalism, combined with a tendency towards naturalism and symbolism, is the defect that spoils at times the mainly realistic effect of his art.

John Galsworthy (1867-1933) was one of the most prominent of the 20th century English realistic writers. His masterpiece is *The Forsyte Saga*, which consists of two trilogies. The first is under the same title *The Forsyte Saga* and the second is entitled *A Modern Comedy*, each including three novels and two iaterludes. In this gigantic work, Galsworthy tells the story of several generations of the bourgeois Forsyte family from 1886 to 1926, unfolding before the reader the gradual decay and decline of the bourgeois class. It is a monumental work of critical realism in English literature of the 20th century. *The Man of Property*, the first novel in the first trilogy, marks the peak of Galsworthy's critical realism. Soames Forsyte, "the man of property" is a typical figure of the Forsyte family, whose principle is to make the accumulation of wealth the sole aim in life and to consider everything in terms of one's property. Soames extends his sense of property not only to material things but also to the physical and spiritual possession of his wife. In the novel, Galsworthy laid bare the oppressive nature of the bourgeois property instinct, and criticized its sense of property because it stifled the natural and justifiable human desire for art and beauty.

George Bernard Shaw (1856-1950) was among the most representative of critical realism in modern English drama. He lived a long life and wrote plays to criticize the evils of capitalism. *Widower's Houses* satirizes bourgeois businessmen whose ill-gotten money is squeezed out of poor, suffering people. *Mrs. Warren's Profession* accuses the bourgeoisie of making profit by fostering prostitution. *The Devils Disciple* derides the much loaded puritan piety. *Major Barbara* exposes British imperialism. *Pygmalion* is a poignant satire on refined bourgeois aristocrats and a lovely portrayal of a simple flower girl. *Heartbreak House* predicts the decline and fall of the bourgeois society of England.

Jane Austen (1775-1817) belonged to the age of Romanticism in terms of chronology. However, her tendency toward realism would place her with the realistic novelists. She wrote six novels in all: *Northanger Abbey*, *Sense and Sensibility*, *Pride and Prejudice*, *Mansfield Park*, *Emma*, and *Persuasion*. Among them *Pride and Prejudice* is the most widely read. It is the story of a young girl who rejects an offer of marriage because the young nobleman who makes it has been rude to her family. It is a very thin plot, but around it the authoress has woven vivid pictures of everyday life of simple country society.

The **Brontë sisters** are the famous talented realistic women novelists, all of whom died young. **Charlotte Brontë**, the eldest, wrote the masterpiece, *Jane Eyre*. Jane, the heroine, was born into a poor parson family and lost his parents shortly after birth. She lived in her aunt's where she was maltreated. Then she was sent to a charity school where she suffered no less. After eight years of hardships there, she got the position of governess in the family of Mr. Rochester, with whom she fell in love. On the wedding day, Jane learned that Rochester had a lunatic wife secretly locked in the attic. She fled from the family. Having gone through many hardships, she returned to Rochester and became his wife on hearing that Rochester became penniless and disabled due to a big fire set by his mad wife. In this novel, the authoress mainly criticized the bourgeois system of education and the uncultivated and narrow-minded English country squires.

Emily Brontë, the second eldest sister, wrote the powerful novel *Wuthering Heights*. It is a story of morbid love, and a strong attack on the bourgeois marriage system. The innocent love between Heathliff and Catherine is poisoned by class prejudice founded on wealth. The former victim, now becoming rich, takes his retaliation by victimizing the son of his former oppressor. The novel shows that love in the bourgeois society is impossible of attainment.

William Dean Howells (1837-1920) was regarded as the champion of literary realism in America. In his critical work *Criticism and Fiction*, he defined realiam as "fidelity to experience", as a quest of the average and the habitual rather than the exceptional or the uniquely high or low. His greatest novel *The Rise of Silas Lapham* is a fine specimen of American realistic writing. The world of Silas Lapham is that of the commonplace Bostonian of the late 19th century. Silas is a new upstart. He starts his paint business from scratch, becomes a millionaire and finally goes bankrupt again because of his honest intention to save others from falling. Here the writer stresses the moral integrity of the individual. Silas, though falling, achieves his moral and ethical "rise".

Henry James (1843-1916) was another important figure of American realism. In his critical work *The Art and Fiction*, he revealed his literary credo that representation of life should be the main object of the novel, which was applied fully to his major novels — *Daisy Miller*, *The Golden Bowl*, *The Ambassadors*, and *The Portrait of a Lady*. In addition to the truthful representation of life, James' novels are noted for their "international theme" and "point of view". Most of his novels deal with the meeting of America and Europe, American innocence in contact and contrast with European decadence. *The Portrait of a Lady* tells about the fate of a splendid American girl, Isabel Archer, arriving in Europe, full of hope, and with a will to live a free and noble life, only to fall prey to the sinister designs of two vulgar and unscrupulous European expatriates, Madame Merle and Gilbert Osmond. "Point of view" is the center of James' aesthetics of the novel. In James' opinion, to correspond to life, the author should make his characters reveal themselves with minimal intervention of the author, that is, illuminate the situation and characters through one or several minds. His works lay emphasis on the inner awareness and inward movements of his characters. Therefore, James is regarded by many to be the first of the modern psychological analysts in the novel.

Mark Twain (1835-1910) is the pseudonym of Samuel Langhorne Clemens, meaning the river man's cry for a sounding of two fathoms. As a realist, Mark Twain is different from Howells and James in that Howells is a genteel realist who concerned himself mainly with the middle class; James is a psychological realist who wrote mostly of the upper class; and Mark Twain is a humorous local colorist who represented social life through portraits of local places which he knew best. His masterpiece *The Adventures of Huckleberry Finn*, with its humor, characterization, realism, and colloquial style, has been regarded as the first modern American novel. Mark Twain's other important works include *The Gilded Age*, *The Adventures of Tom Sawyer*, *The Prince and the Pauper*, and *Life on the Mississippi*.

Harriet Beecher Stowe (1811-1896) is mainly remembered as the authoress of the anti-slavery novel, *Uncle Tom's Cabin*. It is about a horrible world in which the law, the government, the economy, even the church worked for the evil slave system. It was acclaimed the greatest anti-slavery manifesto.

Matthew Arnold (1822-1888), the leading English critic of the second half of the 19th century, was the great proponent of humanism. Many of his ideas are adaptations of the tenets of the older humanism. He thought of poetry as a "criticism of life"and of criticism itself as the effort to "know the best that is known and thought in the world". Arnold admired form, order and measure that constituted the classical qualities. He seeked to judge literature by high standards and used specimens of great poetry as well as his own taste in forming judgements. He said that the greatness of a poet "lies in his powerful and beautiful application of ideas to life. Three of his better known critical essays are *The Function of Criticism* (1865), *The Study of Poetry* (1888), and *On Translating Homer* (1861).

4. Naturalism

Naturalism is a literary movement which is regarded by many as related to but different from, Realism. It began in France in the middle of the 19th century and prevailed in England, France and the United States at the turn of the 20th century. Its founder was Emile Zola (1840-1902), French novelist.

Naturalistic writers held that man's existence is shaped by heredity and environment over which he has no control and about which he can exercise little if any choice. Novels and plays in the movement emphasized the animal nature of man and portrayed characters engrossed in a helpless brutal struggle for survival in a cold world full of the crushing forces of environment and heredity. Unlike realistic writers, naturalists attempted to achieve fidelity to nature by rejecting idealized portrayals of life. Realists observed a general situation and invented incidents which would make that situation vivid, while naturalism followed Zola's principle that a novelist should dissect and analyze his subjects with dispassionate, scientific accuracy and minuteness, and did not allow to invent. The language used in literature, for naturalists, must be the actual language used by the people he was describing. A novelist must not only collect all the possible facts but must present those facts as exactly as they had occurred.

5. The Representatives of Naturalism

Among adherents of naturalism are the American novelists-Stephen Crane, Frank Norris, and Theodore Dreiser. Some works of Earnest Hemingway, Eugene O'Neill, William Faulkner, and Hardy also bear some of the features of naturalism.

Stephen Crane (1871-1900) was a pioneer writer in the naturalistic tradition. His *Maggie: A Girl of the Street* was the first naturalistic novel in America. It relates the story of a good woman's downfall and destruction in a slum environment. Crane's masterpiece, *The Red Badge of Courage*, is a novel of war with the theme of the animal man in a cold manipulating world.

Frank Norris (1870-1902) was another representative of American naturalism. His most well-known work, *The Octopus*, is a novel of social determinism, illustrating how social and economic conditions ruined the lives of innocent, powerless people.

Theodore Dreiser (1871-1945) was the best naturalistic novelist in America. Influenced by Zola, Norris, and Darwinism,

Dreiser learned to regard man merely as an animal driven by greed and lust in a struggle for existence in which only "the fittest", the most ruthless, survive. Life to him is a jungle struggle in which man is a wisp in the wind of social forces with no power whatever to assert his own will. His masterpiece, *Sister Carrie*, is a story of a helpless country girl who catches blindly any opportunity for a better existence at the mercy of forces she can not comprehend. The novel offers a panoramic view of the crude and the savage aspects of social life at the turn of the 20th century.

Emile Zola (1840-1902) was a French novelist and critic, the founder of the Naturalist movement in literature. His *Rougon-Macquart Cycle*, a sequence of 20 novels described in a subtitle as *The Natural and Social History of a Family Under the Second Empire*, includes *Nana* (1880), the life of a courtesan, and *Germinal* (1885), an exposure of mining conditions. As a writer, Zola was in many respects a typical product of his age. This is most evident in his credulous faith in science and his uncritical acceptance of scientific determinism, which was the prevailing philosophy of the latter part of the 19th century in France. He maintained that Naturalism was indigenous to French life and named the 18th-century writer Denis Diderot and the 16th-century essayist Michel de Montaigne among its originators. He believed that human nature was completely determined by heredity. Weakness and vice were the result of an "organic lesion" in one member of a family that was unfailingly transmitted to all his descendants. It was only a fluke if any of them happened, like his own Dr. Pascal Rougon, to escape. Once this was understood, he thought that the inherited weaknesses could be eradicated by the combined efforts of medicine and education, that human nature could be perfected.

At one level, Zola's *Rougon-Macquart Cycle* is a documentary account of French life from the coup d'etate that placed Napoleon Ⅲ on the throne to the defeat of that Battle of Sedan (Sept. 1, 1870) and its aftermath. Zola used his two families — the violent Rougons and the weak Macquarts — to give continuity to the cycle. In the course of it, he managed to study all the main facets of the Second Empire.

Zola used the Second Empire to create what he described as a "microcosm." His aim was to treat it as an emblem of the human condition at one stage of its evolution, to show fallen humanity engaged in the practice of the seven deadly sins. The cycle rests on an elaborate system of symbols. The main Christian doctrines are transposed into Naturalist terms. The "organic lesion" is the Naturalist equivalent of original sin. Tante Dide, the ancestor of both families, is a modern Eve. Sin enters this world not through eating the forbidden apple but through drinking from the forbidden cup, or alcoholism. "Redemption" is to come in the person of the child born of the "free union" between Dr. Pascal Rougon, the Saviour figure, and his niece (an allusion to Zola's liaison with Jeanne Rozerot, a laundress, and the hopes it raised). It is thus important to realize that the three cycles stand for three periods in human history: past, present, and future. It is significant that Zola's inspiration failed almost completely when he endeavored to show the beneficial effects of science in the unfinished *Les Ouatre Evangiles*, which is the cycle of the future.

6. Readings

VANITY FAIR[1]
A Novel Without a Hero
CHAPTER II
In Which Miss Sharp and Miss Sedley Prepare
to Open the Campaign
by William Makepeace Thackeray

When Miss Sharp had performed the heroical act[2] mentioned in the last chapter, and had seen the Dixonary flying over the pavement of the little garden fall at length at the feet of the astonished Miss Jemima, the young lady's countenance, which had before worn an almost livid look of hatred, assumed a smile that perhaps was scarcely more agreeable, and she sank back in the carriage in an easy frame of mind, saying, "So much for the Dixonary; and, thank God, I'm out of Chiswick."

Miss Sedley was almost as flurried at the act of defiance as Miss Jemima had been; for, consider, it was but one minute that she had left school and the impressions of six years are not got over in that space of time. Nay, with some persons those awes and terrors of youth last for ever and ever. I know, for instance, an old gentleman of sixty-eight, who said to me one morning at breakfast, with a very agitated countenance, "I dreamed last night that I was flogged by Dr. Raine." Fancy had carried him back five-and-fifty years in the course of that evening. Dr. Raine and his rod were just as awful to him in his heart, then, at sixty-eight, as they had been at thirteen. If the Doctor, with a large birch, had appeared bodily to him, even at the age of three score and eight, and had said in awful voice, "boy, take down your pant — ?" Well, well, Miss

西方文学

Sedley was exceedingly alarmed at this act of insubordination.

"How could you do so, Rebecca?" at last she said, after a pause.

"Why, do you think Miss Pinkerton will come out order me back to the black-hole?" said Rebecca, laughing.

"No! but —"

"I hate the whole house," continued Miss Sharp, in a fury. "I hope I may never set eyes on it again. I wish it were in the bottom of the Thames, I do; and if Miss Pinkerton were there, I wouldn't pick her out, that I wouldn't. Oh, how I should like to see her floating in the water yonder, turban and all, with her train streaming after her, and her nose like the beak of a wherry."

"Hush!" cried Miss Sedley.

"Why, will the black footman tell tales?" cried Miss Rebecca, laughing. "He may go back and tell Miss Pinkerton that I hate her with all my soul; and I wish he would; and I wish I had a means of proving it, too. For two years I have only had insults and outrage from her. I have been treated worse than any servant in the kitchen. I have never had a friend or a kind word, except from you. I have been made to tend the little girls in the lower schoolroom, and to talk French to the misses until I grew sick of my mother-tongue. But that talking French to Miss Pinkerton was capital fun, wasn't it? She doesn't know a word of French, and was too proud to confess it. I believe it was that which made her part with me; and so thank Heaven for French. Vive la France! Vive l'Empereur! Vive Bonaparte!"[3]

"Oh Rebecca, Rebecca, for shame!" cried Miss Sedlley; for this was the greatest blasphemy Rebecca had as yet uttered; and in those days, in England, to say "Long live Bonaparte!" was as much as to say "Long live Lucifer!"[4] "How can you — how dare you have such wicked, revengeful thoughts?"

"Revenge may be wicked, but it's natural," answered Miss Rebecca. "I'm no angel." And, to say the truth, she certainly was not.

For it may be remarked in the course of this little conversation (which took place as the coach rolled along lazily by the riverside) that though Miss Rebecca Sharp her twice had occasion to thank Heaven, it has been in the first place, for ridding her of some person whom she hated, and secondly, for enabling her to bring her enemies to some sort of perplexity or confusion; neither of which are very amiable motives for religious gratitude, or such as would be put forward by persons of a kind and playable disposition. Miss Rebecca was not, then in the least kind or playable. All the world used her ill, said this young misanthropist, and we may be pretty certain that persons whom all the world treat ill, deserve entirely the treatment they get. The world is a looking-glass and gives back to every man the reflection of his own face. Frown at it, and it will in tum look sourly upon you; laugh at it and with it, and it is a jolly kind companion; and so let all young persons take their choice. This is certain, that if the world neglected Miss Sharp, she never was known to have done a good action in behalf of anybody; nor can it be expected that twenty-four young ladies should all be as amiable as the heroine of this work, Miss Sedley (whom we have selected for the very reason that she was the best-natured of all, otherwise what on earth was to have prevented us from putting up Miss Swartz, or Miss Crump, or Miss Hopkins, as heroine in her place?) — it could not be expected that every one should be of the humble and gentle temper of Miss Amelia Sedley; should take every opportunity to vanquish Rebecca's hard-heartedness and ill-humour; and, by a thousand kind words and offices, overcome, for once at least, her hostility to her kind.

Miss Sharp's father was an artist, and in that quality had given lessons of drawing at Miss Pinkerton's school. He was a clever man; a pleasant companion; a careless student; with a great propensity for running into debt, and a partiality for the tavern. When he was drunk, he used to beat his wife and daughter; and the next morning, with a headache, he would rail at the world for its neglect of his genius, and abuse, with a good deal of cleverness, and sometimes with perfect reason, the fools, his brother painters. As it was with the utmost difficulty that he could keep himself, and as he owed money for a mile round Soho, where he lived, he thought to better his circumstances by marrying a young woman of the French nation, who was by profession an opera-girl. The humble calling of her female parent, Miss Sharp never alluded to, but used to state subsequently that the Entrechats were a noble family of Gascony, and took great pride in her descent from them. And curious it is, that as she advanced in life this young lady's ancestors increased in rank and splendour.

Rebecca's mother had had some education somewhere, and her daughter spoke French with purity and a Parisian accent. It was in those days rather a rare accomplishment, and led to her engagement with the orthodox Miss Pinkerton. For her mother being dead, her father, finding himself not likely to recover, after his third attack of delirium tremens, wrote a manly and pathetic letter to Miss Pinkerton, recommending the orphan child to her protection, and so descended to the grave, after two bailiffs had quarreled over his corpse. Rebecca was seventeen when she came to Chiswick, and was bound over as an articled pupil; her duties being to talk French, as we have seen; and her privileges to live cost free, and, with a few guineas a year, to gather scraps of knowledge from the professors who attended the school.

She was small and slight in person; pale, sandy-haired, and with eyes habitually cast down: when they looked up they were very large, odd, and attractive; so attractive, that the Reverend Mr. Crisp, fresh from Oxford, and curate to the Vicar of Chiswick, the Reverend Mr. Flowerdew, fell in love with Miss Sharp; being shot dead by a glance of her eyes, which was fired all the way across Chiswick Church from the school-pew to the reading-desk. This infatuated young man used sometimes to take tea with Miss Pinkerton, to whom he had been presented by his mamma, and actually proposed something like marriage in an intercepted note, which the one-eyed applewoman was charged to deliver Mrs. Crisp was summoned from Buxton, and abruptly carried off her darling boy; but the idea, even, of such an eagle in the Chiswick dovecote caused a great flutter in the breast of Miss Pinkerton, who would have sent away Miss Sharp, but that She was bound to her under a forfeit, and who never could thoroughly believe the young lady's protestations that she had never exchanged a single word with Mr. Crisp, except under her own eyes on the two occasions when had met him at tea.

By the side of many tall and bouncing young ladies in the establishment, Rebecca Sharp looked like a child. But she had the dismal precocity of poverty. Many a dun had she talked to, and turned away from her father's door; many a tradesman had she coaxed and wheedled into good humour, and into the granting of one meal more. She sat commonly with her father, who was very proud of her wit, and heard the talk of many of his wild companions — often but ill-suited for a girl to hear. But she never had been a girl, she said; she had been a woman since she was eight years old. Oh, why did Miss Pinkerton let such a dangerous bird into her cage?

The fact is, the old lady believed Rebecca to be the meekest creature in the world, so admirably, on the occasions when her father brought her to Chiswick, used Rebecca to perform the part of the ingenue; and only a year before the arrangement by which Rebecca had been admitted into her house, and when Rebecca was sixteen years old, Miss Pinkerton majestically, and with a little speech, made her a present of a doll — which was, by the way, the confiscated property of Miss Swindle, discovered surreptitiously nursing it in school hours. How the father and daughter laughed as they trudged home together after the evening party (it was on the occasion of the speeches, when all the professors were invited), and how Miss Pinkerton would have raged had she seen the caricature of herself which the little mimic, Rebecca, managed to make out of her doll. Becky used to go through dialogues with it; it formed the delight of Newman Street, Gerrard Street, and the artists quarter: and the young painters, when they came to take their gin-and-water with their lazy, dissolute, clever, jovial senior, used regularly to ask Rebecca if Miss Pinkerton was at home: she was well known to them, poor soul! As Mr. Lawrence or President West. Once she had the honour to pass a few days at Chiswick; after which she brought back Jemima, and erected another doll as Miss Jemmy; for though that honest creature had made and given her jelly and cake enough for three children, and a seven-shilling piece at parting, the girl's sense of ridicule was far stronger than her gratitude, and she sacrificed Miss Jemmy quite as pitilessly as her sister.

The catastrophe came, and she was brought to the Mall as to her home. The rigid formality of the place suffocated her: the prayers and the meals, the lessons and the walks, which were arranged with a conventual regularity, oppressed her almost beyond endurance; and she looked back to the freedom and the beggary of the old studio in Soho with so much regret, that everybody, herself included, fancied she was consumed with grief for her father, She had a little room in the garret, where the maids heard her walking and sobbing at night; but it was with rage, and not with grief, She had not been much of a dissembler, until now her loneliness taught her to feign. She had never mingled in the society of women: her father, reprobate as he was, was a man of talent; his conversation was a thousand times more agreeable to her than the talk of such of her own sex as she now encountered. The pompous vanity of the old school mistress, the foolish good humor of her sister, the silly chat and scandal of the elder girls, and the frigid correctness of the governesses equally annoyed her; and she had no soft maternal heart, this unlucky girl, otherwise the prattle and talk of the younger children with whose care she was chiefly entrusted, might have soothed and interested her; but she lived among them two years, and not one was sorry that she went away. The gentle tenderhearted Amelia Sedley was the only person to whom she could attach herself in the least; and who could help attaching herself to Amelia.

The happiness — the superior advantages of the young women round about her, gave Rebecca inexpressible bangs of envy. "What airs that girl gives herself, because she is an earl's granddaughter," she said of one. "how they cringe and bow to that Creole, because of her hundred thousand pounds! I am a thousand times cleverer and more charming than that creature, for all her wealth. I am as well-bred as the earl's granddaughter, for all her fine pedigree; and yet every one passes me by here. And yet, when I was at my father's, did not the men give up their gayest balls and parties in order to pass the evening with me?" She determined at any rate to get free from the prison in which she found herself, and now began to act for herself, and for the first time to make connected plans for the future.

She took advantage, therefore, of the means of study the place offered her; and as she was already a musician and a good linguist, she speedily went through, the little course of study which was considered necessary for ladles in those days. Her music she practiced incessantly, and one day, when the girls were out, and she had remained at home, she was overheard to play a piece so well, the Minerva[5] thought wisely, she could spare herself the expense of a master for the juniors, and intimated to Miss Sharp that she was to instruct them in music for the future.

西方文学

193

The girl refused; and for the first time, and to the astonishment of the majestic mistress of the school. "I am here to speak French with the children," Rebecca said abruptly, "not to teach them music, and save money for you. Give me money, and I will teach them."

Minerva was obliged to yield, and, of course, disliked her from that day. "For five-and-thirty years," she said, and with great justice, "I never have seen the individual who has dared in my own house to question my authority. I have nourished a viper in my bosom."

"A viper — a fiddlestick," said Miss Sharp to the old lady, almost fainting with astonishment. "you took me because I was useful. There is no question of gratitude between us. I hate this place, and want to leave it. I will do nothing here but what I am obliged to do."

It was in vain that the old lady asked her if she was aware she was speaking to Miss Pinkerton? Rebecca laughed in her face, with a horrid sarcastic demoniacal laughter, that almost sent the schoolmistress into fits. "Give me a sum of money," said the girl, "and get rid of me — or, if you like better, get me a good place as governess in a nobleman's family you can do so if you please." And in their further disputes she always returned to this point, "Get me a situation — we hate each other, and I am ready to go."

Worthy Miss Pinkerton, although she had a Roman nose and a turban, and was as tall as a grenadier, and had been up to this time an irresistible princess, had no will or strength like that of her little apprentice, and in vain did battle against her, and tried to overawe her. Attempting once to scold her in public, Rebecca hit upon the before-mentioned plan of answering her in French, which quite routed the old woman. In order to maintain authority in her school, it became necessary to remove this rebel, this monster, this serpent, this firebrand; and hearing about this time that Sir

Pitt Crawley's family was in want of a governess, she actually recommended Miss Sharp for the situation, firebrand and serpent as she was. "I cannot, certainly," she said, "find fault with Miss Sharp's conduct, except to myself: and must allow that her talents and accomplishments are of a high order. As far as the head goes, at least, she does credit to the education system pursued at my establishment. "

And so the schoolmistress reconciled the recommendation to her conscience, and the indentures were cancelled, and the apprentice was free. The battle here described in a few lines, of course, lasted for some months. And as Miss Sedley, being now in her 17th year, was about to leave school, and had a friendship for Miss Sharp ("'tis the only point in Amelia's behaviors," said Minerva, "which has not been satisfactory to her mistress"), Miss Sharp was invited by her friend to pass a week with her at home, before she entered upon her duties as governess in a private family. Thus the world began for these two young ladies. For Amelia it was quite a new, fresh, brilliant world, with all the bloom upon it. It was not quite a new one for Rebecca (indeed, if the truth must be told with respect to the Crisp affair, the tart-woman hinted to somebody, who took an affidavit of the fact to somebody else, that there was a great deal more than was made public regarding Mr. Crisp and Miss Sharp, and that his letter was in answer to another letter). But who can tell you the real truth of the matter? At all events, if Rebecca was not beginning the world, she was beginning it over again.

By the time the young ladies reached Kensington turnpike, Amelia had not forgotten her companions, but had dried her tears, and had blushed very much and been delighted at a young officer of the Life Guards, who spied her as he was riding by, and said, "A dern fine gal, egad! And before the carriage arrived in Russell Square, a great deal of conversation had taken place about the

Drawing-room, and whether or not young ladies wore powder as well as hoops when presented and whether she was to have that honour: to the Lord Mayor's ball she knew she was to go. And when at length home was reached, Miss Amelia Sedley skipped out on Sambo's arm, as happy and as handsome girl as any in the whole big city of London. Both he and coachman agreed on this point, and so did her father and mother, and so did every one of the servants in the house, as they stood bobbing, and curtsying, and smiling, in the hall, to welcome their young mistress.

You may be sure that she showed Rebecca over every room of the house, and everything in every one of her drawers; and her books, and her piano, and her dresses, and all her necklaces, brooches, laces, and gimcracks. She insisted upon Rebecca accepting the white cornelian and the turquoise rings, and a sweet sprigged muslin, which was too small for her now, though it would fit her friend to a nicety: and she determined in her heart to ask her mother's permission to present her white Cashmere shawl to her friend, could she not spare it? And had not her brother Joseph just brought her two from India?

When Rebecca saw the two magnificent Cashmere shawls which Joseph Sedley had brought home to his sister, she said, with perfect truth, "that it must be delightful to have a brother," and easily got the pity of the tender-hearted Amelia, for being alone in the world, an orphan without friends or kindred.

"Not alone," said Amelia; "you know, Rebecca, I shall always be your friend, and love you as a sister — indeed I will."

"Ah, but to have parents, as you have — kind, rich, affectionate parents, who give you everything you ask for; and their love, which is more precious than all! My poor pap could give me nothing, and I had but two frocks in all the world! And then, to have a brother, a dear brother! Oh, How you must love him!"

Amelia laughed.

"What! Don't you love him? You, who say you love everybody?"

"Yes, of course, I do-only-"

"Only what?"

Only Joseph doesn't seem to care much whether I love him or not. He gave me two fingers to shake when he arrived after ten years' absence! He is very kind and good, but he scarcely ever speaks to me; I think he loves his pipe a great deal better than his — but her Amelia checked herself, for why should she speak ill of her brother? "He was very kind to me as a child," she added; "I was but five years old when he went away."

"Isn't he very rich? " Said Rebecca. "They say all Indian nabobs are enormously rich"

"I believe he has a very large income."

"And is your sister-in-law a nine pretty woman?"

"La! Joseph is not married," said Amelia, laughing again.

Perhaps she had mentioned the fact already to Rebecca, but that young lady did not appear to have remembered it; indeed, vowed and protested that she expected to see a number of Amelia's nephews and nieces. She was quite disappointed that Mr. Sedley was not married; she was sure Amelia had said he was, and she doted so on little children.

"I think you must have had enough of them at Chiswick," said Amelia, rather wondering at the sudden tenderness on her friend's part; and indeed in later days Miss Sharp would never have committed herself so far as to advance opinions, the untruth of which would have been so easily detected. But we must remember that she is but nineteen as yet, unused to the art of deceiving, poor innocent creature! And making her own experience in her own person. The meaning of the above series of queries, as translated in the heart of this ingenious young woman, was simply this:—

"If Mr. Joseph Sedley is rich and unmarried, why should I not marry him? I have only a fortnight, to be, sure, but there is no harm in trying." And she determined within herself to make this laudable attempt. She redoubled her caresses to Amelia; she kissed the white cornelian necklace as she put it on and vowed she would never, never part with. When the dinner-bell rang she went downstairs with her arm round her friend's waist, as is the habit of young ladies. She was so agitated at the drawing-room door, that she could hardly find courage to enter. "Feel my heart, how it beats, dear!" said she to her friend.

Notes

1. The novel marks the peak of Wiliam Makepeace Thackeray's critical realism. Building its plot around the lives of the two girls, Becky sharp and Amelia Sedley, the novel presents the life of the ruling classes of England in the early decades of the 19th century, and attacks the social relationship of the bourgeois world by satirizing the individuals in the different strata of the upper society.
2. the heroic act: At the end of Chapter 1, Misss Sharp threw away to the ground the dictionary given to her by Miss Jemima, the younger sister of the headmaster of Miss Pinkerton's academy for young ladies.
3. Vive la France! Vive l'Empereur! Vive Bonaparte!: French, meaning Long live France! Long live the Emperor! Long live Napoleon!
4. Lucifer: Satan
5. Minerra: the godess of wisdom in Greek Mythology, here referring to the woman headmaster in an ironic sense.

THE ART OF FICTION[1]

(Excerpt)

by Henry James

I am far from intending by this to minimize the importance of exactness — of truth of detail. One can speak best from one's own Caste, and I may therefore venture to say that the air of reality (solidity of specification) seems to me to be the supreme virtue of a novel — the merit on which all its other merits (including that conscious moral purpose of which Mr. Besant[2] speak) helplessly and submissively depend. If it be not there they are all as nothing, and if these be there, they owe their effect to the success, with which the author has produced the illusion of life. The cultivation of this success, the study of this exquisite process, form, to my taste, the beginning and the end of the art of the novelist. They are his inspiration, his despair, his reward, his torment, his delight. It is here in very truth that he competes with life; it is here that he competes with his brother the painter in his attempt to render the look of things, the look that conveys their meaning, to catch the colour, the relief, the expression, the surface, the substance of the human spectacle. It is in regard to this that Mr. Besant is well inspired when he bids him take notes. He cannot possibly take too many. He cannot possibly take enough. All life solicits him, and to "render" the simplest surface, to produce the most momentary illusion, is a very complicated business. His case would be easier, and would be more exact, if Mr. Besant had been able to tell him what notes to take. But this, I fear, he can never learn in any manual; it is the business of his life. He has to take a great many in order to select a few, he has to work them up as he can, and even the guides and philosophers who might have most to say to him must leave him alone when it comes to the application of precepts, as we leave the painter in communion with his palette. That his characters "must be clear in outline," as Mr. Besant says — he falls that down to his boots; but how he shall make them so is a secret between his good angel of "description", or that on the contrary the absence of description and the cultivation of dialogue, or the absence of dialogue and the multiplication of "incident," would

rescue him from his difficulties. Noting, for instance, is more possible than that he be of a turn mind for which this odd, literal opposition of description and dialogue, incident and description, has little meaning and light. People often talk of these things as if they
had a kind of internecine distinctness, instead of melting into each
other at everybreath, and being intimately associated parts of one
general effort of expression. I cannot imagine composition existing
in a series of blocks, nor conceive, in any novel worth discussing
at all, of a passage of description that is not in its intention narrative, a passage of dialogue that is not in its intention descriptive, a
touch of truth of any sort that does not partake of the nature of the
incident, or an incident that derives its interest from any other
source than the general and only source of the success of a work of
art-- that of being illustrative. A novel is a living thing, all one and
continuous, like any other organism, and in proportion as it lives
will it be found, I think, that in each of the other parts there is
something of each of the parts. The critic who over the close items
will mark, some frontiers as artificial, I fear, as any that have
been known to history. There is an old-fashioned distinction between the novel of character and the novel of incident which must
have cost many a smile to the intending fabulist who was keen a-
bout his work. It appears to me as little to the point as the equally
celebrated distinction between the novel and the romance to answer as little to any reality. There are bad novels and good novels, as there are bad pictures and good pictures; but that is the
only distinction in which I see any meaning, and I can as little i-
magine speaking of a novel of character as I can imagine speaking
of a picture of character. When one says picture one says of character, when one says novel one says of incident, and the terms
may be transposed at will. What is character but the determination
of incident? What is incident but the illustration of character? What
is either a picture or a novel that is not of character? What else do

we seek in it and find in it? It is an incident for a woman to stand up with her hand resting on a table and look out at you in a certain way; or if it be not an incident I think it will be hard to say what it is. At the same time is an expression of character. If you say you don't see it (character in that-allons donc![3]), this is exactly what the artist who has reasons of his own for thinking he does see it undertakes to show you. When a young man makes up his mind that he had not faith enough after all to enter the church as he intended, that is an incident, though you may not hurry to the end of the chapter to see whether perhaps he doesn't change once more. I do not say that these are extraordinary or startling incidents. I do not pretend to estimate the degree of interest proceeding from them, for this will depend upon the skill of the painter, it sounds almost puerile to say that some incidents are intrinsically much more important than others, and I need not take this precaution after having processed my sympathy for the major ones in remarking that the only classification of the novel that I can understand is into that which has life and that which has it not.

Notes

1. It is James' best-known essay on theory of fiction, which presents the beginnings of modern fictional theory. In this essay, James rejects conventional critical labels and distinctions; he rejects a prior prescriptions and rules about how to write a novel; he rejects limitations on the artist's freedom of choice in respect to subject matter and technique; he rejects trad— tional concepts of plot; and, climatically, he rejects Besant's formulation concerning the conscious moral purpose of the novel.
2. Sir Walter Besant (1836- 1901), English novelist, history and literary critic.
3. French; nonsense.

PYGMALION[1]
from Act III
by George Bernard Shaw

It is Miss Higgins's at-home day. [2] *Nobody has yet arrived.
Her drawing room, in a flat on Chelsea Embankment, has three
windows looking on the river; and the ceiling is not so lofty as it
would be in an older house of the same pretension. The windows
are open, giving access to a balcony with flowers in pots. If
you stand with your face to the windows, you have the fireplace
on your left and the door in the right-hand wall close to the corner nearest the windows.*

Mrs. Higgins was brought up on Morris and Burne Jones, [3]
*and her room, which is very unlike her son's room in Wimpole
street, is not crowded with furniture and little tables and knick-
knacks. In the middle of the room there is a big ottoman; and
this, with the carpet, the Morris wall-papers, and the Morris
chintz window curtains and brocade covers of the ottoman and
its cushions, supply all the ornament, and are much too handsome to be hidden by odds and ends of useless things. A few
good oil-paintings from the exhibitions in the Grosvenor gallery
thirty years ago (the Burne Jones, not the whistler* [4] *side of
them) are on the walls. The only landscape is a Cecil Lawson on
the scale of a Rubens.* [5] *There is a portrait of Mrs. Higgins as
she was when she defied the fashion in her youth in one of the
beautiful rossettian costumes which, when caricatured by people*

*who did not understand, led to the absurdities of popular es-
theticism in the eighteen-seventies.*

*In the corner diagonally opposite the door Mrs. Higgins,
now over sixty and long past taking the trouble to dress out of
the fashion, sits writing at an elegantly simple writingtable
with a bell button within reach of her hand. There is a Chipp-
endable*⁶ *chair further back in the room between her and the window nearest her side. At the other side of the room, further forward, is an Elizabethan chair roughly carved in the taste of Inigo Jones.*⁷ *On the same side a piano in a decorated case. The
corner between the fireplace and the window is occupied by a divan cushioned in Morris chintz.* ·

*It is between four and five in the afternoon. The door is
opened violently ; and Higgins enters with his hat on.*

MRS HIGGINS: [*dismayed*] Henry! [*Scolding him*] What are you
    doing here today? It is my at-home day: you promised not to
    come [*As he bends to kiss her, she takes his hat off, and
    presents it to him*].

HIGGINS: Oh bother! [*He throws the hat down on the table*].

MRS HIGGINS: Go home at once.

HIGGINS: [*kissing her*] I know, mother. I came on purpose.

MRS HIGGINS: But you mustn't, I'm serious, Henry. You offend all
    my friends: they stop coming whenever they meet you.

HIGGINS: Nonsense! I know I have no small talk; but people don't
    mind. [*He sits on the settee*].

MRS HIGGINS: (Oh! don't they? Small talk indeed! What about
    your large talk? Really, dear, you mustn't stay.

HIGGINS: I must. I've a job for you. A phonetic job.

MRS HIGGINS: No use, dear. I'm sorry; but I can't get round your
    vowels; and though I like to get pretty postcards in your pa-

tent shorthand, I always have to read the copies in ordinary writing you so thoughtfully send me.

HIGGINS: Well, this isn't a phonetic job.

MRS HIGGINS: You said it was.

HIGGINS: Not your part of it. I've picked up a girl.

MRS HIGGINS: Does that mean that some girl has picked you up?

HIGGINS: Not at all. I don't mean a love affair.

MRS HIGGINS: What a pity!

HIGGINS: Why?

MRS HIGGINS: Well, you never fall in love with anyone under forty-five. When will you discover that there are some rather nice- looking young women about?

HIGGINS: oh, I can't be bothered with young women. My idea of a lovable woman is somebody as like you as possible. I shall never get into the way of seriously liking young women: some habits lie too deep to be changed. [*rising abruptly and walking about, jingling his money and his keys in his trouser pockets*] Besides, they're all idiots.

MRS HIGGINS: Do you know what you would do if you really loved me, Henry?

HIGGINS: oh bother! What? Marry, I suppose.

MRS HIGGINS: No. Stop fidgeting and take your hands out of your pockets. [*With a gesture of despair, he obeys and sits down again*]. That's a good boy. Now tell me about the girl.

HIGGINS: She's coming to see you.

MRS HIGGINS: I don't remember asking her.

HIGGINS: You didn't, I asked her, If you'd known her you wouldn't have asked her.

MRS HIGGINS: Indeed! Why?

HIGGINS: Well, it's like this. She's common flower girl. I picked her off the kerbstone.

MRS HIGGINS: And invited her to my at-home!

HIGGINS: [*rising and coming to her to coax her*] Oh, that'll be all
   right. I've taught her to speak properly; and she has strict orders as to her behavior. She's to keep to two subjects: the
   weather and everybody's health — Fine day and How do you
   do, you know — and not to let herself go on things in general. That will be safe.
MRS HIGGINS: Safe! To talk about our health! About our insides!
   Perhaps about our outsides! How could you be so silly, Henry?
HIGGINS: [*impatiently*] Well, she must talk about something.
   [*He controls himself and sits down again*]. Oh, she'll be
   all right: don't you fuss. Piokering is in it with me. I've a sort
   of bet on that I'll pass her off as a duchess in six months. I
   started on her some months ago; and she's getting on like a
   house on fire. I shall win my bet. She has a quick ear; and
   she's been easier to teach than my middle-class pupil because she's had to learn a complete new language. She talks
   English almost as you talk French.
MRS HIGGINS: That's satisfactory, at all events.
HIGGINS: Well, it is and it isn't.
MRS HIGGINS: What does that mean?
HIGGINS: You see, I've got her pronunciation all right; but you
   have come to consider not only how a girl pronounces, but
   what she pronounces; and that's where —
   They are interrupted by the parlor-maid, announcing
   guests.
THE PARLOR-MAID: MRS and Miss Eynsford Hill. [*She with-*
   draws].
HIGGINS: Oh Lord! [*He rises; snatches his hat from the table;
   and makes for the door; but before he reaches it his mother
   introduces him*].
[*Mrs And Miss Eynsford Hill are the mother and daughter who*

sheltered from the rain in Covent Garden. The mother is well bred, and has the habitual anxiety of straitened means. The daughter has acquired a gay air of being very much at home in society; the bravado of genteel poverty.]

MRS EYNSFORD HILL: [*to Mrs. Higgins*] How do you do? [*They shake hands*].

MRSS EYNSFORD HILL: How do you do? [*She shakes*].

MRS HIGGINS: [*introducing*] My son Henry.

MRS EYNSFORD HILL: Your celebrated son! I have so longed to meet you, Professor Higgins.

HIGGINS: [*glumly, making no movement in her direction*] delighted. [*he backs against the piano and bows brusquely*].

MISS EYNSORD HILL: [*going to him with confident familiarity*] How do you do?

HIGGINS: [*staring at her*] I've seen you before somewhere. I haven't the ghost of a notion where; but I've heard your voice. [*Drearily*] It doesn't matter. You'd better sit down.

MRS HIGGINS: I'm sorry to say that my celebrated son has no manners. You mustn't mind him.

MRS EYNSFORD HILL: [*gaily*] I don't. [*She sits in the Elizabethan chair*].

MRS EYNSFORD HILL: [*a little bewildered*] Not at all. [*She sits on the ottoman between her daughter and Mrs. Higgins, who has turned her chair away from the writing-table*].

HIGGINS: Oh, have I been rude? I didn't mean to be. He goes to the central window, through which, with his back to the company, he contemplates the river and the flowers in Battersea park on the opposite bank as if they were a frozen desert. The parlor-aid returns, ushering in Pickering.

THE PARLOR-MAID. Colonel Pickering. [*She withdraws.*]

PICKERING: How do you do, Mrs. Higgins?

MRS HIGGINS: So glad you've come. Do you know Mrs. Eynsford

Hill and Miss Eynsford Hill? [*Exchange of bows. The colonel brights the Chippendale chair a little forward Mrs. Hill and Mrs. Higgins, and sits down*].

PICKEFIING: Has Henry told you what we've come for?

HIGGINS: [*over his shoulder*] We were interrupted: damn it!

MRS HIGGINS: Oh Henry, Henry, really!

MRS EYNSFORD HILL: [*half rising*] Are we in the way?

MRS HIGGINS: [*rising and making her sit down again*] No, no. You couldn't have come more fortunately: we want you to meet a friend of ours.

HIGGINS: [*turning hopefully*] Yes, by George![8] we want two or three people. You'll do as well as anybody else.

The parlor-maid returns, ushering Freddy.

The PARLOR-MAID. Mr. Eynsford Hill.

HIGGINS: [*almost audibly, past endurance*] God of Heaven! Another of them.

FREDDY: [*shaking hands with Mrs. Higgins*] Ahdedo?

MRS HIGGINS: Very good of you to come. [*Introducing*] colonel Pickering.

FREDDY: [*bowing*] Ahdedo?

MRS HIGGINS: I don't think you know my son, Professor Higgins.

FREDDY: [*going to Higgins*]Ahdedo?

HIGGINS: [*looking at him much as if he were a pickpocket*]I'll take my oath I've met you before somewhere. Where was it?

FREDDY: I don't think so.

HIGGINS: [*resignedly*]It doesn't matter, anyhow. Sit down.

He shakes Freddy's hand, and almost slings him on to the ottoman with his face to the window; then comes round to the other side of it.

HIGGINS: Well, here we are, anyhow! [*He sits down on the ottoman next Mrs. Eynsford Hill, on her left*]. And now, what the devil are we going to talk about until Eliza comes?

MRS HIGGINS: Henry: you are the life and soul of the Royal
　　　　Society's soirees;[9] but really you're rather trying on more
　　　　commonplace occasions.
HIGGINS: Am I? Very sorry. [*Beaming suddenly*] I suppose I am,
　　　　you know. [*Uproariously*] Ha, ha!
MISS EYNSFORD HILL: [*who considers Higgins quite eligible
　　　　matrimonially*] I sympathize. I haven't any small talk If peo-
　　　　ple would only be frank and say what they really think!
HIGGINS: [*relapsing into gloom*] Lord forbid!
MRS EYNSFORD HILL: [*taking up her daughter's cue*] But why?
HIGGINS: What they think they ought to think is bad enough, Lord
　　　　knows; but what they really think would break up the whole
　　　　show. Do you suppose it would be really agreeable if I were
　　　　to come out now with what I really think?
MISS EYNSFORD HILL: [*gaily*] Is it so very cynical?
HIGGINS: Cynical! Who the dickens said it was cynical? I mean it
　　　　wouldn't be decent.
MRS EYNSFORD HILL: [*seriously*] Oh! I'm sure you don't mean
　　　　that, Mr. Higgins.
HIGGINS: You see, we're all savages, more or less. We're sup-
　　　　posed to be civilized and cultured — to know all about poetry
　　　　and philosophy and art and science, and so on; but how many
　　　　of us know even the meanings of these names? [*To Miss
　　　　Hill*] What do you know of poetry? [*To Mrs. Hill*] What do
　　　　you know of science? [*Indicating Freddy*] What does he
　　　　know of art or science or anything else? What the devil do you
　　　　imagine I know of philosophy?
MRS HIGGINS: [*warningly*] Or of manners, Henry?
THE PARLOR-MAID: [*opening the door*] Miss Doolittle. [*She
　　　　withdraws*].
HIGGINS: [*rising hastily and running to Mrs. Higgins*] Here
　　　　she is, mother. [*He stands on tiptoe and makes signs over,*

*his mother's head to Eliza to indicate to her which lady is
her hostess*.

    *Eliza, who is exquisitely dressed, produces an impres-
sion of such remarkable distinction and beauty as she enters
that they all rise, quite fluttered. Guided by Higgins'
signals, she comes to Mrs. Higgins with studied grace.*

LIZA: *[speaking with pedantic correctness of pronunciation and
great beauty of tone]* How do you do, Mrs. Higgins? *[She
gasps slightly in making sure of the H in Higgins, but is
quite successful]*. Mr. Higgins told me I might come.

MRS HIGGINS: *[cordially]* Quite right: I'm very glad indeed to
see you.

PICKERING: How do you do, Miss Doolittle?

LIZA: *[shaking hands with him]* Colonel Pickering, is it not?

MRS EYNSFORD HILL: I fell sure we have met before, Miss
Doolittle. I remember your eyes.

LIZA: How do you do? *[She sits down on the ottoman gracefully
in the place just left vacant by Higgins]*.

MRS EYNSFORD HILL: *[introducing]* My daughter Clara.

LIZA: How do you do?

CLARA: *[Impulsively]* HOW do you do? *[She sits down on the
ottoman besides Eliza, devouring her with her eyes]*.

FREEDDY: *[coming to their side of the ottoman]* I've certainly
had the please.

MRS EYNSFORD HILL: *[introducing]* My son Freddy.

LIZA: How do you do?

    *Freddy bows and sits down in the Elizabethan chair, infatuat-
ed.*

HIGGINS: *[suddenly]* By George, yes: it all comes back to me!
[They stare at him]. Covenden Garden! *[Lamentably]*
What a damned thing!

MRS HIGGINS: Henry, please! *[He is about to sit on the edge of the table*]. Don't sit on my writing-table; you'll break it.

HIGGINS: [*sulkily*] Sorry.

He goes to the divan, stumbling into the fender and over the fire-irons on his way; extricating himself with muttered imprecations; and finishing his disastrous journey by throwing himself so impatiently on the divan that he almost breaks it. Mrs. Higgins looks at him, but controls herself and says nothing.

A long and painful pause ensues.

MRS HIGGINS: [*at last, conversationally*] Will it rain, do you think?

LIZA: The shallow depression in the west of these islands is likely to move slowly in an easterly direction. There are no indications of any great change in the barometrical situation.

FREDDY: Ha! Ha! How awfully funny!

LIZA: What is wrong with that, young man? I bet I got it right.

FREDDY: Killing!

MRS EYNSFORD HILL: I'm sure I hope it won't turn cold. There's so much influenza about. It runs right through our whole family regularly every spring.

LIZA: [*darkly*] My aunt died of influenza: so they said.

MRS EYNSFORD HILL: [*clicks her tongue sympathetically*]!!!

LIZA: [*in the same tragic tone*] But it's my belief they done the old woman in.

MRS HIGGINS: [*puzzled*] Done her in?

LIZA: Y-e-e-e-es, Lord love you! Why should she die of influenza? She had come through diphtheria right enough the year before. I saw her with my own eyes, Fairly blue with it, she was. They all thought she was dead; but my father he kept ladling gin down her throat till she came to sudden that she bit the bowl off the spoon.

MRS EYNSFORD HILL: [*startled*] Dear me!

LIZA: [*piling up the indictment*] What call would a woman with that strength in her have to die of influenza? What become of her new straw hat that should have come to me? Somebody pinched it; and what I say is, them as pinched it done her in.

MRS EYNSFORD HILL: What does doing her in mean?

HIGGINS: [*hastily*] Oh, that's the new small talk. To do a person in means to kill them.

MRS EYNSFORD HILL: [*to Eliza, horrified*] You surely don't believe that your aunt was killed?

LIZA: Do I not! Them she lived with would have killed her for a hat pin, let alone a hat.

MRS EYNSFORD HILL: But it can't have been right for your father to pour spirits down her throat like that. It might have killed her.

LIZA: Not her. Gin was mother's milk to her. Besides, he'd poured so much down his own throat that he knew the good of it.

MRS EYNSFORD HILL: Do you mean that he drank?

LIZA: Drank! My word! Something chronic.

MRS EYNSFORD HILL: How dreadful for you!

LIZA: Not a bit. It never did him no harm what I could see. But then he did not keep it up regular. [*cheerfully*] On the burst, as you might say, from time to time. And always more agreeable when he had a drop in. When he was out of work, my mother used to give him fourpence and tell him to go out and not come back until he'd drunk himself cheerful and lov-ing-like. There's lots of women have to make their husbands drunk to make them fit to live with. [*Now quite at her ease*] You see, it's like this. If a man has a bit of a conscience, it always takes him when he's sober, and then it makes him happy. [*To Freddy, who is in convulsions of suppressed laughter*] Here! What are you sniggering at?

FREDDY: The new small talk. You do it so awfully well.

LIZA: If I was doing it proper, what was you laughing at? [*To Higgins*] Have I said anything I oughtn't?

MRS HIGGINS: [*interposing*] Not at all, Miss Doolittle.

LIZA: Well, that's a mercy, anyhow. [*Expansively*] What I always say is —

HIGGINS: [*rising and looking at his watch*] Ahem!

LIZA: [*looking round at him; taking the hint; and rising*]Well: I must go. [*They all rise. Freddy goes to the door*]. So pleased to have met you. Goodbye. [*She shakes hands with Mrs. Higgins*].

MRS HIGGINS: Goodbye.

LIZA: Goodbye, Colonel Pickering.

PICKERING: Goodbye, Miss Doolittle. [*They shake hands*].

LIZA: [*nodding to the others*] Goodbye, all.

FREDDY: [*opening the door for her*] Are you walking across the Park, Miss Doolittle? If so —

LIZA: [*with perfectly elegant diction*] Walk! Not bloody likely. [*Sensation*]. I am going in a taxi. [*She goes out*].

Pickering gasps down and sits down. Freddy goes out on the balcony to catch another glimpse of Eliza.

MRS EYNSFORD HILL: [*suffering from shock*] Well, I really can't get used to the new ways.

CLARA: [*throwing herself discontentedly into the Elizabethan chair*] Oh, it's all right, mamma, quite right. People will think we never go anywhere or see anybody if you are so old-fashioned.

MRS EYNSFORD HILL: I daresay I am very old-fashioned; but I do hope you won't begin using that expression, Clara. I have got accustomed to hear you talking about men as rotters, and calling everything filthy and beastly; though I do think it horrible and unladylike. But this last is really too much. Don't you think so, Colonel Pickering?

PICKERING: Don't ask me. I've been away in India for several years; and manners have changed so much that I sometimes don't know whether I'm at a respectable dinner-table or in ship's forecastle.

CLARA: It's all a matter of habit. There's no right or wrong in it. Nobody means anything by it. And it's so quaint, and gives such a smart emphasis to things that are not in themselves very witty I find the new small talk delight and innocent.

MRS EYNSFORD HILL: [*rising*] Well, after that, I think it's time for us to go.

Pickering and Higgins rise.

CLARA: [*rising*] Oh yes: we have three at-homes to go to still. Goodbye, Mrs. Higgins. Goodbye, Colonel Pickering. Goodbye, Professor Higgins.

HIGGINS: [*coming grimly at her from the divan, and accompanying her to the door*] Goodbye. Be sure you try on that small talk at the three at-homes. Don't be nervous about it. Pitch it in strong.

CLARA: [*all smiles*] I will. Goodbye. Such damned nonsense, all this early Victorian prudery!

HIGGINS: [*tempting her*] Such damned nonsense!

CLARA: Such bloody nonsense!

MRS EYNSFORD HILL: [*convulsively*] Clara!

CLARA: Ha! Ha! [*She goes out radiant, conscious of being thoroughly up to date, and is heard descending the stairs in a stream of silvery laughter*].

FREDDY: [*to the heavens at large*] Well, I ask you — [*He gives it up, and comes to Mrs. Higgins*]. Goodbye.

MRS HIGGINS: [*shaking hands*] Goodbye. Would you like to meet Miss Doolittle again?

FREDDY: [*eagerly*] Yes, I should, most awfully.

MRS HIGGINS: Well, You know my days.

FREDDY: Yes. Thanks awfully. Goodbye. [*He goes out*].

MRS EYNSFORD HILL: [*to Pickering*] It's no use. I shall never be able to bring myself to use that word.

PICKERING: Don't. It's not compulsory, you know. You'll get on quite well without it.

MRS EYNSFORD HILL: Only, Clara is so down on me if I am not positively reeking with the latest slang. Goodbye.

PICKERING: Goodbye [*They shake hands*].

MRS EYNSFORD HILL: [*to Mrs. Higgins*] You mustn't mind.

Clara: [*Pickering, catching from her lowered tone that this is not meant for him to hear, discreetly joins Higgins at the window*]. We're so poor! And she gets so few parties, poor child! She doesn't quite know. [*Mrs. Higgins, seeing that her eyes are moist, takes her hand sympathetically and goes with her to the door*]. But the boy is nice. Don't you think so?

MRS HIGGINS: Oh, quite nice. I shall always be delighted to see him.

MRS EYNSFORD HILL: Thank you, dear. Goodbye. [*She goes out.*]

Notes

1. The play is a poignant satire on high life. The story goes like this: Henry Higgins, a linguist, meets a flower girl named Eliza Doolittle, and makes a bet with Pickering, another linguist, that he can train the flower girl to behave herself as a duchess in six months. After a period of training, Eliza is present at a reception and conducts well like a princess. Higgins succeeds in his bet, but Eliza, a girl of dignity, leaves him and is ready to marry a young man by the name of Freddy. In the above act, Higgins arranges for Eliza to make a show of her improved behavior and pronuncia-

tion at his mother's party.

2. at-home day: Special day for receiving guest.

3. Morris and Burne Jones: British artists of the late 19th century.

4. Whistler: a paintist like Burne Tones.

5. a Cecil Lawson on the scale of a Rubens: A landscape by Cecil Lawson which is of the size of Rubens'. Cecil Lawson (1851-1882): British painter. Rubens (1577-1640): Italian painter.

6. Chippendale (1718-1779): a famous carpenter.

7. Inigo Jones (1573-1652): a famous carpenter.

8. By George!: I swear by St. George. Saint George: the patron saint in England.

9. soirees: (French) social party.

Considerations:

1. What is the "new small talk"? What is the "sanguinary element" in that "small talk"? In what way is the "small talk" like the fairy tale of the Emperor's new clothes?

2. Though this scene seems comically exaggerated, what elements of "truth" or "reality" are in it? What does it suggest about society and its "rules"?

AN AMERICAN TRAGEDY[1]
Chapter Ⅲ
by Theodore Dreiser

Two letters, which arrived at this time and simultaneously, but accentuated the difficulty of all this.

Pine Point Landing, June 10th.

CLYDE MYDLE:[2]

How is my pheet phing? All wytie?[3] It's just glorious up here. Lots of people already here and more coming every day. The Casino[4] and golf course over at Pine Point are open and lots of people about. I can hear Stuart ancl Grant[5] with their launches going up toward Gray's Inlet now. You must hurry and come up, dear. It's too nice for words. Green roads to gallop through, and swimming and dancing at the Casino every afternoon at four. Just back from a wonderful gallop on Dickey[6] and going again after luncheon to mail these letters. Bertine[7] says she'll write you a letter today or tomorrow good for any weekend or any old time,[8] so when Sonda[9] says come, you come, you hear, else Sonda whip hard. You baddie, good boy.[10]

Is he working hard in the baddie old factory? Sonda wisses he here wiss her instead.[11] We'd ride and drive and swim and dance. Don't forget your tennis racquet and golf dabs. There's a dandy course on the Casino Grounds.

This morning when I was riding a bird flew right up under Dickey's heels. It scared him so that he bolted and Sonda got all switched and scratched. Isn't clydie[12] sorry for his Sonda?

She is writing lots of notes today. After lunch and the ride to catch the down mail, Sonda and Bertine and Nina[13] going to the Casino. Don't you wish you were going to be there? We could dance to "Tautly." Sonda just loves that song. But she has to dress now. More tomorrow, baddie boy. And when Bertine writes, answer right away. See all 'ose dots? Kisses.[14] Big and little ones. All for baddie boy. And wite[15] Sonda every day and she'll write 'oo.

More kisses.

To which Clyde responded eagerly and in kind[16] in the same hour, But almost the same mail, at least the same day, brought the following letter from Roberta.

Blitz. [17] June 10th,

DEAR CLYDE:

 I am nearly ready for bed, but I will write you a few lines. I had such a tiresome journey coming up that I was nearly sick. In the first place I didn't want to come much (alone) as you know. I feel too upset and uncertain about everything, although I try not to feel so now that we have our plan and you are going to come for me as you said.

 (*At this point, while nearly sickened by the thought of the wretched country world in which she lived, still, because of Roberta's unfortunate and unavoidable relation to it, he now experienced one of his old time twinges of remorse and pity in regard to her. For after all, this was not her fault. She had so little to look forward to — nothing but her work or a commonplace marriage. For the first time in many days, really, and in the absence of both, he was able to think clearly — and to sympathize deeply, if gloomily. For the remainder of the letter read*:)

 But it's very nice here now. The trees are so beautifully green and the flowers in bloom. I can hear the bees in the orchard whenever I go near the south windows. On the way up instead of coming straight home I decided to stop at Homer[18] to see my sister and brother-in-law, since I am not so sure now when I shall see them again, if ever, for I am resolved that they shall see me respectable, or never at all any more. You mustn't think I mean anything hard or mean by this. I am just sad. They have such a cute little home there, Clyde-pretty furniture, a victrola[19] and all, and Agnes[20] is so very happy with Fred.[21] I hope she always will be. I couldn't help thinking of what a dear place we might have had, if only my dreams had come true. And nearly all the time I was there Fred kept teasing me as to why I don't get married, until I said, "Oh, well, Fred, you mustn't be too sure that I won't one of these days. All good things come to him who waits, you know.""Yes, unless you just turn ou   be a waiter," was the way he hit me back.

But I was truly glad to see mother again, Clyde. She's so loving and patient and helpful. The sweetest, dearest mother that ever, ever was. And I just hate to hurt her in any way. And Tom and Emily[22] too. They have had friends here every evening since I've been here — and they want me to join in, but I hardly feel well enough now to do all the things they want me to do — play cards and games — dance.

(At this point Clyde could not help emphasizing in his own mind the shabby home world of which she was a part and which so recently he had seen — that rickety house! Those toppling chimneys! Her uncouth father. And that in contrast to such a letter as this other from Sondra.)

Father and mother and Tom and Emily just seem to hang a-round and try to do things for me. And I feel remorseful when I think how they would feel if they knew, for, of course, I have to pretend that it is work that makes me feel so tired and depressed as I am sometimes. Mother keeps saying that I must stay a long time or quit entirely and rest and get well again, but she just don't know of course — poor dear. If she did! I can't tell you how that makes me feel sometimes, Clyde. Oh, dear!

But there, I mustn't put my sad feelings over on you either. I don't want to, as I told you, if you will only come and get me as we've agreed. And I won't be like that either, Clyde. I'm not that way all the time now. I've started to get ready and do all the things it'll take to do in three weeks and that's enough to keep my mind off everything but work. But you will come for me, won't you, dear? You won't disappoint me any more and make me suffer this time like you have so far, for, oh, how long it has been now — ever since I was here before at Christmas time, really. But you were truly nice to me. I promise not to be a burden on you, for I know you don't really care for me any more and so I don't care much what happens now, so long as I get out of this: But I truly promise not to be a burden on you.

But as for what I came for. The family think they[23] are clothes for a party down in Lycurgus and that I must be having a wonderful time. Well, it's better that way than the other. I may have to come as far as Fonda to get some things, if I don't send Mrs. Anse, the dressmaker, and if so, and if you wanted to see me again before you come, although I don't suppose you do, you could. I'd like to see you and talk to you again if you care to, before we start. It all seems so funny to me, Clyde, having these clothes made and wishing to see you so much and yet knowing that you would rather not do this. And yet I hope you are satisfied now that you have succeeded in making me leave Lycurgus and come up here and are having what you call a good time. Are they so very much better than the ones we used to have last summer, when we went about to the lakes and everywhere? But whatever they are, Clyde, surely you can afford to do this for me without feeling too bad. I know it seems hard to you now, but you don't want to forget either that if I was like some that I know, I might and would ask more. But as I told you I'm not like that and never could be. If you don't really want me after you have helped me out like I said, you can go.

Please write me, Clyde, a long, cheery letter, even though you don't want to, and tell me all about how you have not

thought of me once since I've been away or missed me at all —
you used to, you know, and how you don't want me to come back
and you can't possibly come up before two weeks from Saturday
if then. [24]

Oh, dear, I don't mean the horrid things I write, but I'm so
blue and tired and lonely that I can't help it at times. I need
some one to talk to — not just any one here, because they don't
understand, and I can't tell anybody.

But there, I said I wouldn't be blue or gloomy or cross and
yet I haven't done so very well this time, have I? But I promise
to do better next time — tomorrow or next day, because it re-
lieves me to write to you, Clyde. And won't you please write me
just a few words to cheer me up while I'm waiting, whether you
mean it or not, I need it so. And you will come, of course. I'll
be so happy and grateful and try not to bother you too much in
any way.

Your lonely
BERT. [25]

And it was the contrast presented by those two scenes which
finally determined for him the fact that he would never marry Roberta — never — nor even go to her at Blitz, or let her come back
to him here, if he could avoid that, For would not his going, or her
return, put a period to all the joys that so recently in connection
with Sondra had come to him here — make it impossible for him to
be with Sondra at 12th Lake this summer — make it impossible for
him to run away with and marry her? In God's name was there no
way? No outlet from this horrible difficulty which now confronted
him?

And in a fit of despair, having found the letters in his room on
his return from work one warm evening in June, he now threw him-

self upon his bed and fairly groaned, The misery of this! The horror of his almost insoluble problem! Was there no way by which she could be persuaded to go away — and stay — remain at home, maybe for a while longer, while he sent her ten dollars a week, or twelve, even — a full half of all his salary? Or could she go to some neighboring town — Fonda, Gloversville, Schenectady — she was not so far gone but what she could take care of herself well enough as yet,[26] and rent a room and remain there quietly until the fatal time, when she could go to some doctor or nurse? He might help her to find some one like that when the time came, if only she would be willing not to mention his name.

But this business of making him come to Blitz, or meeting her somewhere, and that within two weeks or less, He would not, he would not, He would do something desperate if she tried to make him do that — run away — or — maybe go up to 12th Lake before it should be time for him to go to Bills, or before she would think it was time, and then persuaded Sondra if he could — but oh, what a wild, wild chance was that — to run away with and marry him, even if she wasn't quite eighteen — and then — and then — being married, and her family not being able to divorce them, and Roberta not being able to find him, either, but only to complain — well, couldn't he deny it — say that it was not so — that he had never had any relationship, other than that which any department head might have with any girl working for him, He had not been introduced to the Gilpins,[27] nor had he gone with Roberta to see that Dr. Glenr[28] near Gloversville, and she had told him at the time, she had not mentioned his name.

But the nerve of trying to deny it!

The courage it would take. The courage to try to face Roberta when, as he knew, her steady, accusing, horrified, innocent blue eyes would be about as difficult to face as anything in all the world.

And could he do that? Had he the courage? And would it all work out satisfactorily if he did? Would Sondra believe him — once she heard?

But just the same in pursuance of this idea, whether finally he executed it or not, even though he went to Twelfth Lake, he must write Sondra a letter saying that he was coming. And this he did at once, writing her passionately and yearningly. At the same time he decided not to write Roberta at all. Maybe call her on long distance, since she had recently told him that there was a neighbor nearby who had a telephone, and if for any reason he needed to reach her, he could use that. For writing her in regard to all this, even in the most guarded way, would place in her hands, and at this time, exactly the type of evidence in regard to this relationship which she would most need, and especially when he was so determined not to marry her. The trickery of all this! It was low and shabby, no doubt. Yet if only Roberta had agreed to be a little reasonable with him, he would never have dreamed of indulging in any such low and tricky plan as this. But, oh, Sondra! Sondra! And the great estate that she had described, lying along the west shore of Twelfth Lake. How beautiful that must be! He could not help it! He must act and plan as he was doing! He must!

And forthwith he arose and went to mail the letter to Sondra. And then while out, having purchased an evening paper and hoping via the local news of all whom he knew, to divert his mind for the time being, there, upon the first page of the times-Union of Albany, was an item which read:

ACCIDENTAL DOUBLE TRAGEDY AT PASS LAKE — UP-TURNED CANCE AND FLOATING HATS REVEAL PROBABLE LOSS OF TWO LIVES AT RESORT NEAR PITTSFIELD — UNIDEN-TIFIED BODY OF GIRL REOOVERED — THAT OF OOMPANION STILL MISSING.

Because of his own great interest in canoeing, and indeed in any form of water life, as well as his own particular skill when it came to rowing, swimming, diving, he now read with interest.

Pancoast, Mass, June 7th ... What proved to be a fatal boat ride for two, apparently, was taken here day before yesterday by an unidentified man and girl who came presumably from Pittsfield to spend the day at Pass Lake, which is fourteen miles north of this place.

Tuesday morning a man and a girl, who said to Thomas Lucas, who conducted the Casino Lunch and Boat House there, that they were from Pittsfield, rented a small rowboat about ten o'clock in the morning and with a basket, presumably containing lunch, departed for the northern end of the lake. At seven o'clock last evening, when they did not return, Mr. Lucas, in company with his son Jeffrey, made a tour of the lake in his motor boat and discovered the rowboat upside down in the shallows near the north shore but no trace of the occupants. Thinking at the time that it might be another instance of renters having decamped in order to avoid payment, he returned the boat to his own dock.

But this morning, doubtful as to whether or not an accident had occurred, he and his assistant, Fred Walsh, together with his son, made a second tour of the north shore and finally came upon the hats of both the girl and the man floating among some rushes near the shore. At once a dredging party was organized, and by three o'clock today the body of the girl, concerning whom nothing was known here, other than that she came here with her companion, was brought up and turned over to the authorities. That of the man has not yet been found, The water in the immediate vicinity of the accident in some places being over thirty feet deep, it is not certain whether the trolling and dred-

西方文学

ging will yield the other body or not, In the case of a similar accident which took place here some fifteen years ago, neither body was ever recovered.

To the lining of the small jacket which the girl wore was sewed the tag of a Pittsfield dealer, Also in her shoe lining was stamped the name of Jacobs of this same city. But other than these there was no evidence as to her identity, It is assumed by the authorities here that if she carried a bag of any kind it lies at the bottom of the lake.

The man is recalled as being tall, dark, about thirty-five years of age, and wore a light green suit and straw hat with a white and blue band, The girl appears to be not more than twenty-five, five feet five inches tall, and weighs 150 pounds. She wore her hair, which was long and dark brown, in braids about her forehead. On her left middle finger is a small gold ring with an amethyst setting. The police of Pittsfield and other cities in this vicinity have been notified, but as yet no word as to her identity has been received.

This item, commonplace enough in the usual grist of summer accidents, interested Clyde only slightly. It seemed odd, of course, that a girl and a man should arrive at a small lake anywhere, and setting forth in a small boat in broad daylight thus lose their lives. Also it was odd that afterwards no one should be able to identify either of them. And yet here it was. The man had disappeared for good. [29] He threw the paper down, little concerned at first, and turned to other things — the problem that was confronting him really — how he was to do. But later — and because of that, and as he was putting out the light before getting into bed, and still thinking of the complicated problem which his own life here presented, he was struck by the thought (what devil's whisper? — what evil hint of an evil spirit?) — supposing that he and Roberta — no, say he and Sondra — （no, Sondra could swim so well, and so could he） — he and Roberta were in a small boat, somewhere and it should capsize at the very time, say, of this dreadful complication which was so harassing him? What an escape? What a relief from a gigantic and by now really destroying problem! On the other hand — hold — not so fast! — for could a man even think of such a solution in connection with so difficult a problem as his without committing a crime in his heart, really — a horrible, terrible crime? He must not even think of such a thing. It was wrong — wrong — terrible wrong. And yet, supposing, — by accident, of course — such a thing as this did occur? That would be the end, then, wouldn't it, of all his troubles in connection with Roberta? No more terror as to her — no more fear and heartache even as to Sondra. A noiseless, pathless, quarrelless solution of all his present difficulties, and only joy before him forever. Just an accidental, unpremeditated drowning — and then the glorious future which would be his!

But the mere thinking of such a thing in connection with Roberta at this time （why was it that his mind persisted in identifying her with it?） was terrible, and he must not, he must not, allow such a thought to enter his mind. Never, never, never! He must not. It was horrible! Terrible! A thought of murder, no less! Murder?!!! Yet so wrought up[30] had he been, and still was, by the letter which Roberta had written him, as contrasted with the one from Sondra — so delightful and enticing was the picture of her life and his as she now described it, that he could not for the life of him quite expel that other and seemingly easy and so natural a solution of all his problem — if only such an accident could occur to him and Roberta. For after all he was not planning any crime, was he? Was he not merely thinking of an accident that, had it occurred or could it but occur in his case ... Ah — but that "could it but occur." There was the dark and evil thought about which he must not, he must not think, HE MUST NOT. And yet — and yet . . . He was an excellent swimmer and could swim ashore, no doubt — whatever the distance. Whereas Roberta, as he knew from swimming with her at one beach and another the previous summer, could not swim. And then — and then — well and then, unless he chose to help her, of course . . .

As he thought, and for the time, sitting in the lamplight of his own room between nine-thirty and ten at night, a strange and disturbing creepiness as to flesh and hair and fingertips assailed him. The wonder and the horror of such a thought! And presented to him by this haper in this way. Wasn't that strange? Besides, up in that lake country to which he was now going to Sondra, were many, many lakes about everywhere — were there not? Scores up there where Soodra was. Or so she had said. And Roberta loved the out-of-doors and the water so — although she could not swim — could not swim. And they or at least he was going where lakes were, or they might, might they not — and if not, why not? Since both had talked of some 4th of July[31] resort in their planning, their final departure — he and Roberta.

But, no! No! The mere thought of an accident such as that in connection with her, however much he might wish to be rid of her — was sinful, dark and terrible! He must not let his mind run on any such things for even a moment. It was too wrong — too vile — too terrible! Oh, dreadful thought. To think it should have come to him! And at this time of all times — when she was demanding that he go away with her!

Death!

Murder!

The murder of Roperta!

But to escape her of course — this unreasonable, unshakable, unchangeable demand of hers! Already he was quite cold, quite damp — with the mere thought of it. And now — when — when' — !But he must not think of that! The death of that unborn child, too!!

But how could any one even think of doing any such thing with calculation — deliberately? And yet — many people were drowned like that — boys and girls-men and women — here and there — everywhere the world over in the summer time. To be sure, he would not want anything like that to happen to Roberta. And especially at this time. He was not that kind of a person, whatever else he was. He was not. he was not. He was not. The mere thought now caused a damp perspiration to form on his hands and face. He was not that kind of a person. Decent, sane people did not think of such things. And so he would not either — from this hour on.

In a tremulous state of dissatisfaction with himself — that any such grisly thought should have dared to obtrude itself upon him in this way — he got up and lit the lamp — re-read this disconcerting item in as cold and reprobative way as he could achieve, feeling that in so doing he was putting anything at which it hinted far from him once and for all. Then having done so, he dressed and went out of the house for a walk — up Wykeagy Avenue, along Central Avenue, out Oak, and then back on Spruce[32] and to Central again — feeling that he was walking away from the insinuating thought or suggestion that had so troubled him up to now. And after a time, feeling better, freer, more natural, more human, as he so much wished to feel — he returned to his room, once more to sleep, with the feeling that he had actually succeeded in eliminating completely a most insidious and horrible visitation.[33] He must never think of it again! He must never think of it again. He must never, never, never think of it — never.

And then falling into a nervous, feverish doze soon thereafter, he found himself dreaming of a savage black dog that was trying to bite him. Having escaped from the fangs of the creature by waking in terror, he once more fell asleep. But now he was in some very strange and gloomy place, a wood or a cave or narrow canyon between deep hills, from which a path, fairly promising at first, seemed to lead. But soon the path, as he progressed along it, became narrower and narrower and darker, and finally disappeared entirely. And then, turning to see if he could not get back as he had come, there directly behind him were arrayed an entangled mass of snakes that at first looked more like a pile of brush. But above it waved the menacing heads of at least a score of reptiles, forked tongues and agate eyes. And in front now, as he turned swiftly, a horned and savage animal — huge, it was — its heavy tread crushing the brush — blocked the path in that direction. And then, horrified and crying out in hopeless desperation, once more he awoke — not to sleep again that night.

Notes

1. *An American Tragedy* is perhaps Dreiser's most impressive work. It is, as Dreiser once noted, not only a tragedy, but an American tragedy.

   The central character in the novel, Clyde Griffiths, is the son of a street evangelist in Kansas City. At the age of 16, he becomes a bellboy in a hotel. After an automobile accident for which he is culpable, he flees to Chicago, where he encounters his wealthy uncle, Samuel Griffiths. The uncle employs him in his collar factory in Lycurgus, a small town in New York State. Shortly after that Clyde seduces Roberta Alden, a working girl fresh from the country; almost simultaneously he is madly pursued by Sondra Finehley, daughter of a wealthy boss. Gradually he turns cold toward Roberta. When Roberta reveals that she is pregnant and demands marriage, he decides to get rid of her. He tries to force Roberta, to have an abortion, but the doctor refuses. He is greatly worried and doesn't know what to do. Learning the news about the death of a man and a girl caused by an upturned canoe, he plans to murder Roberta. He takes her boating on a deserted lake and strikes her with his camera, which causes the boat to capsize. In spite of Roberta's cries for help, Clyde swims a-shore. Soon after the discovery of Roberta's body, Clyde is arrested while seeking pleasure with Sondra. After a lengthy trial Clyde is sentenced to death.

2. CLYDE MYDIE: CLYDE MY DEAR

3. How is my pheet phing? All wylie?: how is my sweet thing? All right?

4. Casino: a public room or building for music, dancing, etc. , and in some places for gambling.

5. Stuart and Grand: Sondra's friends.

6. Dickey: name of a horse.

7. Bertiue: a friend of Sondra's.

8. she'll write you a letter today or tomorrow good for any weekend or any old time: she'll write you a letter of invitation today or tomorrow which you can use for any weekend or any time. Here "any old time" simply means "any time"("old" is used as an intensifier).

9. Sonda: Sondra's pet name.

10. You baddie, good boy: you bad, good boy. (That is, you are a boy both bad and good).

11. Sonda wisses he was here wiss her instead: Sonda wishes he was here with her instead.

12. Clydie: Clyde's pet name.

13. Nina: a friend of Sondra's.

14. See all'ese dots? Kisses. : See all those dots? They are marks representing kisses.

15. wire: write.

16. in kind: in the same way (that is, with kisses).

17. Blitz: the place where Roberta's family lived.

18. Homer: name of a town.

19. Victrola: (trademark of) a plonograph.
20. Agnes: Roberta's sister.
21. Fred: Roberta's brother-in-law.
22. Tom and Emily: Roberta's younger brother and sister.
23. they: Roberta wanted to have some clothes made in Blitz.
24. if then: if indeed you intend to come up then.
25. Bert: Roberta's pet name.
26. she was not so far gone but what she could take care of herself well e-
    nough as yet: she was not very much advanced in pregnancy, and so she
    could take care of herself well enough as yet.
27. the Gilpins: the family whose room Roberta rented.
28. Dr. Glenn: When Roberta found herself pregnant she went to this doctor
    for help.
29. for good: for ever.
30. so wrought up: so excised.
31. 4th of July: Independence Day in the United States, an occasion for pub-
    lic celebrations and festivals.
32. Wykeagy venue, Central Avenue, Oak and Spruce: names of streets in
    Lycurgus.
33. a most insidious, horrible visitation: a most insidious horririble idea.

Consideration

1. Describe Clyde's feelings when both letters reached him.
2. Describe Clyde's response when Sondra refused to elope with
   him.
3. Discuss the character of Clyde Griffiths.
4. What were the root causes which led to Clyde's destruction?

Chapter VII Modernism

1. The Rise of Modernism

Modernism was a complex and diverse international literary movement, originating at about the end of the 19th century and reaching its maturity in the mid 20th. It was rooted in the social upheavals and promoted by the new ideas and thoughts such as Nietzsche's philosophy of subconsciousness, Sigmund Freud's psychoanalysis, Bergson's intuitionism, and Darwinism.

It is usually regarded that the time between the publication of Baudelaire's *The Flower of Evils* (1857) and World War I was the originating period of modernism. During this time, free capitalism was on its way to monopolistic capitalism. The innate social contradictions in capitalist countries were becoming increasingly acute and complex. In accordance to the unreasonable development of social economy was the cultural life, which also tended to be more and more irrational. It was from the social and cultural irrationality that arose the modernist literature, which fully developed between the two world wars.

World War I broke out in 1914 and lasted till 1918. It fought chiefly among imperialist countries for a redivision of the colonies. The war was a massive manslaughter and brought disaster to the human race.

After the war, the problems of the capitalist world were far from being solved. On the contrary, eeonomic crisis in all the imperialist countries deepened. The crisis culminated in a worldwide economic disaster in the 1930s — the Great Depression. The nations of the world, especially the United States, were affected by it. Everywhere prices were falling, workers got unemployed, political alignments were altered, and international tensions mounted. All aspects of Western culture, including art, literature, education, and science, were shaken and given new directions.

This worldwide economic disaster gave rise to a most ugly phenomenon — Hitler and his Nazi party came into power in Germany. The result was even more horrible and disastrous for mankind: World War II. In the war, more than 17 million members of the armed forces of the various countries were killed. Although the war turned out to be a victory for democracy over fascism, it strained the economic capabilities of the major nations and left many countries on the verge of collapse.

The economic crisis and the great tragedy of the two world wars shook people's trust and belief in the future and values of capitalism. A large group of writers took up pens to express people's frustration and perplexity, especially to present how people were distorted and dislocated under the irrational forces of the modern world.

Modernism is mainly the product of the social upheavals. But it was profoundly influenced by new ideas and philosophy. The persons to whom the modernists were indebted most were Sigmund Freud, Nietszche, and Bergson.

Sigmund Freud (1856-1939) was an Austrian physician and

neurologist. He was the father of psychoanalysis, a new school of psychology embodying revolutionary and controversial views of human behavior. His books entitled *The Interpretation of Dreams*, *Three Contributions to the Sexual Theory*, and *The Ego and Id* had a profound influence upon the modernist movement. In his theory, the unconscious is emphasized and human sexuality is given prime importance in analyzing human behavior. His discovery opened up a new dimension for the modernists, who later strove to explore this new "inner"reality in many of their works of art.

Friedrich Nietzsche (1844-1900) was a German philosopher. In his philosophy, he focused on the individual, not society, and admired only the superhero who refused to be bound by the prevailing social paradigms of nationalism, Christianity, faith in science, loyalty to the state, or bourgeois civilized comfort. Nietzsche's insistence on the individual's complete freedom in a world that lacked transcendental law, and his attack on the unimaginative mediocrity of mass society in the modern industrial world made him a powerful influence in the early years of the 20th century.

Menri Bergson (1859-1941) was a French philosopher. He attacked scientific rationality as artificial and unreal because it froze everything in conceptual space and it ignored the whole dimension of life as it is actually experienced. For Bergson, reality was a fluid, living force that could only be apprehended by consciousness. Instead of quantitative and logical inquiry, he proposed intuiting the "immediate data of consciousness" as an alternate, nonscientific means of knowledge. In 1927, Bergson received the Nobel Prize for literature, both for the creative imagination shown in his own work and for his literary influence.

After the 1950s, Modernism began to lose its wail, but its artistic technique has been still exerting influence on contemporary writers. Therefore, the time between the 1950s and the present day is generally regarded by some western critics as the period of postmodernism, which is related to but different from Modernism.

2. The Features of Modernism

Based on different social realities and influenced by different ideas and thoughts, Modernism has been made up of many facets — symbolism, surrealism, existentialism, and so on. These minor schools differ from each other, but only in subtle ways. They have certain features in common. As a whole, Modernism, is characterized by a conscious rejection of established rules, traditions and conventions both in content and in form.

In content, the search for identity is the frequent common theme. To modernists, the world is an irrational machine full of forces at random, from whose control man can by no means escape; man is an indifferent, selfish and cruel animal who is unable to understand each other; nature is like a horrible prison in which man's freedom is not allowed. In such a world of chaos, man loses his identity. He does not know who he is and where he belongs. Modernists deny rationalism and science, and stress the importance of intuition, instinct, and subconsciousness in literary creation. They are subjective idealists who concentrate on the representation of the "inner reality" of the character. Their works are tragic, nihilistic, and mysterious.

In form, Modernism is the synonym of revolution. Not any of the previous periods in history has ever seen so many experiments in form and style. In fact, modernists are formalists, holding that content and form are identical. In stressing form, modernists advocate "art for art's sake". To them, art should be separated from life and politics. It serves nothing but itself.

3. Post-modernism

Post-modernism intensifies the modernist feeling of the world as a random, contingent and chaotic place. Modernists tend to try to control the meaningless and disorder through the agency of art, hoping to transcend it by shaping it and giving it an art form, whereas post-modernists tend to accept the world as it is and skeptical of their self integrity and their own ability to give shape and significance to the immense panorama of futility and anarchy, and they open themselves up to that disorder and contingency which no art can mediate. They regard these features of modern existence as standard and locate themselves within the messiness of their world. Rejecting modernist nostalgia for an organic wholeness and feeling that life's quandaries are not resolvable, post-modernists attempt to generate meaning in the face of chaos and absurdity. For them uncertainty is the rule. Because they believe that the self constitutes part and parcel of the world, involvement, immersion and participation become their ethic.

4. Symbolism and Imagism

Symbolism, the first literary school of Modernism, is the

line of demarcation between traditional literature and modern writings. It rose against Realism in France in the mid-19th century, flourished in the 1920s to 1940s in England, the U S, and other European countries, and has lingered on until the present day. In 1857, Charles Baudelaire, the founder of French symbolism, published *The Flowers of Evils*, the first work of symbolism. Later in the 1880s, symbolism grew into a conscious literary movement with Arther Rimbaud, Paul Verlaine and Stephane Mallarme as the leading advocates.

Symbolism does not believe in the doctrine of Realism that art represents reality. It sees the immediate, unique, and personal emotional response as the proper subject of art, and its full expression as the ultimate aim of art. Since the emotions experienced by a poet in a given moment are unique to that person and that moment are finally both fleeting and incommunicable, the poet is reduced to the use of a complex and highly private kind of symbolization in an effort to give expression to an evanescent and ineffable feeling. The result is a kind of writing consisting of a series of symbols lacking apparent logical relation, which are put together in a pattern characterised by an indefiniteness as great as the indefiniteness of the experience itself and the conscious effort to use words for their evocative musical effect without very much attention to precise meaning.

Symbolism developed into Imagism, a poetic movement in England and the United States from 1909 to 1917. The imagists put forth the following tenets: 1) to regard any subject as acceptable for poetry; 2) to suggest rather than to state ideas, expressing them concisely; 3) to emphasize images, choosing those that are specific rather than abstract; 4) to use exact words from common speech, avoiding those that are overused; and 5) to create new rhythms to express new moods (free verse). The leading spokesmen of the movement are the Irish poet William Butler Yeats and the American poets T. S. Eliot and Ezra Pound.

Symbolism also made some achievement in drama. The outstanding plays of symbolism include *L'Oiseau Bleu* (*The Blue Bird*) by Maeterlinck (Belgian), *The Sunken Bell* by G. Hauptmann (German), and *Riders to the Sea* by John Synge (Irish).

Charles Baudelaire (1821-1867) was the predecessor and inspirer of the symbolist poets in France, Germany, and elsewhere; a blasphemer in whom some Catholics see a profoundly Catholic poet; a dandy who could assert that his poems concerned only the aesthetic sensibilities and yet confessed, more privately, that in them he had placed his entire heart; a literary critic who insisted that the artist's task is to evoke and clarify the experiences of the individual consciousness, with its wealth of overtones and gossamer cross-paths and its transcendence of time and space. His collection of poems under the gaudy title *Flowers of Evil* includes several litanies to Satan and several poems, in which the poet attempted to create a world of beauty through evils of both social reality and human nature.

William Butler Yeats (1865-1939) was an Irish poet, critic, and playwright. As a poet, his greatness lies in his ability to communicate the power and significance of his symbols by experimenting with different kinds of rhythm and language. Yeats' career of poetic creation can roughly be divided into two periods, the first including poems such as "The Stolen Child", "The Rose of the World", which have drawn their subjects from the heroic legends of old Ireland and the folk traditions of the modern Irish countryside, and are characterized by esoteric language and mysticism; the second containing poems like "The Tower", "The Winding Stair", and "Sailing to Byzantium", which mainly deal with the Irish nationalism and individual psychology in less formal and simpler language. As a critic, Yeats developed a symbolist theory of his own which constitutes an impressive and coherent scheme of aesthetics and poetics. In the essays collected under the title *Ideas of Good and Evil* and in scattered articles, Yeats elaborated his views that art is not a criticism of life but a revelation of a hidden life and that there is a great memory which can be evoked by symbols, for our memories are part of one great memory, the Memory of Nature herself. Yeat's plays are *The Land of Heart's Desire*, *The Hour Glass* and *Dedidre*. In 1923, Yeats was awarded the Nobel Prize.

Ezra Pound (1885-1972), American poet and critic, was often called "the poet's poet" because of his profound influence on 20th century writing in English. Pound believed that poetry is the highest of arts. He challenged many of the common views of his time and spent 12 years in an American mental hospital. Pound's major work was the *Cantos*, which was published in ten sections between 1925 and 1969, and then as a one-volume collected edition, *The Cantos of Ezra Pound I-CXVII* (1970). In 1908 he travelled widely in Europe, working as a journalist. His first book of poems, *A Lume Spento*, appeared in 1908. After its publication Pound settled in London, where he founded with Richard Aldington (1892-1962) and others the literary 'Imagism', and edited its first anthology, *Des Imagistes* (1914). The movement was influenced by thoughts of Rémy de Gourmont whose book, *The Natural Philosophy of Love* (1904), Pound translated later, and T. E. Hulme (1883-1917), who stressed the importance of fresh language and true perception on nature. In his cautions, published in *Poetry* in 1913, Pound wrote: "Don't use such an expression as 'dim lands of peace'. It dulls the image. It mixes an abstraction with the concrete. It comes from the writer's not realizing that the natural object is always the adequate symbol. "

T. S. Eliot (1888-1965) was one of the most important figures of the 20th century. He was not only a great poet but an outstanding critic and playwright. When· he was still young at Harvard, he became interested in the French symbolists and began to wrote symbolic poems, the most well-known of which is "The Love Song of J. Alfred Prufrock", an expression of the poet's sense of both personal emptiness and of the emptiness and vulgarity of the 20th century through a repressed, weak, balding man who measures life by coffee spoons. In 1914 Eliot went to Europe, where he met Ezra Pound, the founder of the Imagism. Under the influence of the imagists tenets (a free choice of subject matter, conciseness of diction, clarity of images, and musical rhythm) and with the help of Pound, Eliot published his most memorable poem *The Waste Land* (1922), a succession of unrelated images combining to form an impression of the spiritual crisis of postwar Europe. Eliot's other important poems include *Hollow Men* (1925), *Ash Wednesday* (1930), and *Four Quartets* (1943), the last two turning to religious themes. Eliot's verse dramas contain *Sweeney Agonistes*, *Murder in the Cathedral*, *The Cocktail Party*, and *The Confidential Clerk*, all of which are concerned with religion. Eliot's collections of critical essays include *The Sacred Wood*, *Essays on Style and Order*, *Homage to John Dryden*, *The Use of Poetry and The Use of Criticism*, *Selected Essays*, and *After Strange Gods*, the basic themes of which concerned the relationship between tradition and individual talent, and between the past, the present, and the future. Eliot won the Nobel Prize for literature in 1948.

John Millington Synge (1871-1909) was a famous Irish Symbolist playwright. As a young man he traveled in several European countries, studying and engaging in poetry and drama writing. In 1899, having taken W. B. Yeats' advice, Synge returned to Ireland and lived among farmers and fishermen on The Aran Island for many years, during which he collected folk legends and mastered folk language that provided his works with a strong local flavor. In all his life Synge wrote six plays including, *The Playboy of the Western World*, *Riders to the Sea*, *In the Shadow of the Glen*, *The Tinker's Wedding*, and *Deirdre of the Sorrows*, all of which except the last one deal with the life of farmers and fishermen. *Riders to the Sea* is Synge's most representative work of symbolism. It is about the tragedy of a fishing family which has lost its three male generations in the sea. Here the sea is the symbol of nature full of cruelty and power, against which human beings are constantly fighting and yet to which human beings can do nothing.

Arther Rimbaud (1854-1891) was born at Charleville and educated at the Charleville College. For most of his life, Rimbaud

西方文学

was a vagabond, wandering in England, Germany, Italy, the Dutch East Indies, and the interior of Africa. A few months before his death, a diseased knee led to the amputation of a leg, and he died in hospital at Marseilles. In 1873 he published *Une Saison en Enfer*, a miscellany of snatches of verse and prose in which Rimbaud probes agonizingly his states of mind and soul. It attracted little attention then; but as author of that and *Les Illuminations* (1886), Rimbaud has since become one of the masters of the symbolist movement in poetry, with a powerful hold on writers, English as well as others, in the 20th century.

Maurice Maeterlinck (1862-1949) was born at Ghent and educated at the university of Ghent where he studied law and practiced for a while, before he was drawn into the circle of the Symbolists. From 1889 he published poems and verse plays, his first enduring success being *Pelleas and Melisande* (1892). For two or three decades there after Maeterlinck became a world figure with plays and such prose works as *The Treasure of the Humble* (essays, 1897) and *The Life of the Bee* (1901). His theatre reputation reached its height with *The Blue Bird* (1909) which enchanted children by the fairytale story of Tytyl and Mytyl and impressed adults by its mystical element. *Monna Vanna* (1902) stirred some excitement and moral disfavor by a scene in which the heroine was to be imagined as naked under her cloak, and some short plays including *The Death of Tintageles* (1899) were in vogue in England and elsewhere in the early years of the 20th century. Maeterlinck created atmosphere by leaving sentences incomplete or symbolism unexplained, and was for a time noted as the exponent of "the drama of the unspoken work" which was in its own day successfully absorbed. He was lauded as "the Belgian Shakespeare".

THE LOVE SONG OF J. ALFRF D PRUFROCK[1]
by T. S. Eliot

S'io credesse che mia risposta fosse
A persona che mai tornasse al mondo,
Questa fiamma staria senza piu scosse.
Ma perciocche hiammai di questo fondo
Non torno vivo clcun, s'l'odo li vero,
Senza tema d'infamia ti rispondo. [2]

Let us go then, you[3] and I,
When the evening is spread out against the sky
Like a patient etherised upon a table;[4]
Let us go, through certain half-deserted streets,
The muttering retreats
Of restless nights in one-night cheap hotels
And sawdust restaurants with oyster-shells;[4]
Streets that follow like a tedious argument
Of insidious intent
To lead you to an overwhelming question . . .
Oh, do not ask, "What is it?"
Let us go and make our visit.
In the room the women come and go
Talking of Michelangelo.

The yellow fog that rubs its back upon the window-panes,
Licked its tongue into the corners of the evening,
Lingered upon the pools that stand in drains,
Let fall upon its back the soot that falls from chimneys,
Slipped by the terrace, made a sudden leap,

And seeing that it was a soft October night,
Curled once about the house, and fell asleep.

And indeed there will be times[5]
For the yellow smoke that slides along the street,
Rubbing its back upon the windowpanes;
There will be time, there will be time
To prepare a face to meet the faces that you meet;
There will be time to murder and create,
And time for all the works and days of hands
That lift and drop a question on your plate;
Time for you and time for me,
And time yet for a hundred indecisions,
And for a hundred visions and revisions,
Before the taking of a toast and tea.
In the room the women come and go
Talking of Michelangelo.

And indeed there will be time
To wonder, "Do I dare?" and, "do I dare?"
Time to turn back and descent the stair,
With a bald spot in the middle of my hair —
(They will say: "How his hair is growing thin!")
My morning coat, my collar mounting firmly to the chin,
My necktie rich and modest, but asserted by a simple pin —
(They will say: "But how his arms and legs are thin!")
Do I dare
Disturb the universe?
In a minute there is time
For decisions and revisions which a minute will reverse.

For I have known them all already, known them all; —
Have known the evenings, mornings, afternoons,
I have measured out my life with coffee spoons;

I know the voices dying with a dying fall
Beneath the music from a farther room.
So how should I presume?

And I have known the eyes already, known them all —
The eyes that fix you in a formulated phrase,
And when I am formulated, sprawling on a pin,
When I am pinned and wriggling on the wall,
Then how should I begin
To spit out all the butt-ends of my days and ways?
And how should I presume? . . . And I have known the arms al-
     ready, known them all — Arms that are braceleted and
     white and bare (but in the lamplight, downed with light
     brown hair!）
Is it perfume from a dress
That makes me so digress?
Arms that lie along a table, or wrap about a shawl.
And should I then presume?
And how should I begin?

Shall I say, I have gone at dust through narrow streets
And watched the smoke that rises from the pipes
Of lonely men in shirt-sleeves, leaning out of windows? . . .

I should have been a pair of ragged claws
Scuttling across the floors of silent sea.

And the afternoon, the evening, sleeps so peacefully!
Smoothed by long fingers,
Asleep . . . tired . . . or it malingers,
Stretched on the floor, here beside you and me.
Should I, after tea and cakes and ices,
Have the strength to force the moment to its crisis?
But though I have seen my head (grown slightly bald) brought
     in upon a platter,[6]

I am no prophet — and here's no great matter;
I have seen the moment of my greatness flicker,
And I have seen the eternal Footman hold my coat, and snicker,
And in short, I was afraid.

And would it have been worth it, after all,
After the cups, the marmalade, the tea,
Among the porcelain, among some talk of you and me,
Would it have been worthwhile,
To have bitten off the matter with a smile,
To have squeeze the universe into a ball
To roll it toward some overwhelming question,
To say:"I am Lazarus, come from the dead,[7]
Come back to tell you all, I shall tell you all" —
If one, settling a pillow by her head,
Should say:"That is not what I meant at all.
That is not it, at all."

And would it have been worth it, after all,
Would it have been worth while,
After the sunsets and the dooryards and the sprinkled streets,
After the novels, after the teacups, after the skirts that trail a-
    long the floor —
And this, and so much more? —
It is impossible to say just what I mean!
But as if a magic lantern threw the nerves in patterns on a
    screen:
Would it have been worthwhile
If one, settling a pillow or throwing off a shawl,
And turning toward the window, should say:
    "That is not it at all,
    That is not what I mean, at all."
No! I am not Prince Hamlet, nor was meant to be;

Am an attendant lord[8] , one that will do
To swell a progress, start a scene or two,
Advise the prince; no doubt, an easy tool,
Deferential, glad to be of use,
Politic, cautious, and meticulous;
Full of high sentence[9] , but a bit obtuse;
At times, indeed, almost ridiculous —
Almost, at times, the Fool.

I grow old ... I grow old ...
shall wear the bottoms of my trousers rolled.

Shall I part my hair behind? Do I dare to eat a peach?
I shall wear white flannel trousers, and walk upon the beach.
I have heard the mermaids[10] singing, each to each.

I do not think that they will sing to me.
I have seen them riding seaward on the waves
Combing the white hair of the waves blown back

We have lingered in the chambers of the sea
By sea-girls wreathed with seaweed red and brown
Till human voices wake us, and we drown.

Notes

1. A symbolist poem that has been called the first masterpiece of modernism in English. In the form of a dramatic monologue it presents with irony and pathos the musings of an aging young man, uncertain, unable to commit to the love he desires or to life at all, a figure representative of the frustrations in modern life and of the aridity of a sterile upper-class culture.

2. This stanza is taken from Dante's *Inferno*, meaning "If I thought that my reply would be to one who would ever return to the world, this flame would stay without further movement; but since none has ever renamed a-live from this depth, if what I hear is true, I answer you without fear of

infamy."

3. "You" probably refers to his soul.
4. The evening is compared to a patient lying numb on a table of operation.
5. A reference to "Works and Days", a poem by the Greek Hesiod, on the rural life and labors of a peasant.
6. The prophet John the Baptist was beheaded and his head brought in a platter to Salome, the daughter of Heodias. Mathew 14.
7. Jesus raised Lazarus from the dead. John 11.
8. To be part of a royal procession.
9. Judgment, pronouncement.
10. Mythical alluring creatures, half woman and half fish.

Considerations

1. In the opening line of this poem, when Prufrock speaks of "you and I," he is referring only to two conflicting sides of himself. A battle is going on inside him making him virtually incapable of decisive action. How does the situation at the outset of the poem illustrate his indecision? Where else do you find evidence of this characteristic? What sort of person would he like to be?

2. Can the poem be considered a love song? Explain the irony of the title.

5. Futurism

Futurism was a literary and artistic movement which flourished chiefly in Italy and France between 1908 and the 1920s. Early in 1909 Futurism was officially launched with the publication of *Le Figaro*, a manifesto by the Italian poet F. T. Marinetti, the leader of the Futurist movement, which was antagonistic to traditional values and ideas and derided it as "pastism". Marinetti and his followers were advocates of violence, both physical and in ideas and imagination: they affected to despise virtue, beauty, and compassion, idolized machinery and all the paraphernalia of modern industry, and preached a debased philosophy degrading women and gnawing at the foundations of Christianity.

Between 1912 and 1914, Marinetti visited England, where he lectured frequently and caused a sensation with his poetry readings. In his writings and lectures, Marinetti outlined his aesthetic for Futurist poetry: it abandons conventional syntax and verb forms; transforms or deforms words "at liberty"; introduces total freedom in the use of images; expresses a "most rapid brutal and immediate lyricism ... a telegraphic lyricism" ; renders "all the sounds and even the most cacophonous noises of modern life"; and employs a typography (e. g. twenty kinds of type on a single page) that suggests the "bursts of style. " Futurists had as offspring such "anti-art" groups as the Dadaists and surrealists. In England the vorticists and P. Wyndham Lewis's short-lived periodical *Blast* owed something to Marinetti.

6. Expressionism

Expressionism originated as an artistic technique in painting at the beginning of the 20th century, grew into a literary movement in Germany during the First World War, and reached its zenith in Germany and the United States in the 1930s. Then expressionism lost its wail, but it did not disappear and lingered until the 1950s, when came into being the Theatre of the Absurd, the sequel of expressionism.

Expressionists were mainly concerned with subjective impressions. They advocated the presentation of the objective world through the internal impressions and moods of characters. Therefore, they often concentrated on the probing of the inner world of the character, and their works are marked by the presentation of the objective outer world by means of distortion. In painting, for instance, "childhood" might be shown not through a conventional representational picture of children at play or at school but by seemingly unarticulated and exaggerated physical details that suggest "childhood" or convey the impression that the artist has the concept "child".

As an organized literary movement expressionism was strongest in the theatre. The major figures in the European expressionistic drama include the Swedish dramatist Strindberg, the German dramatists Wedekind, George Kaiser, and Ernst Toller, and Czech dramatist Karel Capek. Their drama was marked by unreal atmosphere, a nightmarish quality of action, distortion and oversimplification, the de-emphasis of the individual (characters are likely to be called "Father", "Man" or "Bank Clerk" to embody some social mood or to represent a certain occupation), antirealistic stage settings, and staccato, telegraphic dialogue. The expressionistic drama was strongly influential on the American dramatists Eugene O'Neill and Elmer Rice. Rice's *The Adding Machine* uses moving stages and other nonrealistic devices to express the mechanical world seen by one cog named Mr. Zero. Elements of expressionism can also be seen in the plays of Thornton Wilder, Arthur Miller, and Tennessee Williams. The transfer of the quality of expressionistic drama is to be found in the works of Franz Kafka, in the antirealistic novels of Kurt Vonnegut, Jr. and Thomas Pynchon, in Joyce's *Finnegans Wake*, and in modern poetry, particularly T. S. Eliot's *The Waste Land*, which is expressionistic in its revolt against realism, distortion of the objects of the outer world, and its violent dislocation of time sequence and spatial logic in an effort to show the world as it appears to a troubled mind.

John August Strindberg (1849-1912) was an outstanding Swedish playwright. He was a prolific writer and his dramatic work totals fifty-eight plays, which, together with his more than sixty novels, fill the fifty-five volumes of his collected works. Strindberg's earlier plays such as *Master Olof*, *Father* and *Miss Julie* present the author as a critical realist and naturalist, and his later plays employ extensive nonrealistic devices, showing the author as an expressionist. His play *Play Dream* is regarded as the first work of expressionism, expressing his grief, dream and illusion. *The Ghost Sonata* is Strindberg's another famous expressionistic play, which is constructed in an absurd and fantastic plot with ghosts and mummies as well as the living as the characters, displaying the "madhouse" of the world filled with deception and trickery.

Franz Kafka (1883-1924) was an Austrian writer of expressionism. His achievement mainly lies in his three novels (*The Trial*, *The Castle*, and *America*) and a series of short stories. Kafka was a peculiar figure that has long fascinated contemporary writers. This is chiefly because of his peculiar style, which is marked by a timely combination of down-to-earth, matter-of-fact realism and a nightmare imagination that lifts daily events to an allusively symbolic and infinitely interpretable level; and his ability to find familiar images to convey the most prevalent themes of modern literature: the helpless yearning towards meaning in a universe that will not respond, and the oppressive alienation of individual living in modern industrial society. Kafka's characters speak every language and react in a commonsense way when such a response is utterly grotesque in the given situation. A young businessman is changed overnight into a giant beetle (*The Metamorphosis*) or charged with undefined crimes and finally executed (*The Trial*); a would-be land surveyor is unable to communicate with the castle that employs him and keeps sending incomprehensible messages. This miraculous level of existence hidden behind everyday life is the obverse of the heroes' vain attempts to maintain control over the impossible.

Eugene O'Neill (1888-1953) America's greatest playwright, has become a major influence on the development of the modern American theatre. In his literary career, he kept exploring difficult subjects and experimenting with a variety of dramatic styles. Starting with realistic writing in such plays as *Beyond the Horizon* and *Anna Christie*, he shifted to expressionistic writing in *The Emperor Jones*, wherein the uneasy conscience of a fleeting Negro dictator is dramatised by symbolic scenes and sound effects. In *The Hairy Ape* some of the scenery and much of the dialogue and action are realistic. In some scenes, however, masked characters, marionette-like processions, monologues, and chaotic effects lift the action into the realm of fantasy. This expressionistic mingling of the realistic and the fantastic is employed to project modern man's loss of self-identity and despair in an indifferent and impersonal universe. O'Neill's other plays that deserve to be mentioned are *Desire Under the Elms*, *Mourning Becomes Electra*, *The Iceman Cometh*, and *Long Day's Journey into Night*, all concerning modern man's helplessness and impotence. O'Neill was a prize-winning playwright. He received the Pulitzer Prize four times and was awarded the Nobel Prize in 1936.

George Kaiser (1878-1945) was born and educated in Magdeburg. He worked in Argentina and spent some time in Spain and Italy before returning to Germany, from which he went into exile in Switzerland after the Nazis usurped power. During the vogue in the 1920s for Expressionism in drama, his plays — *From Morn to Midnight* (1912), *The Coral* (1917), *Gas I* (1918), and Gas *II* (1920) — were internationally applauded as were those of his younger contemporary Ernst Toiler. Though Kaiser's aim was to contribute to the drama of ideas, he was less a productive thinker than a stage craftman more successful in dramatic action than in rational presentation.

Ernst Toiler (1893-1939) was born in Prussia of Jewish parentage and educated in Bromberg. He studied law at Grennoble, and joined the German army as a volunteer in 1914, but was invalided in 1916, having in the meantime developed pacifist convictions. He became a communist and his revolutionary activities led to a five-year prison sentence. He left Germany in 1932 and went to the U S. The triumphs of Fascism in Europe caused him great distress and he committed suicide in New York. His plays had a vogue in England in the 1920s and among those the best-known were *Masses and Men* (1920), and *The Machine Wreckers* (1922).

A COUNTRY DOCTOR
by Franz Kafka

I was in great perplexity; I had to start on an urgent journey; a seriously ill patient was waiting for me in a village ten miles off; a thick blizzard of snow filled all the wide spaces between him and me; I had a gig, a light gig with big wheels, exactly right for our country roads; muffled in furs, my bag of instruments in my hand, I was in the courtyard all ready for the journey; but there was no horse to be had, no horse. My own horse had died in the night, worn out by the fatigues of this icy winter; my servant girl was now running round the village trying to borrow a horse; but it was hopeless, I knew it, and I stood there forlornly, with the snow gathering more and more thickly upon me, more and more unable to move. In the gateway the girl appeared, alone, and waved the lantern; of course, who would lend a horse at this time for such a journey? I strode through the courtway once more; I could see no way out; in my confused distress I licked at the dilapidated door of the year-long uninhabited pigsty. It flew open and flapped to and fro on its hinges. A steam and smell as of horses came out of it. A dim stable lantern was swinging inside from a rope. A man, crouching on his hams in that low space, showed an open blue-eyed face. "Shall I yoke up?" he asked, crawling out on all fours. I did not know what to say and merely stooped down to see what else was in the sty. The servant girl was standing beside me. "You never know what you're going to find in your own house," she said, and we both laughed. "Hey there, Brother, hey there, Sister!" called the groom, and two horses, enormous creatures with powerful flanks, one after the other, their legs tucked close to their bodies, each well-shaped head lowered like a camel's, by sheer strength of bootlicking squeezed out through the door hole which they filled entirely. But at once they were standing up, with their long legs and their bodies steaming thickly. "Give him a hand," I said, and the willing girl hurried to help the groom with the harnessing. Yet hardly was she beside him when the groom clapped hold of her and pushed his face against hers. She screamed and fled back to me; on her cheek stood out in red the marks of two rows of teeth. "You brute," I yelled in fury, "do you want a whipping?" but in the same moment reflected that the man was a stranger; that I did not know where he came from, and that of his own free will he was helping me out when everyone else had failed me. As if he knew my thoughts he took no offense at my threat but, still busied with the horses, only turned round once towards me. "Get in," he said then, and indeed: everything was ready. A magnificent pair of horses, I observed, such as I had never sat behind, and I climbed in happily. "But I'll drive, you don't know the way," I said. "Of course," said he, "I'm not coming with you anyway, I'm staying with Rose." "No," shrieked Rose, fleeing into the house with a jus-tified presentiment that her fate was inescapable; I heard the door chain rattle as she put it up; I heard the key turn in the lock; I could see, moreover, how she put out the lights in the entrance hall and in further flight all through the rooms to keep herself from being discovered. "You're coming with me," I said to the groom, "or I won't go, urgent as my journey is. I'm not thinking of paying for it by handing the girl over to you." "Gee up!" he said; clapped his hands; the gig whirled off like a log in a freshet; I could just hear the door of my house splitting and bursting as the groom charged at it and then I was deafened and blinded by a storming rush that steadily buffeted all my senses. But this only for a mo-ment, since, as if my patient's farmyard had opened out just before

my courtyard gate, I was already there; the horses had come quietly to a standstill; the blizzard had stopped; the moonlight all around; my patient's parents hurried out of the house, his sister behind them; I was almost lifted out of the gig; from their confused ejaculations I gathered not a word; in the sick room the air was almost unbreathable; the neglected stove was smoking; I wanted to push open a window; but first I had to look at my patient. Gaunt, without any fever, not cold, not warm, with vacant eyes, without a shirt, the youngster heaved himself up from under the feather bedding, threw his arms around my neck, and whispered in my ear. "Doctor, let me die." I glanced round the room; no one had heard it; the parents were leaning forward in silence waiting for my verdict; the sister had set a chair for my handbag; I opened the bag and hunted among my instruments; the boy kept clutching at me from his bed to remind me of his entreaty; I picked up a pair of tweezers, examined them in the candlelight and laid them down again. "Yes," I thought blasphemously, "in cases like this the gods are helpful, send the missing horse, add to it a second because of the urgency, and to crown everything bestow even a groom —"
And only now did I remember Rose again; what was I to do, how could I rescue her, how could I pull her away from under that groom at ten miles' distance, with a team of horses I couldn't control. These horses, now, they had somehow slipped the reins loose, pushed the window open from the outside, I did not know how; each of them had stuck a head in at a window and, quite unmoved by the startled cries of the family, stood eyeing the patient. "Better go back at once," I thought, as if the horses were summoning me to the return journey, yet I permitted the patient's sister, who fancied that I was dazed by the heat, to take my fur coat from me. A glass of rum was poured out for me, the old man clapped me on the shoulder, a familiarity justified by this offer of his treasure. I shook my head; in the narrow confines of the old man's thoughts I

felt ill; that was my only reason for refusing the drink. The mother stood by the bedside and cajoled me towards it; I yielded, and, while one of the horses whinnied loudly to the ceiling, laid my head to the boy's breast, which shivered under my wet beard. I confirmed what I already knew, the boy was qiute sound, something a little wrong with his circulation, saturated with coffee by his solicitous mother, but sound and best turned out of bed with one shove. I am no world reformer and so I let him lie. I was the district doctor and I did my duty to the uttermost, to the point where it became almost too much. I was badly paid and yet generous and helpful to the poor. I had still to see that Rose was alright, and then the boy might have his way and I wanted to die too. What was I doing there in that endless winter! My horse was dead, and not a single person in the village would lend me another. I had to get my team out of the pigsty; if they hadn't chanced to be horses I should have had to travel with swine. That was how it was. And I nodded to the family. They knew nothing about it, and, had they known, would not have believed it. To write prescriptions is easy, but to come to an understanding with people is hard. Well, this should be the end of my visit, I had once more been called out needlessly, I was used to that, the whole district made my life a torment with my night bell, but that I should have to sacrifice Rose this time as well, the pretty girl who had lived in my house for years almost without my noticing her — that sacrifice was too much to ask, and I had somehow to get it reasoned out in my head with the help of what craft I could muster, in order not to let fly at this family, which with the best will in the world could not restore Rose to me. But as I shut my bag and put an arm out for my fur coat, the family meanwhile standing together, the father sniffing at the glass of rum in his hand, the mother, apparently disappointed in me — why, what do people expect? — biting her lips with tears in her eyes, the sister fluttering a blood-soaked towel, I was somehow ready to admit conditionally that the boy might be ill after all. I went towards him, he welcomed me smiling as if I were bringing him the most nourishing invalid broth — ah, now both horses were whinnying together; the noise, I suppose, was ordained by heaven to assist my examination of the patient — and this time I discovered that the boy was indeed ill. In his right side, near the hip, was an open wound as big as the palm of my hand. Rose-red, in many variations of shade, dark in the hollows, lighter at the edges, softly granulated, with irregular clots of blood, open as a surface mine to the daylight. That was how it looked from a distance, but on a closer inspection there was another complication. I could not help a low whistle of surprise. Worms, as thick and as long as my little finger, themselves rose-red and blood-spotted as well, were wriggling from their fastness in the interior of the wound towards the light, with small white heads and many little legs. Poor boy, you were past helping. I had discovered your great wound; this blossom in your side was destroying you. The family was pleased; they saw me busying myself; the sister told the mother, the mother told the father, the father told several guests who were coming in, through the moonlight at the open door, walking on tiptoe, keeping their balance with outstretched arms. "Will you save me?" whispered the boy with a sob, quite blinded by the life within his wound. That is what people are like in my district. Always expecting the impossible from the doctor. They have lost their ancient beliefs; the parson sits at home and unravels his vestments, one after another; but the doctor is supposed to be omnipotent with his merciful surgeon's hand. Well, as it pleases them; I have not thrust my services on them; if they misuse me for sacred ends, I let that happen to me too; what better do I want, old country doctor that I am, bereft of my servant girl! And so they came, the family and the village elders, and stripped my clothes off me; a school choir with the teacher at the head of it stood before the house and sang these words to an utterly simple tune:

    Strip his clothes off, then he'll heal us,

    If he doesn't, kill him dead!

    Only a doctor, Only a doctor.

Then my clothes were off and I looked at the people quietly, my fingers in my beard and my head cocked to one side. I was altogether composed and equal to the situation and remained so, although it was no help to me, since they now took me by the head and feet and carried me to the bed. They laid me down in it next to the wall, on the side of the wound. Then they all left the room; the door was shut; the singing stopped; clouds covered the moon; the bedding was warm around me; the horses' heads in the opened windows wavered like shadows. "Do you know," said a voice in my ear, "I have very little confidence in you. Why, you were only blown in here, you didn't come on your own feet. Instead of helping me, you're cramping me on my death bed. What I'd like best is to scratch your eyes out." "right," I said, "It's a shame. And yet I am a doctor. What am I to do? Believe me, it is not too easy for me either." "Am I supposed to be content with this apology? Oh, I must be, I can't help it. I always have to put up with things. A fine wound is all I brought into the world; that was my sole endowment." "My young friend," said I, "Your mistake is: you have not a wide enough view. I have been in all the sickrooms, far and wide, and I tell you: your wound is not so bad. Done in a tight corner with two strokes of the ax. Many a one proffers his side and can hardly hear the ax in the forest, far less that it is coming nearer to him." "Is that really so, or are you deluding me in my fever? . . . It is really so, take the word of honor of an official doctor." And he took it and lay still. But now it was time for me to think of escaping. The horses were still standing faithfully in their places. My clothes, my fur coat, my bag were quickly collected; I didn't want to waste time dressing; if the horses raced home as they had come, I should only be springing, as it were, out of this bed into my own. Obediently a horse backed away from the window; I threw my bundle into the gig; the fur coat missed its mark and was caught on a hook only by the sleeve. Good enough I swung myself on to the horse. With the reins loosely trailing, one horse barely fastened to the other, the gig swaying behind, my fur coat last of all in the snow. "Get up!" I said, but there was no galloping; slowly, like old men, we crawled through the snowy wastes; a long time echoed behind us the new but faulty song of the children:

O be joyful, all you patients,
The doctor's laid in bed beside you!

Never shall I reach home at this rate; my flourishing practice is done for; my successor is robbing me, but in vain, for he cannot take my place; in my house the disgusting groom is raging; Rose is the victim; I do not want to think about it any more. Naked, exposed to the frost of this most unhappy of ages, with an earthly vehicle, unearthly horses, old man that I am, I wander astray. My fur coat is hanging from the back of the gig, but I cannot reach it, and none of my limber pack of patients lifts a finger. Betrayed! Betrayed! A false alarm on the night bell once answered — it cannot be made good, not ever.

Considerations

1. Identify four challenges that confront the doctor.
2. What frustrations accompany each challenge?
3. Why could this story be called a nightmare?
4. What themes do you find in this story?

7. Existentialism

Existentialism was originally applied to a group of attitudes current in philosophical, religious, and artistic thought during and after the Second World War, which emphasizes existence rather than essence and sees the inadequacy of the human reason to explain the enigma of the universe as the basic philosophical question. In its modern expression it had its beginning in the writings of the 19th-century Danish theologian, Soren Kierkegaard, and developed into its mature form and popularity under the influence of the French novelist-philosopher Jean-Paul Sartre.

Basically the existentialist assumes that existence precedes essence, that the significant fact is that we and things in general exist, but that these things have no meaning for us except we can create meaning through acting upon them. The existentialist's point of meaninglessness in the outer world produces in them a discomfort, an anxiety, aloneness in the face of human limitations and a desire to invest experience with meaning by acting upon the world, although efforts to act in a meaningless, "absurd" world lead to anguish, greater loneliness, and despair. As an individual existing actively, one is totally free to make his own choice in the presence of established ideas and institutions but also wholly responsible for what he makes for himself. A man becomes a man only because he thinks his own thoughts, lives his own life and keeps his own individuality. This freedom and responsibility are the sources for one's most intense anxiety. Such a philosophical attitude tends to result in nihilism and hopelessness, as, indeed, it has with many of the literary existentialists.

Existentialist writings are noted for its distinct philosophy. They do not care much about the complexity of the novel plot, and they stress the philosophic analysis of the mind. Following Sartre's philosophy that "man is alone in a godless universe," existentialist writers tend to display a meaningless world filled with anxiety, loneliness, acute discomfort, and despair. In technique, they take interest in metaphors and implications. In diction, they prefer simple, precise, direct and colloquial language, trying to achieve the effect of proverbs. Their tone is objective and indifferent, which is in accordance with the characters they depict. These existential qualities find expression in the novels of Franz Kafka, Dostoyevsky, Camus, and Simone de Beauvoir, and in the plays and novels of Sartre and Samel Beckett, and the plays of Eugine Ionesco.

Jean-Paul Sartre (1905-1980) is one of those rare authors who have been outstandingly successful in a great variety of genres. His publications embrace short stories, novels, plays, essays, psychology, philosophy, and public affairs. In his philosophical work *Being and Nothingness*, he sets his existentialist theories that man is totally free; that each man's project is fundamentally the endeavor to realize himself fully like a solid object; and that man's life has no meaning or purpose beyond the goal he sets for himself. In accordance with his philosophy, Sartre created a large number of literary works that are often concerned with sordid aspects of human existence. His novel *Nausea*, written in the form of diary, expresses the intellectual's perplexity between the years of the two world wars. *The Wall*, the title piece of his collection of short stories, depicts the mental activities of a soldier in prison waiting for his execution, and illustrates that the fear of death is the wall between life and death, through which one can break and obtain the freedom of living. *The Flies*, based on the Greek myth, is Sartre's best play. Agamemnon, on his return home from the Trojan War, is killed by his wife and her lover, which brings millions of flies swirling over the city. Agamemnon's son killed his mother and her lover in return, and takes the responsibility for all the chaos, leaving his home city with the flies and relieving his city people of the trouble. Here Sartre eulogizes the freedom of choice that results in heroism and lofty human value.

Albert Camus (1913-1961) is often linked with the contemporary philosopher Jean-Paul Sartre as an existentialist writer, and indeed as a novelist, a playwright, and an essayist, he is widely known for his analysis of two concerns basic to existentialism: its distinctive assessment of the human condition and its search for authentic values. One famous theme in his works is that of the "absurd": the absurdly grotesque discrepancy between human being's brief, material existence and their urge to believe in larger meanings — to "make sense of a world which has no discernible sense. In his famous novel, *The Stranger*, Camus described a thirty-year-old clerk named Meursault who is a stranger to all conventional reactions. He attends his mother's funeral without grief; he makes love to and is going to marry his mistress just because he can know no reason why he should not; he goes swimming and shoots an Arab for no conscious reason. Meursault is finally condemned to death not for murder but for this alienation, and his failure to respond to society's expectations of proper behavior. The novel reaffirms the importance of life lived moment by moment, in a total awareness that life creates whatever meaning exists, and its impact comes from the contrast between the immediacy of the physical experience described, and the objective meaninglessness of that experience.

THE GUEST[1]
by Albert Camus

The schoolmaster was watching the two men climb toward him. One was on horseback, the other on foot. They had not yet tackled the abrupt rise leading to the schoolhouse built on the hillside. They were toiling onward, making slow progress in the snow among the stones, on the vast expanse of the high, deserted plateau. From time to time the horse stumbled. Without hearing anything yet, he could see the breath issuing from the horse's nostrils. One of the men, at least, knew the region. They were following the trail although it had disappeared days ago under a layer of dirty white snow. The schoolmaster calculated that it would take them half an hour to get onto the hill. It was cold; he went back into the school to get a sweater.

He crossed the empty, frigid classroom. On the blackboard the four rivers of France, drawn with four different colored chalks, had been flowing toward their estuaries for the past three days. Snow had suddenly fallen in mid-October after eight months of drought without the transition of rain, and the twenty pupils, more or less, who lived in the villages scattered over the plateau had stopped coming. With fair weather they would return. Daru now heated only the single room that was his lodging, adjoining the classroom and giving also onto the plateau to the east. Like the class windows, his window looked to the south too. On that side the school was a few kilometers from the point where the plateau began to slope toward the south. In clear weather could be seen the purple mass of the mountain range where the gap opened onto the desert. Somewhat warmed, Daru returned to the window from which he had first seen the two men. They were no longer visible. Hence they must have tackled the rise. The sky was not so dark, for the snow had stopped falling during the night. The morning had opened with a dirty light which had scarcely become brighter as the ceiling of clouds lifted. At two in the afternoon it seemed as if the day were merely beginning. But still this was better than those three days when the thick snow was falling amidst unbroken darkness with little gusts of wind that rattled the double door of the classroom. Then Daru had spent long hours in his room, leaving it only to go to the shed and feed the chickens or get some coal. Fortunately the delivery truck from Tadjid,[2] the nearest village to the north, had brought his supplies two days before the blizzard. It would return in forty-eight hours.

Besides, he had enough to resist a siege, for the little room was cluttered with bags of wheat that the administration left as a stock to distribute to those of his pupils whose families had suffered from the drought. Actually they had all been victims because they were all poor. Every day Daru would distribute a ration to the children. They had missed it, he knew, during these bad days. Possibly one of the fathers or big brothers would come this afternoon and he could supply them with grain. It was just a matter of carrying them over to the next harvest. Now shiploads of wheat were arriving from France and the worst was over. But it would be hard to forget that poverty, that army of ragged ghosts wandering in the sunlight, the plateaus burned to a cinder month after month, the earth shriveled up little by little, literally scorched, every stone bursting into dust under one's foot. The sheep had died then by thousands and even a few men, here and there, sometimes without anyone's knowing.

In contrast with such poverty, he who lived almost like a monk in his remote schoolhouse, nonetheless satisfied with the little he had and with the rough life, had felt like a lord with his white-washed walls, his narrow couch, his unpainted shelves, his well, and his weekly provision of water and food. And suddenly this snow, without warning, without the foretaste of rain. This is the way the region was, cruel to live in, even without men — who didn't help matters either. But Daru had been born here. Every-where else, he felt exiled.

He stepped out onto the terrace in front of the schoolhouse. The two men were now halfway up the slope. He recognized the horseman as Balducci, the old gendarme[3] he had known for a long time. Balducci was holding on the end of a rope an Arab who was walking behind him with hands bound and head lowered. The gen-darme waved a greeting to which Daru did not reply, lost as he was in contemplation of the Arab dressed in a faded blue jellaba,[4] his feet in sandals but covered with socks of heavy raw wool, his head surmounted by a narrow, short chéche.[5] They were approach-ing. Balducci was holding back his horse in order not to hurt the Arab, and the group was advancing slowly.

Within earshot, Balducci shouted: "One hour to do the three kilometers from El Amour!" Daru did not answer. Short and square in his thick sweater, he watched them climb. Not once had the Ar-ab raised his head. "Hello," said Daru when they got up onto the terrace. "Come in and warm up." Balducci painfully got down from his horse without letting go the rope. From under his bristling mus-tache he smiled at the schoolmaster. His little dark eyes, deep-set under a tamed forehead, and his mouth surrounded wrinkles made him look attentive and studious. Daru took the bridle, led the horse to the shed, and came back to the two men, who were now wait-ing for him in the school. He led them into his room. "I am going to heat up the classroom," he said. "We'll be more comfortable there". When he entered the room again, Balducci was on the couch. He had undone the rope tying him to the Arab, who had squatted near the stove. His hands still bound, the chéche pushed back on his head, he was looking toward the window. At first Daru noticed only his huge lips, fat, smooth, almost Negroid; yet his nose was straight, his eyes were dark and full of fever. The chéche revealed an obstinate forehead and, under the weathered skin now rather discolored by the cold, the whole face had a restless and rebellious look that struck Daru when the Arab, turning his face toward him, looked him straight in the eyes. "Go into the other room," said the schoolmaster, "and I'll make you some mint tea.""Thanks,"Balducci said. "What a chore! How I long for retirement." And addressing his prisoner in Arabic:"Come on, you." The Arab got up and, slowly, holding his bound wrists in front of him, went into the classroom.

With tea, Daru brought a chair. But Balducci was already enthroned on the nearest pupil's desk and the Arab had squatted against the teacher's platform facing the stove, which stood between the desk and the window. When he held out the glass of tea to the prisoner, Daru hesitated at the sight of his bound hands, "He might perhaps be untied.""Sure,"said Balducci. "That was for the trip." He started to get to his feet. But Daru, setting the glass on the floor, had knelt beside the Arab. Without saying anything, the Arab watched him with his feverish eyes. Once his hands were free, he rubbed his swollen wrists against each other, took the glass of tea, and sucked up the burning liquid in swift little sips.

"Good,"said Daru. "And where are you headed?" Balducci withdrew his mustache from the tea. "Here, son."

"Odd pupils! And you're spending the night?"

"No. I'm going back to El Ameur. And you will deliver this fellow to Tinguit. He is expected at police headquarters," Balducci was looking at Daru with a friendly little smile.

"What's this story?" asked the schoolmaster. "Are you pulling my leg?"

"The orders? I'm not ... " Daru hesitated, not wanting to hurt the old Corsican. "I mean, that's not my job. "

"What! What's the meaning of that? In wartime people do all kinds of jobs. "

"Then I'll wait for the declaration of war!" Balducci nodded.

"O. K. But the orders exist and they concern you too. Things are brewing, it appears. There is talk of a forthcoming revolt. We are mobilized, in a way. "

Daru still had his obstinate look.

"Listen, son," Balducci said. "I like you and you must understand. There's only a dozen of us at El Ameur to patrol throughout the whole territory of a small department and I must get back in a hurry. I was told to hand this guy over to you and return without delay. He couldn't be kept there. His village was beginning to stir; they wanted to take him back. You must take him to Tinguit tomorrow before the day is over. Twenty kilometers shouldn't faze a husky fellow like you. After that, all will be over. You'll come back to your pupils and your comfortable life. "

Behind the wall the horse could be heard snorting and pawing the earth. Daru was looking out the window. Decidedly, the weather was clearing and the light was increasing over the snowy plateau. When all the snow was melted, the sun would take over again and once more would burn the fields of stone. For days, still, the unchanging sky would shed its dry light on the solitary expanse where nothing had any connection with man.

"After all," he said, turning around toward Balducci, "what did he do?" And, before the gendarme had opened his mouth, he asked: "Does he speak French?"

"No, not a word. We had been looking for him for a month,

but they were hiding him. He killed his cousin. "

"Is he against us?"

"I don't think so. But you can never be sure."

"Why did he kill?"

"A family squabble, I think. One owed the other grain, it seems. It's not at all clear. In short, he killed his cousin with a billhook. You know, like a sheep, kreezk!"

Balducci made the gesture of drawing a blade across his throat and the Arab, his attention attracted, watched him with a sort of anxiety. Daru felt a sudden wrath against the man, against all men with their rotten spite, their tireless hates, their blood lust. But the kettle was singing on the stove. He served Balducci more tea, hesitated, then served the Arab again, who, a second time, drank avidly. His raised arms made the jellaba fall open and the school-master saw his thin muscular chest.

"Thanks, kid,"Belducci said, "And now, I'm off."

He got up and went toward the Arab, taking a small rope from his pocket.

"What are you doing?"Daru asked dryly.

Balducci, disconcerted, showed him the rope.

"Don't bother."

The old gendarme hesitated. "It's up to you. Of course, you are armed?"

"I have my shotgun."

"Where?"

"In the trunk."

"You ought to have it near your bed."

"Why? I have nothing to fear."

"You're crazy, son. If there's an uprising, no one is safe, we're all in the same boat."

"I'll defend myself. I'll have time to see them coming."

Balducci began to laugh, then suddenly the mustache covered

the white teeth.

"You'll have time? O. K. That's just what I was saying. You have always been a little cracked. That's why I like you, my son was like that."

At the same time he took out his revolver and put it on the desk.

"Keep it; I don't need two weapons from here to El Ameur."

The revolver shone against the black paint of the table. When the gendarme turned toward him, the schoolmaster caught the smell of leather and horseflesh.

"Listen, Balducci," Daru said suddenly, "every bit of this disgusts me, and first of all your fellow here. But I won't hand him over. Fight, yes, if I have to. But not that."

The old gendarme stood in front of him and looked at him severely.

"You're being a fool," he said slowly. "I don't like it either. You don't get used to putting a robe on a man even after years of it, and you're even ashamed — yes, ashamed. But you can't let them have their way."

"I won't hand him over," Baru said again.

"It's an order, son, and I repeat it."

"That's right. Repeat to them what I've said to you: I won't hand him over."

Balducci made a visible effort to reflect. He looked at the Arab and Daru. At last he decided.

"No, I won't tell them anything. If you want to drop us, go ahead; I'll not denounce you. I have an order to deliver the prisoner and I'm doing so. And now you'll just sign this paper for me."

"There's no need. I'll not deny that you left him with me."

"Don't be mean with me. I know you'll tell the truth. You're from hereabouts and you are a man. But you must sign, that's the rule."

"No, son. Those are the orders."

Daru openecd his drawer, took out a little square bottle of purple ink, the red wooden penholder with the "sergeant-major" pen he used for making models of penmanship, and signed. The gendarme carefully folded the paper and put it into his wallet. Then he moved toward the door.

"I'll see you off," Daru said.

"No," said Balduoci. "There's no use being polite. You insulted me."

He looked at the Arab, motionless in the same spot, sniffed peevishly, and turned away toward the door. "Good-by, son,"he said. The door shut behind him. Balducci appeared suddenly outside the window and then disappeared. His footsteps were muffled by the snow. The horse stirred on the other side of the wall and several chickens fluttered in fright. A moment later Balducci reappeared outside the window leading the horse by the bridle. He walked toward the little rise without tuming around and disappeared from sight with the horse following him. A big stone could be heard bouncing down. Daru walked back toward the prisoner, who, without stirring, never took his eyes off him. "What," the schoolmaster said in Arabic and went toward the bedroom. As he was going through the door, he had a second thought, went to the desk, took the revolver, and stuck it in his pocket. Then, without looking back, he went into his room.

For some time he lay on his couch watching the sky gradually close over, listening to the silence. It was this silence that had seemed painful to him during the first days here, after the war. He had requested a post in the little town at the base of the foothills separating the upper plateaus from the desert. There, rocky walls, green and black to the north, pink and lavender to the south, marked the frontier of eternal summer. He had been named to a post farther north, on the plateau itself. In the beginning, the solitude and the silence had been hard for him on these wastelands peopled only by stones. Occasionally furrows suggested cultivation, but they had been dug to uncover a certain kind of stone good for building. The only plowing here was to harvest rocks. Elsewhere a thin layer of soil accumulated in the hollows would be scraped out to enrich paltry village gardens. This is the way it was: bare rock covered three quarters of the region. Towns sprang up, flourished, then disappeared; men came by, loved one another or fought bitterly, then died. No one in this desert, neither he nor his guest, mattered. And yet, outside this desert neither of them, Daru knew, could have really lived.

When he got up, no noise came from the classroom. He was amazed at the unmixed joy he derived from the mere thought that the Arab might have fled and that he would be alone with no decision to make. But the prisoner was there. He had merely stretched out between the stove and the desk. With eyes open, he was staring at the ceiling. In that position, his thick lips were particularly noticeable, giving him a pouting look. "Come," said Daru. The Arab got up and followed him. In the bedroom, the schoolmaster pointed to a chair near the table under the window. The Arab sat down without taking his eyes off Daru.

"Are you hungry?"

"Yes," the prisoner said.

Daru set the table for two. He took flour and oil, shaped a cake in a frying pan, and lighted the little stove that functioned on bottled gas. While the cake was cooking, he went out to the shed to get cheese, eggs, dates, and condensed milk. When the cake was done he set it on the window sill to cool, heated some condensed milk diluted with water, and beat up the eggs into an omelette. In one of his motions he knocked against the revolver stuck in his right pocket. He set the bowl down, went into the classroom, and put the revolver in his desk drawer. When he came back to the

room, night was falling. He put on the light and served the Arab.
"Eat," he said. The Arab took a piece of the cake, lifted it eagerly to his mouth, and stopped short.

"And you?"he asked.

"After you. I'll eat too. "

The thick lips opened slightly. The Arab hesitated, then bit into the cake determinedly.

The meal over, the Arab looked at the schoolmaster. "Are
you the judge?"

"No, I'm simply keeping you until tomorrow. "

"Why do you eat with me?"

"I'm hungry. "

The Arab fell silent. Daru got up and went out. He brought
back a folding bed from the shed, set it up between the table and
the stove, perpendicular to his own bed. From a large suitcase
which, upright in a comer, served as a shelf for paper, he took
two blankets and arranged them on the camp bed. Then he
stopped, felt useless, and sat down on his bed. There was nothing
more to do or to get ready. He had to look at this man. He looked
at him, therefore, trying to imagine his face bursting with rage. He
couldn't do so. He could see nothing but the dark yet shining eyes
and the animal mouth.

"Why did you kill him?" he asked in a voice whose hostile
tone surprised him.

The Arab looked away.

"He ran away. I ran after him. "

He raised his eyes to Daru again and they were full of a sort of
woeful interrogation. "Now what will they do to me?"

"Are you afraid?"

He stiffened, turning his eyes away.

"Are you sorry. "

The Arab stared at him openmouthed. Obviously he did not

understand. Dam's annoyance was growing. At the same time he felt awkward and self conscious with his big body wedged between the two beds.

"Lie down there," he said impatiently. "That's your bed."

The Arab didn't move. He called to Daru:

"Tell me!"

The schoolmaster looked at him.

"Is the gendarme coming back tomorrow?"

"I don't know."

"Are you coming with us?"

"I don't know. Why?"

The prisoner got up and stretched out on top of the blankets, his feet toward the window. The light from the electric bulb shone straight into his eyes and he closed them at once.

"Why?" Daru repeated, standing beside the bed.

The Arab opened his eyes under the blinding light and looked at him, trying not to blink.

"Come with us," he said.

In the middle of the night, Daru was still not asleep. He had gone to bed after undressing completely; he generally slept naked. But when he suddenly realized that he had nothing on, he hesitated. He felt vulnerable and the temptation came to him to put his clothes back on. Then he shrugged his shoulders; after all, he wasn't a child and, if need be, he could break his adversary in two. From his bed he could observe him, lying on his back, still motionless with his eyes closed under the harsh light. When Daru turned out the light, the darkness seemed to coagulate all of a sudden. Little by little, the night came back to life in the window where the starless sky was stirring gently. The schoolmaster soon made out the body lying at his feet. The Arab still did not move, but his eyes seemed open. A faint wind was prowling around the schoolhouse. Perhaps it would drive away the clouds and the sun would reappear.

During the night the wind increased. The hens fluttered a little and then were silent. The Arab turned over on his side with his back to Daru, who thought he heard him moan. Then he listened for his guest's breathing, become heavier and more regular. He listened to that breath so close to him and mused without being a-ble to go to sleelp. In this room where he had been sleeping alone for a year, this presence bothered him. But it bothered him also by imposing on him a sort of brotherhood he knew well but refused to accept in the present circumstances. Men who share the same rooms, soldiers or prisoners, develop a strange alliance as if, having cast off their armor with their clothing, they fraternized ev-ery evening, over and above their differences, in the ancient com-munity of dream and fatigue. But Daru shook himself; he didn't like such musings, and it was essential to sleep.

A little later, however, when the Arab stirred slightly, the schoolmaster was still not asleep. When the prisoner made a sec-ond move, he stiffened, on the alert. The Arab was lifting himself slowly on his arms with almost the motion of a sleepwalker. Seat-ed upright in bed, he waited motionless without tuming his head to-ward Daru, as if he were listening attentively. Daru did not stir; it had just occurred to him that the revolver was still in the drawer of his desk. It was better to act at once. Yet he continued to observe the prisoner, who, with the same slithery motion, put his feet on the ground, waited again, then began to stand up slowly. Daru was about to call out to him when the Arab began to walk, in a quite natural but extraordinarily silent way. He was heading toward the door at the end of the room that opened into the shed. He lifted the latch with precaution and went out, pushing the door behind him but without shutting it. Daru had not stirred. "He is running a-way," he merely thought. "Good riddance!" Yet he listened atten-tively. The hens were not fluttering; the guest must be on the plateau. A faint sound of water reached him, and he didn't know what it was until the Arab again stood framed in the doorway, closed the door carefully, and came back to bed without a sound. Then Daru turned his back on him and fell asleep. Still later he seemed, from the depths of his sleep, to hear furtive steps around the schoolhouse. "I'm dreaming! I'm dreaming!" he repeated to himself. And he went on sleeping.

When he awoke, the sky was clear; the loose window let in a cold, pure air. The Arab was asleep, hunched up under the blankets now, his mouth open, utterly relaxed. But when Daru shook him, he started dreadfully, staring at Daru with wild eyes as if he had never seen him and such a frightened expression that the schoolmaster stepped back. "Don't be afraid. It's me. You must eat. " The Arab nodded his head and said yes. Calm had returned to his face, but his expression was vacant and listless.

The coffee was ready. They drank it seated together on the folding bed as they munched their pieces of the cake. Then Daru led the Arab under the shed and showed him the faucet where he washed. He went back into the room, folded the blankets and the bed, made his own bed and put the room in order. Then he went through the classroom and out onto the terrace. The sun was already rising in the blue sky; soft, bright light was bathing the deserted plateau. On the ridge the snow was melting in spots, The stones were about to reappear. Crouched on the edge of the plateau, the schoolmaster looked at the deserted expanse. He thought of Balducci. He had hurt him, for he had sent him off in a way as if he didn't want to be associated with him. He could still hear the gendarme's farewell and, without knowing why, he felt strangely empty and vulnerable. At that moment, from the other side of the schoolhouse, the prisoner coughed. Daru listened to him almost despite himself and then, furious, threw a pebble that whistled through the air before sinking into the snow. That man's stupid crime revolted him, but to hand him over was contrary to honor. Merely thinking of it made him smart with humiliation. And he cursed at one and the same time his own people who had sent him this Arab and the Arab too who had dared to kill and not managed to get away. Daru got up, walked in a circle on the terrace, waited motionless, and then went back into the schoolhouse.

The Arab, leaning over the cement floor of the shed, was washing his teeth with two fingers. Daru looked at him and said "Come." He went back into the room ahead of the prisoner. He slipped a hunting-jacket on over his sweater and put on walking-shoes. Standing he waited until the Arab had put on chèche and sandals. They went into the classroom and the schoolmaster pointed to the exit, saying: "Go ahead." The fellow didn't budge. "I'm coming," said Daru. The Arab went out. Daru went back into the room and made a package of pieces of rusk, dates, and sugar. In the classroom, before going out, he hesitated a second in front of his desk, then crossed the threshold and locked the door. "That's the way," he said. He started toward the east, followed by the prisoner. But, a short distance from the schoolhouse, he thought he heard a slight sound behind them. He retraced his steps and examined the surroundings of the house; there was no one there. The Arab watched him without seeming to understand. "Come on," said Daru.

They walked for an hour and rested beside a sharp peak of limestone. The snow was melting faster and faster and the sun was drinking up the puddles at once, rapidly cleaning the plateau, which gradually dried and vibrated like the air itself. When they resumed walking, the ground rang under their feet. From time to time a bird rent the space in front of them with a joyful cry. Daru breathed in deeply the fresh morning light. He felt a sort of rapture before the vast familiar expanse, now almost entirely yellow under its dome of blue sky. They walked an hour more, descending toward the south. They reached a level height made up of crumbly rocks. From there on, the plateau sloped down, eastward, toward a low plain where there were a few spindly trees and, to the south, toward outcroppings of rock that gave the landscape a chaotic look.

Daru surveyed the two directions. There was nothing but the sky on the horizon. Not a man could be seen. He turned toward the Arab, who was looking at him blankly. Daru held out the package to him. "Take it," he said. "There are dates, bread, and sugar. You can hold out for two days. Here are a thousand francs too." The Arab took the package and the money but kept his full hands at chest level as if he didn't know what to do with what was being given him. "Now look," the schoolmaster said as he pointed in the direction of the east, "there's the way to Tinguit. You have a two-hour walk. At Tinguit you'll find the administration and the police. They are expecting you." The Arab looked toward the east, still holding the package and the money against his chest. Daru took his elbow and turned him rather roughly toward the south. At the foot of the height on which they stood could be seen a faint path. "That's the trail across the plateau. In a day's walk from here you'll find pasturelands and the first nomads. They'll take you in and shelter you according to their law." The Arab had now turned toward Daru and a sort of panic was visible in his expression. "Listen," he said. Daru shook his head; "No, be quiet. Now I'm leaving you." He turned his back on him, took two long steps in the direction of the school, looked hesitantly at the motionless Arab, and started off again. For a few minutes he heard nothing but his own step resounding on the cold ground and did not turn his head. A moment later, however, he turned around. The Arab was still there on the edge of the hill, his arms hanging now, and he was looking at the schoolmaster. Daru felt something rise in his throat. But he swore with impatience, waved vaguely, and started off again. He had already gone some distance when he again stopped and looked. There was no longer anyone on the hill.

Daru hesitated. The sun was now rather high in the sky and was beginning to beat down on his head. The schoolmaster retraced his steps, at first somewhat uncertainly, then with decision. When he reached the little hill, he was bathed in sweat. He climbed it as fast as he could and stopped, out of breath, at the top. The rock-fields to the south stood out sharply against the blue sky, but on the plain to the east a steamy heat was already rising. And in that slight haze, Daru, with heavy heart, made out the Arab walking slowly on the road to prison.

A little later, standing before the window of the classroom, the schoolmaster was watching the clear light bathing the whole surface of the plateau, but he hardly saw it. Behind him on the blackboard, among the winding French rivers, sprawled the clumsily chalked-up words he had just read. "You handed over our brother. You will pay for this." Daru looked at the sky, the plateau, and beyond, the invisible lands stretching all the way to sea. In this vast landscape he had loved so much, he was alone.

Notes

1. Camus's stories depict human being in situations where personal involvement is necessary, and where the important values of independence, tolerance, compassion, and justice are difficult to preserve. "The Guest," from his collection of short stories *Exile and the Kingdom* (1957), is set on a high plateau near the Atlas Mountains in Algeria, at the beginning of the rebellion that resulted in Algeria's independence from France.

2. Tadjid: a city on the Algerian plateau, south of the Mediterranean Sea and north of the Sahara.

3. gendarme: police.

4. jelllaba: loose cloak with a hood.

5. chéche: a cap with a tassel.

Considerations

1. Explain the relationship between where Daru lives and his personality. What is most important to Daru? Why does he feel exiled from the rest of the world?
2. To what extent, if any, is the end tragic? Why does Camus use the words "had loved" instead of "loved" in describing the landscape?
3. An allegory is a story in which characters, events, and settings represent abstract qualities. The author of an allegory expects readers to look for a meaning below the surface of the story. To what extent can this story be considered an allegory? Consider Daru's physical environment as symbolic of Camus's universe and Daru himself as symbolic of the human condition.

8. The Theatre of the Absurd

The Theatre of the Absurd, the sequel of existentialism, is a term referring to the works of some European and American playwrights of the 1950s and 1960s. The word "absurd" originated from the works of Camus and the term was invented by the British critic Martin Esslin.

This kind of drama presents a view of the absurdity of the human condition by the abandoning of usual or rational devices and by the use of nonrealistic form. It expounds an existential ideology and views its task as essentially metaphysical. Conceived in perplexity and spiritual anguish, the Theatre of the Absurd portrays not a series of connected incidents telling a story but a pattern of images presenting people as bewildered beings in an incomprehensible universe. It ignores or distorts conventional structure, plot and characterization. Its characters may appear in different forms and identities, and many of them change their sex, age or personality; its presentation may have no fixed or determinable setting; its sequence of time is fluid and indefinite; its language is often dislocated, with plenty of jargons, cliches, and repetitions. As a whole, the "absurd" plays often appear to be ridiculous and comic, but in fact, they are imbued with philosophical implications and suggestions.

The first true example of the Theatre of the Absurd was Eugene Ionesco's *The Bald Soprano* (1905). The most widely acclaimed play of this school is Samuel Beckett's *Waiting for Godot* (1953). Other playwrights in the school include Jean Genet, Arthur Adamor, Edward Albee, Arthur Kopit, and Harold Pinter.

Samuel Beckett (1906-1989) is an Irish writer. His novels and plays are filled with the sparest, starkest representation of the human conditions in all its "absurd" emptiness. Beckett's world is haunted by an absence of meaning at the core. His characters engage in a desperate attempt to find or to create meaning for themselves. Born into a world without reason, they live out their lives waiting for an explanation that never comes and whose existence may be only a figment of their imagination. In *Waiting for Godot*, we find two clownlike tramps, talking, quarreling, falling down, contemplating suicide, and generally filling up time with conversation that ranges from vaudeville patter to meta-physical speculation as they wait under a tree for a Godot who they think will make a great difference to their meaningless life but who never comes. As to who Godot is, nobody knows. The power of the play lies in its uncertainty and mysteriousness, which project the existential anguish at the inexplicable human condition.

Eugene Ionesco (1912-) the contemporary well-known French playwright, is one of the typical representatives of the Theatre of the Absurd. He objects to the didactisim of plays, especially to that of realistic plays, and advocates a kind of irrational drama that abandons the conventional elements such as coherent plot, setting, characterization, and language. In his plays, he put his anti-theatre theory into practice and dramatized the absurdity of human experience and the meaninglessness of cliches. In his most famous play *The Bald Soprano*, there is no central plot, nor characters of individual features. It is merely a succession of meaningless talks between some married couples, who, in fact, could not communicate with each other in a real sense. The Martins, for instance, do not realize that they are husband and wife living in the same house and having given birth to a daughter until they have talked for a long time as strangers to each other. Such absurdity of human experience is enhanced by the title that is in no way related to the content of the play.

Edward Albee (1928-) is the most important contemporary American playwright of the "absurd". His plays on the absurdity of human life built very much on a frail illusion and spiritual emptiness. Albee's major success is *Who's Afraid of Virginia*

Woolf? — a three-act play about a night of drunken verbal conflict between a middle-aged professor and his wife, in which a state of compassion is finally achieved after the "death" of their imaginary child. Albee's other important plays include *The Zoo Story*, *The American Dream*, and *Tiny Alice*. *The American Dream* expressed disenchantment with American middle-class values through the description of the appalling relationship of a family members. *Tiny Alice* is the story of a rich woman who seduces a Catholic lay brother into marriage and then murders him.

THE ZOO STORY*
(Excerpt)
by Edward Albee

THE PLAYERS

PETER: *A man in his early forties, neither fat nor gaunt, neither handsome nor homely. He wears tweeds, smokes a pipe, carries hornrimmed glasses. Although he is moving into middle age, his dress and his manner would suggest a man younger.*

JERRY: *A man in his late thirties, not poorly dressed, but carelessly. What was once a trim and lightly muscled body has begun to go to fat; and while he is no longer handsome, it is evident that he once was. His fall from physical grace should not suggest debauchery; he has, to come closest to it, a great weariness.*

THE SCENE

It is Central Park; a Sunday afternoon in summer; the present. There are two park benches, one toward either side of the stage; they both face the audience. Behind them; foliage, trees, sky. At the beginning, Peter is seated on one of the benches.

Stage Directions; As the curtain rises. Peter *is seated on the bench stage-right. He is reading a book. He stops reading, cleans his glasses, goes back to reading.* Jerry *enters.*

JERRY: I've been to the zoo. (Peter *doesn't notice*) I said, I've been to the zoo. MISTER, I'VE BEEN TO THE ZOO!

PETER: He? . . . ? What? . . . I'm sorry, were you talking to me?

JERRY: I went to the zoo, and then I walked until I came here. Have I been walking north?

JERRY: (*Pointing past the audience*) Is that 5th Avenue?

PETER: Why yes; yes, it is.

JERRY: And what is that cross street there; that on, to the right?

PETER: That? Oh, that's 74th Street.

JERRY: And the zoo is around 75th Street; so, I've been walking north.

PETER (*Anxious to get back to his reading*) Yes; it would seem so.

JERRY: Good old north.

PETER: (*Lightly, by reflex*) Ha, ha.

JERRY: (*After a slight pause*) But not due north.

PETER: I . . . well, no, not due north; but, we . . . call it north. It's northerly.

JERRY: (*Watches as* PETER, *anxious to dismiss him, prepares his pipe*) Well, boy; you're not going to get lung cancer, are you?

PETER: (*Looks up, a little annoyed, then smiles*) NO, sir. Not from this.

JERRY: No, sir. What you'll probably get is cancer of the mouth, and then you'll have to wear one of those things Freud wore after they took one whole side of his jaw away. What do they call those things?

PETER: (*Uncomfortable*) A prosthesis?

JERRY: The very thing! A prosthesis. You're an educated man, aren't you? Are you a doctor?

PETER: Oh, no; no. I read about it somewhere; *Time* magazine, I think. (*He turns to his book*)

JERRY: Well, *Time* magazine isn't for blockheads.

PETER: No, I suppose not.

JERRY: (*After pause*) Boy, I'm glad that's 5th Avenue there.

PETER: (*Vaguely*) Yes.

JERRY: I don't like the west side of the park much.

PETER: Oh? (*Then, slightly wary, but interested*) Why?

JERRY: (*Off hand*) I don't know.

PETER: Oh. (*He returns to his book*)

JERRY: (*He stands for a few seconds, looking at* PETER, *who finally looks up again, puzzled*) Do you mind if we talk?

PETER: (*Obviously minding*) Why ... no, no.

JERRY: Yes you do; you do.

PETER: (*Puts his book down, his pipe out and away, smiling*) No, really; I don't mind.

JERRY: Yes you do.

PETER: (*Finally decided*) No; I don't mind at all. Really.

JERRY: It's ... It's a nice day.

PETER: (*Stares unnecessarily at the sky*) Yes, yes, it is; lovely.

JERRY: I've been to the zoo.

PETER: Yes, I think you said so ... didn't you?

JERRY: You'll read about it in the papers tomorrow, if you don't see it on your TV tonight. You have TV, haven't you?

PETER: Why yes, we have two; one for the children.

JERRY: You're married!

PETER: (*With pleased emphasis*) Why, certainly.

JERRY: It isn't a law, for God's sake.

PETER: No ... no, of course not.

JERRY: And you have a wife.

PETER: (*Bewildered by the seeming lack of communication*)
Yes!

JERRY: And you have children.

PETER: Yes; two.

JERRY: Boys?

PETER: No, girls ... both girls.

JERRY: But you wanted boys.

PETER: Well ... naturally, every man wants a son, but ...

JERRY: (*Lightly mocking*) But that's the way the cookie crumbles?

PETER: (*Annoyed*) I wasn't going to say that.

JERRY: And you're not going to have any more kids, are you?

PETER: (*A bit distantly*) No. No more. (*Then back, and irksome*)
Why did you say that? How would you know about that?

JERRY: The way you cross your legs, perhaps; something in the
voice. Or maybe I'm just guessing. Is it your wife?

PETER: (*Furious*) That is none of your business! (*A silence*) Do
you understand? (JERRY *nods.* PETER *is quiet now*) Well,
you're right. We'll have no more children.

JERRY: (*Softly*) That *is* the way the cookie crumbles.

PETER: (*Forgiving*) Yes ... I guess so.

JERRY: Well, now; what else?

PETER: What were you saying about the zoo ... that I'd read a-
bout it, or see?

JERRY: I'll tell you about it, soon. Do you mind if I ask you questions?

PETER: Oh, not really.

JERRY: I'll tell you why I do it; I don't talk to many people — except to say like: give me a beer. Or where's the John. Or what time does the feature go on, or keep your hands to yourself, buddy. You know — things like that.

PETER: I must say I don't . . .

JERRY: But every once in a while I like to talk to somebody, really talk; like to get to know somebody, know all about him;

PETER: (*Lightly laughing, still a little uncomfortable*) And am I the guinea pig for today?

JERRY: On a sun-drenched afternoon like this? Who better than a nice married man with two daughters and . . . uh . . . a dog? (PETER *shakes his head, sadly*) Oh, that's shame. But you look like an animal man. CATS? (PETER *nods his head, ruefully*) Cats! But, that can't be your idea. No, sir. Your wife and daughters? (PETER *nods his head*) Is there anything else I should know?

PETER: (*He has to clear his throat*) There are . . . there are two parakeets. One . . . uh . . . one for each of my daughters.

JERRY: Birds.

PETER: My daughters keep them in a cage in their bedroom.

JERRY: Do they carry disease? The birds?

PETER: I don't believe so.

JERRY: That's too bad. If they did you could set them loose in the house and the cats could eat them and die. Maybe. (PETER *looks blank for a moment, then laughs*) And what else? What do you do to support your enormous household?

PETER: (*Still cheerful*) Now look here!

JERRY: Oh. Come on.

PETER: Well. I make around eighteen thousand a year, but I don't carry more than forty dollars at any one time . . . in case you're a ... a holdup man ... ha, ha, ha.

JERRY: (*Ignoring the above*) Where do you live? (PETER *is reluctant*) Oh, look; I'm not going to rob you, and I'm not going to kidnap your parakeets, your cats, or your daughters,

PETER: (*Too loud*) I live between Lexington and Third Avenue. On Seventy-4th Street.

JERRY: That wasn't so hard. Was it?

PETER: I didn't mean to seem ... ah ... it's that you don't really carry on a conversation; you just ask questions. And I'm ... I'm normally ... uh ... reticent. Why do you just stand there?

JERRY: I'll start walking around in a little while, and eventually I'll sit down. (*Recalling*) Wait until you see the expression on his face.

PETER: What? Whose face? Look here; is this something about zoo?

JERRY: (*Distantly*) The what?

PETER: The zoo; the zoo. Something about the zoo.

JERRY: The zoo?

PETER: You mentioned it several times.

JERRY: (*Still distant, but returning abruptly*) The zoo? Oh, yes; the zoo. I was there before I came here. I told you that. Say, what's the dividing line between upper middle-class and lower-upper-middle-class.

PETER: My dear fellow. I ...

JERRY: Don't my dear follow me.

PETER: (*Unhappily*) Was I patronizing? I believe I was; I'm sorry. But, you see. Your question about the classes bewildered me.

JERRY: And when you're bewildered you become patronizing?

PETER: I ... I don't express myself too well. Something. (*He attempts a joke on himself*) I'm in publishing. Not writing.

JERRY: (*Amused, but not at the humor*) So be it. The truth is: I was being patronizing.

PETER: Oh, now; you needn't say that. (*It is at this point that JERRY may begin to move about the stage with slowly increasing determination and authority. But pacing himself, so that the long speech about the dog comes at the high point*)

JERRY: All right. Who are your favorite writers? Baudelaire and J. P. Marquand.

PETER: (*Wary*) Well, I like a great many writers; I have a considerable ... catholicity of taste, if I may say so. Those two men are fine, each in his way. (*Warming up*) Baudelaire, of course ... uh ... is by far the finer of the two, but Marquand has a place ... in our ... uh ... national ...

JERRY: Skip it.

PETER: I ... sorry.

JERRY: Do you know what I did before I went to the zoo today? I walked all the way up 5th Avenue from Washington Square; all the way.

PETER: Oh, you live in the Village! (*This seems to enlighten* PETER)

JERRY: No. I don't. I took the subway down to the Village so I could walk all the way up 5th Avenue to the zoo. It's one of those things a person has to do; sometimes a person has to go a very long distance out of his way to come back a short distance correctly.

PETER: (*Almost pouting*) Oh, I thought you lived in the Village.

JERRY: What were you trying to do? Make sense out of things? Bring order? The old pigeonhole bit? Well, that's easy: I'll tell you. I live in a four-story brownstone rooming-house on the upper West Side between Columbus Avenue and Central Park West. I live on the top floor; rear; west. It's a laughably small room, and one of my walls is made of beaverboard; this beaverboard separates my room from another laughably small room. So I assume that the two rooms were once one room, a small room, but not necessarily laughable. The room beyond my beaverboard wall is occupied by a colored queen who always keeps his door open; well, not always but always when he's plucking his eyebrows, which he does with Buddhist concentration. The colored queen has rotten teeth, which is rare, and he has a Japanese kimono which is also pretty rare; and he wears this kimono to and from the John in the hall, which is pretty frequent. I mean, he goes to the John a lot. He never bothers me, and he never brings anyone up to his room. All he does is pluck his eyebrows, wear his kimono and go to the John. Now, the two front rooms on my floor are a little larger, I guess; but they're pretty small, too. There's a Purto Rican family in one of them, a husband, a wife, and some kids; I don't know how many. These people entertain a lot. And in the other front room, there's somebody living there, but I don't know who it is. I've never seen who it is. Never. Never ever.

Notes

* It was Albee's first play, written in 1958. It is short, has a small cast, deals with human encounter and the search for communion. In Central Park, the poorly dressed Jerry tries to have a good talk with Peter, manager of a publishing house. But Peter pays no heed to him. To arouse Peter's reaction, Jerry bursts into talking about his exciting experiences with his dog. Peter still makes no response, and even gets angry at his disturbance. In order to break the situation of non-communion, Jerry forces Peter to grapple. He squeezes a knife into Peter's hand and launches himself on to the knife. Jerry gets the single encounter with Peter at the lost of his life.

西方文学

9. Surrealism

Surrealism is a movement in art and literature that developed from Dadaism. Dadaism was founded by Tristan Tzara in Zurich during World War I. It was a nihilistic movement in art and literature which protested against logic, restraint, social convention, and literature itself. The word "dada" is a nonsense word which represents the disgust the Dadaists felt for the traditional middle-class values (patriotism, religion, morality, and rationalism) that they blamed for World War I. For Dadaists the important thing was to bring about a "revolution of the mind" in which ordinary habits of seeing yielded to a different, "surreal" or "superreal" vision. Surrealism, like Dadaism, emphasizes the expression of the imagination as realized in dreams and presented without conscious control. It began in France under the leadership of André Breton, who published his *Surrealist Manifesto* in 1924. The surrealism demonstrates the marked influence of Freudian theory concerning the unconscious and its relation to dreams. It calls for the exploration of hidden and neglected areas of the human psyche, and the resolution of the apparently contradictory states of dream and reality.

Surrealism, as a literary movement, has flourished most robustly in France. It centers on poetry and its representatives are the French poets Breton, Aragon, and Eluard, and the English poet Dylan Thomas. Literary surrealism finally reached the United States after the Second World War and became an important feature in the work of Robert Lowell and many younger writers like Philip Lamantia, John Ashbery, Frank O'Hara, and others.

Surrealistic writers hold that beyond the realistic world there is an unconscious world, which is more true than the real one, and hence poets should concern themselves with dreams, fancies, and coincidences, which are supposed to correspond to the unconscious. In technique, surrealistic writers advocate the automatic processes, the spontaneous coupling of unrelated objects as occur in dreams. Their works present unexpected images and pursue the miraculous and chance effect, thus making understanding very difficult. Their language lacks logic and standard.

André Breton (1896-1966) was a French poet, essayist, critic, and editor, chief promoter and one of the founders of the Surrealist movement. As a medical student, Breton was interested in mental illness; his reading of the works of Sigrnund Freud (whom he met in 1921) introduced him to the concept of the unconscious. Influenced by psychiatry and symbolist poetry, he joined the Dadaists. In 1919, with Louis Aragon and Philippe Soupault, he cofounded the review *Littérature* (*Literature*); in its pages, Breton and Soupault published "Les Champs Magnétiques" (1920; "Magnetic Fields"), the first example of the Surrealist technique of automatic writing. In 1924, Breton's *Manifeste du Surréalisme* (*Manifesto of Surrealism*) defined Surrealism as "pure psychic automatism, by which it is intended to express... the real process of thought. It is the dictation of thought, free from any control by the reason and of any aesthetic or moral preoccupation." Surrealism aimed to eliminate the distinction between dream and reality, reason and madness, objectivity and subjectivity. Breton's novel *Nadja* (1928) merged everyday occurrences with psychological aberrations. *L'Immaculée*

Conception (1930; *Immanent Conception*), written with Paul Eluard, attempted to convey a verbal impression of different types of mental disorder. *Les Vases Communicants* (1932; "The Communicating Vessels") and *L'Amour Fou* (1937; *Mad Love*) explored the connection between dream and reality. Breton also wrote theoretical and critical works, including *Les Pas Perdus* (1924; *The Lost Steps*), *Légitime Défense* (1926; *Legitimate Defense*), *Le Surréalisme et le Peinture* (1926; *Surrealism and Painting*), *Ou'est-ce que le Surréalisrne?* (1934; *What is Surrealism?*), and *La Clé des Champs* (1953; *The Key to the Fields*).

The Surrealist movement eventually became politically involved in the ferment of the 1930s, and Breton and several colleagues joined the Communist Party. His second Surrealist manifesto, published in 1930, explored the philosophical implications of Surrealism. Breton broke with the Communist Party in 1935 but remained committed to Marxist ideals. With Leon Trotsky in Mexico he founded the Federation de l'Art Revolutionnaire Independent in 1938. During the German occupation of France, Breton escaped to the United States. In 1942 at Yale University he organized a Surrealist exposition and issued yet another Surrealist manifesto. In 1946 Breton returned to France, where, the following year, he produced another Surrealist Exhibition. His *Poémes* (*Poems*) appeared in 1948 in Paris, and *Selected Poems* was published in London in 1969.

Paul Eluard (1895-1952) was one of the founders of the surrealist movement and one of the important lyrical poets of the 20th century experiments with new verbal techniques, theories on the relation between dream and reality, and the free expression of thought processes produced *Capitale de la Douleur* (*Capital of Sorrow*), his first important work, which was followed by *La Rose Publique* (*The Public Rose*) and *Les Yeux Fertiles* (*The Fertile Eyes*). The poems in these volumes are generally considered the best to have come out of the surrealist movement. Eluard also explored, with André Breton, the paths of mental disorders in *L'Immaculée Conception*. Eluard's later work reflects his political militance and a deepening of his underlying attitudes: the rejection of tyranny, the search for happiness. In 1942 he joined the Communist Party. His poems dealing with the sufferings and brotherhood of man, *Poésie et Vérité* (*Poetry and Truth*), *Au Rendez-Vous Allemand* (*To the German Rendezvous*), and *Dignes de Vivre* (*Worthy of Living*), were circulated clandestinely during World War Ⅱ and served to strengthen the morale of the Resistance. After the war his *Tout Dire* (*Say Everything*) and *Le Phénix* added, in simple language and vivid imagery, to the great body of French popular lyrical poetry.

Aragon Louis (1897-1982) was a poet, a novelist, and an essayist who was a political activist and spokesman for communism.

Through the Surrealist poet André Breton, Aragon was introduced to avant-garde movements such as Dadaism; and together with Philippe Soupault, he and Breton founded the Surrealist review *Littérature* (1919; *Literature*). Aragon's first poems, *Feu de Joie* (1920; *The Fire of Joy*) and *Le Mouvement Perpétuel* (1925; *The Perpetual Movement*), were followed by a novel, *Le Paysan de Paris* (1926; *The Peasant of Paris*); *The Night-Walker*, 1950). In 1927 his search for an ideology led him to the Communist Party, with which he was identified thereafter as he came to exercise a continuing authority over its literary and artistic expression. In 1930 he visited the Soviet Union, and in 1933 his political commitment resulted in a break with the Surrealists. The four volumes of his long novel series, *Le Monde Réel* (1933-1944; *The Real World*), describe in some historical perspective the class struggle of the proletariat marching toward social revolution. Aragon continued to employ a traditional Social Realism in another long novel, *Les Communistes* (1949-1951; *The Communists*), a bleak chronicle of the party from 1939 to 1940. His next three novels — *La Semaine Sainte* (1958; *The Saint Week*), La Mise à Mort (1965; *Going to Death*), and *Blanche ou l'Oubli* (1967; *White or Forgotten*), became a veiled autobiography, laced with pleas for the Communist Party. They reflected the newer novelistic techniques of the day.

Dylan Thomas (1914-1953) was an original poet of great power and beauty. His famous *Eighteen Poems* were noted for the strange violence of their imagery and their powerfully suggestive obscurity. His images were most carefully ordered in a patterned sequence, and his major theme was the unity of all life, the continuing process of life and death and new life which linked the generations to each other. Thomas saw the workings of biology as a magical transformation producing unity out of diversity, and again and again in his poetry he sought a poetic ritual to celebrate this unity ("The force that through the green fuse drives the flower / Drives my green age"). He saw men and women locked in a round of identities — with the beginning of growth also the first movement toward death, the beginning of love leading to procreation, new growth, and so in turn to death again and to life again, and because of this view he comforted himself with the unity of man and nature, of past and present, of life and death, and so "refused to mourn the death of a child. " In his best poems the closely woven imagery is organized to present aspects of this theme. His more open-worked poems of reminiscence and autobiographical emotion, such as *Poem in October*, communicate more immediately to the reader through their fine lyrical feeling and compelling use of simple natural images.

Robert Lowell (1917-1977) was considered one of the leading poets of his generations. His early work, which was formal and highly symbolic, often focuses on the history of New England and of his own family, subjects which continued to interest him throughout his life. *Land of Unlikeness* (1944), his first book, dealt especially with his temporary conversion to Catholicism; *Lord Weary's Castle* (1946) was awarded the Pulitzer prize. It was not until *Life Studies* (1959), however, that he began to exhibit the loose form and sharp irony which characterize his mature work. The poems and prose pieces in *Life Studies* are highly autobiographical, and the book is usually identified as one of the major works of the Confessional school. He did not confine himself to purely personal subjects; *For the Union Dead* (1964) and *Near the Ocean* (1967), for example, linked an understanding of the self to an understanding of politics and history.

西方文学

DO NOT GO GENILE
INTO THAT GOOD NIGHT

by Dylan Thomas

Do not go gentle into that good night,
Old age should burn and rave at close of day;
Rage, rage against the dying of the light,

Though wise men at their end know dark is right,
Because their words had forked no lightening they
Do not go gentle into that good night.

Good men, the last wave by, crying how bright
Their frail deeds might have danced in a green bay,
Rage, rage against the dying of the light.

Wild men who caught and sang the sun in flight,
And learn, too late, they grieved it on its way,
Do not go gentle into that good night.

Grave men, near death, who see with blinding sight
Blind eyes could blaze like meteors and be gay,
Rage, rage against the dying of the light.

And you, my father, there on the sad height,
Curse, bless, me now with your fierce tears, I pray.
Do not go gentle into that good night.
Rage, rage against the dying of the light.

Considerations

1. In stanzas 2-4 Dylan Thomas describes the way in which certain types of men have faced death and why they reacted in that way. Why does he mention this in a poem about the

death of his father?

2. In line 5, what is meant by "Because their words had forked no lightening"?
3. What is Thomas' attitude toward his father's death?
4. This is one of the most powerful examples of the use of the villanelle form. Do the repeated lines seem forced?

10. Stream of Consciousness

Stream of consciousness is a manner of writing which is widely used in modern arts especially in novels. It originated from the chaos of modern life and was directly influenced by modern psychology. The phrase "stream of consciousness" first appeared in *Principles of Psychology* by William James, an American psychologist, who believed that the human mind was a continuous stream that could not be cut off. This belief catered to some writers at the turn of the century, who took interest in depicting the inner thoughts of the character. In the 1920s, the technique was widely employed in the realms of novels, poetry, and drama, and became an conscious independent school in novels.

In the writings of this school, the character's perceptions, thoughts, impressions, and emotions were presented as occurring in random form without regard to logical sequences or syntax. Writers of this school avoided artificial omniscience and let their characters reveal themselves through their minds without the intervention of the author. The author's withdrawal from the novel led to the common use of the technique of "interior monologue" to convey the movement of the conscious. Molly Bloom's reflections depicted in the closing pages of James Joyce's *Ulysses* is a celebrated example of interior monologue in which the author seems not to exist and the reader directly "overhears" the thought flowing through the character's mind.

The writers of this school includes James Joyce, Virginia Woolf, Dorothy Richardson, William Faulkner, and Marcel Proust.

James Joyce (1882-1941) was an Irishman, who after some early shifts in career became well known as a founder of the "stream of consciousness" school of novel writing. He wrote poetry and short stories. But his fame mainly rests on his novels: *Ulysses*, *Finnegans Wake*, and *A Portrait of the Artist as a Young Man*.

Ulysses is a strange novel. Its nearly eight hundred pages record the mental activities of three Dubliners in about nineteen hours — Leopold Bloom, his wife Molly, and the artist Stephen Dedalus. Bloom leaves his wife and returns to her again. Hence the title Ulysses, the hero in Homer's *Odyssey* who leaves his wife Penelope to fight the Trojan War and returns to her after an absence of 20 years. But unlike the Greek Ulysses, the modern Ulysses is a coward. This novel is formless, plotless, recording the thought fleeting flashes of the mind as they rise regardless of the time sequence. It is written in a variety of styles, ranging all the way from the simplest colloquialisms to highly poetical passages, from the very vulgar to the very beautiful to correspond with the mood of the moment.

Finnegans Wake is even more unusual. It coins up new

words, strange combinations of old words given no meanings, and uses many different languages. The whole novel makes hardly one intelligible statement. The novel records the dream of old Finnegans in which the entire history of Dublin and even the world is displayed, suggesting that the human history is the circulation of the sexual desire that creates human beings and war that destroys life.

A Portrait of the Artist as a Young Man is an autobiographical novel. It projects the developing mind and consciousness of a certain Stephen Dedalus, who is shaped by his environment but at the same time rebels against it. It depicts Stephen in his maturity, still trying to seek his identity. The depiction is done with the mind.

Virginia Woolf (1882-1941) represents the much more readable novelists of the stream of consciousness school. She was a woman of sharp sensitivity who, in one of her frequent mental depressions, committed suicide during an air war in England. Woolf was a fine artist and critic. She cast away the accepted techniques of presentation and claimed that "Let us record the atoms as they fall upon the mind in the order in which they fall". *Mrs. Dalloway*, Woolf's masterpiece, recounts the mental reflections of Claissa Dalloway in a single day, but sufficient to revivify her past life story. The work *Orlando* is a unique but brilliant fantastic biography. The hero Orlando lives from the Elizabethan Age to the present day, and changes into a woman in the 19th century.

William Faulkner (1897-1962) has been considered America's greatest novelist in the 20th century. He wrote about

America's south and used the method of the stream of consciousness and multiple-narrators. In his writings, he created a Mississippi community modeled on his own country by the name Yoknapatwapha. His works has been termed the Yoknapatwapha saga, as they seem to be one connected story telling the rise and fall histories of a number of southern aristocratic families expressing the spiritual deterioration of the modern life.

Faulkner wrote altogether 18 novels and three volumes of short stories, the most well-known of which are *The Sound and the Fury*; *Absalom, Absalom*! *As I Lay Dying*; and *Go Down, Moses*.

The Sound and the Fury is a sad story of the Compsons. Mr. Compson is disenchanted with life and society and escapes into alcoholism and cynicism. He is spiritually effete and has little love to spare for his children. Of the four children, Caddy is the only one capable of loving, but she loses her virginity. The youngest brother, Benjy, is an idiot. The first part of the book is told by him full of sound and fury, signifying nothing. The second son, Quentin, lives in the ideal world of his youth with his dreams of love, honor, and integrity and when he fails to keep off the intrusion of the harsh world, he commits suicide. The life of the eldest brother, Jason, is empty and meaningless. He falls in a morbid love with his sister, Caddy. When Caddy gets married he commits suicide, too.

Marcel Proust (1871-1922), the great French novelist of stream of consciousness, is known for the one work: the enormous, fifteen-volume exploration of time and consciousness called *Remembrance of Things Past*. This novel has no clear and continuous plot line building to a dénouement, nor (until the last volume) could the reader detect a consistent development of the central character, Marcel. Only at the end does the narrator recognize the meaning and value of what has preceded. The overall theme of the novel is search of lost time. The narrator, a "Marcel" who suggests but is not identical with the author, is an old man weakened by a long illness who puzzles over the events of his past, trying to find in them a significant pattern. He begins with his childhood, ordered within the comfortable security of accepted manners and ideals in the family home at Combay. In succeeding volumes he goes out into the world, experiences love and disappointment, discovers the disparity between idealized images of places and their crude, sometimes banal reality, and is increasingly overcome by disillusionment with himself and society. Until the end of the novel, Marcel remains an extremely sensitive person impelled by the major experiences of his life — love, betrayal, art, separation, and death — to discard his earlier naive perspective and seek out a largely intuited meaning for life.

Dorothy Miller Richardson (1878-1957) is regarded as the first of the stream of consciousness. She was born in Abingdon, Berkshire, and worked as a teacher and as a clerk. She has repeatedly been referred to by other writers as an important innovator in the history of the Modern English novel; yet her work has received only limited attention from critics and scarcely any from the general reader. Though she was scornful of the term "stream of consciousness" as applied to her method, and little less so of "interior monologue", the terms have continued to be used of her twelve-volume novel, *Pilgrimage*, devoted to what may best be called the life-in-the-mind of Miriam Henderson. The narrative throughout resembles a wide plain in which events are no more than slight undulation, yet it is in its way deserving of tolerant and patient contemplation.

MRS. DALLOWAY
(Excerpt)
by Virginia Woolf

She had reached the Park gates.[1] She stood for a moment, looking at the omnibuses in Piccadilly.[2]

She would not say of any one in the world now that they were this or were that. She felt very young; at the same time unspeakably aged. She sliced like a knife through everything; at the same time was outside, looking on. She had a perpetual sense, as she watched the taxi cabs, of being out, out, far out to sea and alone; she always had the feeling that it was very, very dangerous to live even one day. Not that she thought herself clever, or much out of the ordinary. How she had got through life on the few twigs of knowledge Fraulein Daniels'[3] gave them she could not think. She knew nothing; no language, no history; she scarcely read a book now, except memoirs in bed; and yet to her it was absolutely absorbing; all this; the cabs passing; and she would not say of Perter[4], she would not say of herself, I am this, I am that.

Her only gift was knowing people almost by instinct, she thought, walking on. if you put her in a room with some one, up went her back like a cat's or she purred. Devonshire House, Bath House[5], the house with the china cockatoo[6], she had seen them all lit up once; and remembered Sylyia, Fred, Sally Seton — Such hosts of people; and dancing all night; and the waggons plodding past to market; and driving home across the Park. She remembered once throwing a shilling into the Serpentine[7]. But every one remembered; what she loved was this, here, now, in front of her; the fat lady in the cab. Did it matter then, she asked herself, walking towards Bond Street[8], did it matter that she must inevitably cease completely; all this must go on without her; did she resent it; or did it not become consoling to believe that death ended absolutely? But that somehow in the streets of London, on the ebb and flow of things, here, there, she survived, Peter survived, lived in each other, she being part, she was positive, of the trees at home; of the house there, ugly, rambling all to bits and pieces as it was;[9] part of people she had never met; being laid out like a mist between the people she knew best, who lifted her on their branches as she had seen the trees lift the mist, but it spread ever so far, her life herself. But what was she dreaming as she looked into Hatchard's shop window?[10] What was she trying to recover? What image of white dawn in the country, as she read in the book spread open:

Fear no more the heat O' the sun.

Nor the Furious winter's rages.[11]

This late age of the world's experience had bred in them all, all men and women, a well of tears. Tears and sorrows; courage and endurance; a perfectly upright and stoical bearing. Think, for example, of the woman she admired most, Lady Bexbotough[12], opening the bazaar.

There were Jorrock's Jaunts and Jollities; there were Soapy Sponge and Mrs. Asquith's Memoirs and Big Game Shooting in Nigeria[13], all spread open. Ever so many books there were; but none that seemed exactly right to take to Evelyn Whitbread[14] in her nursing home. Nothing that would serve to amuse her and make that indescribably dried-up little woman look, as Clarissa came in, just for a moment cordial; before they settled down for the usual interminable talk of women's ailments. How much she wanted it —

西方文学

303

that people should look pleased as she came in, Clarissa thought and turned and walked back towards Bond Street, annoyed, because it was silly to have other reasons for doing things. Much rather would she have been one of those people like Richard who did things for themselves, whereas, she thought, waiting to cross, half the time she did things not simply, not for themselves; but to make people think this or that; perfect idiocy she knew (and now the policeman held up his hand) for no one was ever for a second taken in. Oh if she could have had her life over again. She thought, stepping on to the pavement, could have looked even differently!

She would have been, in the first place, dark like Lady Bexboroagh, with a skin of crumpled leather and beautiful eyes. She would have been, like Lady Bexborough, slow and stately; rather large; interested in politics like a man; with a country house; very dignified, very sincere. Instead of which she had a narrow peastick figure; a ridiculous little face, beaked like a bird's. That she held herself well was true; and had nice hands and feet; and dressed well, considering that she spent little. But often now this body she wore (she stopped to look at a Dutch picture), this body, with all its capacities, seemed nothing — nothing at all. She had the oddest sense of being herself invisible; unseen; unknown; there being no more marrying, no more having of children now, but only this astonishing and rather solemn progress with the rest of them, up Bond Street, this being Mrs. Dalloway not even Clarissa any more; this being Mrs. Richard Dalloway.

Bond Street fascinated her; Bond Street early in the morning in the season; its flags flying; its shops; no splash; no glitter; one roll of tweed in the shop where her father had bought his suits for fifty years; a few pearls; salmon on an iceblock.

"That is all," she said, looking at the fishmonger's. "That is all", she repeated, pausing for a moment at the window of a glove shop where, before the War[15], you could buy almost perfect gloves. And her old Uncle William used to say a lady is known by her shoes and her gloves. He had turned on his bed one morning in the middle of the War. He had said, "I have had enough." Gloves and shoes, she had a passion for gloves; but her own daughter, her Elizabeth, cared not a straw for either of them.

Not a straw, she thought, going on up Bond Street to a shop they kept flowers for her when she gave a party. Elizabeth really cared for her dog most of all. The whole house this morning smelt of tar. Still, better poor Grizzle[16] than Miss Kilman[17]; better distemper and tar and all the rest of it than sitting me wed in a stuffy bedroom with a prayer book! Better anything, she was inclined to say. But it might be only a phase, as Richard said, such as all girls go through. It might be falling in love. BUt why with Miss Kilman? Who had been badly treated of course; one must make allowances for that, and Richard said she was very able, had a really historical mind. Anyhow they were inseparable, and Elizabeth, her own daughter, went to communion[18]; and how she dressed, how she treatded people who came to lunch she did not care a bit, it being her experience that the religious ecstasy made people callous (so did causes); dulled their feelings, for Miss Kilman would do anything for the Russians, starved herself for Austrians, but in private inflicted positive torture, so insensitive was she, dressed in a green mackintoeh coat, year in year out she wore that coat; she perspired; she was never in the room five minutes without making you feel her superiority, your inferiority; how poor she was; how rich you were; how she lived in a slum without a cushion or a bed or a rug or whatever it might be, all her soul rusted with that grievance sticking in it, her dismissal from school during the War — poor embittered unfortunate creature! For it was not her one hated but the idea of her, which, undoubtedly had gathered in to itself a great deal that was not Miss Kilman: had beoome one of

those specters'with which one battles in the night; one of those,
specters who stand astride us and suck up half our life-blood, dom-
inators and tyrants; for no doubt with another throw of the dice,
had the black been uppermost and not the white, she would have
loved Miss Kilman! But not in his world. No.

It rasped her, though, to have stirring about in her this brutal
monster! To hear twigs cracking and feel hooves planted down in
the depths of that leafencurnbered forest, the soul; never to be
content quite, or quite secure, for at any moment the brute would
be stirring, this hatred, which especially since her illness, had
power to make her feel scraped, hurt in her spine; gave her physical pain, and made all pleasure in beauty, in friendship, in being
well, in being loved and making her home delightful rock, quiver,
and bend as if indeed there were a monster grubbing at the roots,
as if the whole panoply of content were nothing but self love! This
hatred! Nonsense, nonsense! She cried to herself, pushing through
the swing doors of Mulberry's the florists. She advanced, light,
tall, very upright, to be greeted at once by button-faced Miss Py-
ro, whose hands were always bright red, as if they had been stood
in cold water with the flowers.

There were flowers: delphiniums, sweet peas, bunches of ti-
lao; and camations, masses of camations. There were roses;
there were irises. Ah yes — so she breathed in the earthy garden
sweet smell as she stood talking to Miss Pym who owed her help,
and thought her kind, for kind she had been years ago; very kind,
but she looked older, this year, turning her head from side to side
among the irises and roses and nodding tufts of lilac with her eyes
half closed, snuffing in, after the street uproar, the delicious
scent, the exquisite coolness. And then, opening her eyes, how
fresh like frilled linen clean from a laundry laid in wicker trays the
roses looked; and dark and prim the red camations, holding their
heads up; and all the sweet peas spreading in their bowls, tinged

violet, snow white, pale — as if it were the evening and girls in muslin frocks came out to pick sweet peas and roses after the superb summer's day, with its almost bule-biack sky, its delphiniums, its camation, its arum lilies was over; and it was the moment between six and seven when every flower — roses, camations, irises, lilac — glows; white, violet, red, deep orange; every flower seems to bum by itself, softly, purely in the misty beds; and how she loved the grey-white moths spinning and out over the cherry pie, over the evening primroses!

And as she began to go with Miss Pym from jar to jar, shooting, nonsense, nonsense, she said to herself, more and more gently, as if this beauty, this scent, this colour, and Miss Pym liking her, trusting her, were a wave which she let flow over her and surmount that hatred, that monster, sumount it all; and it lifted her up and up when — oh! A pistol shot in the street outside!

"Dear, those motor cars," said Miss Pym, going to the window to look, and coming back and smiling apologetically with her hands full of sweep peas, as if those motor cars, those tyres of motor cars, were all her fault.

Notes

1. Park gates: here referring to the gates of St. James Park in London.
2. Piccadilly: a street in London, a traditional center of fashionable shops, clubs and hotels.
3. Fraulein Dauielle: referring to the (German) governess who taught her (Mrs. Dalloway) in her childhood. "Fraulein" = German word for "Miss".
4. Peter: Peter Walsh, Mrs. Dalloway's former lover.
5. Devonshire Home, Bath Home: referring to the buildings she remembered she had seen some time in the past.
6. china cookatoo: a large crested parrot made of porcelain.
7. the Srepentine: ornamental water in Hyde Park, London.

8. Bond Street: a street in the West End of London.

9. ugly, rambling all to bits and pieces as it was: referring to the ugly house, big but somewhat old and dilapidated, where she lived.

10. Hatchard's shop window: shop window of Hatchard's (name of a shop).

11. "Fear no more the heat O' the sun / Nor the furious wintor's rages": the first two-lines of the dirge on Imogen in Shakespeare's *Cymbeline* which Mrs. Dalloway remembered to have read.

12. Lady Bexborough: an aristocratic lady Mrs. Dalloway knew and admired, who was asked to open the bazaar (somewhere some time ago).

13. Jorroek's Jaunts and Jollities, Soapy Sponge, Mrs. Asquith's Memoirs and Big Game Shooting in Nigeria: There are books for popular reading in the 1920s that came to Mrs. Dalloway's mind at the moment. Mrs. (Margot) Asquith (1864-1945) was wife of Herbert Henry Asquith (1852-1928), a well-known English statesman.

14. Evelyn Whitbread: Mrs. Dalloway's friend, wife of Hugh Whitbread, a coal merchant.

15. before the War: obviously referring to the First World War (1914-1918).

16. Grizzle: the dog at the Dalloway's.

17. Miss Kilman: servant at the Dalloway's.

18. communion: celebration of the Lord's Supper.

11. Black Humor

Black Humor is a term derived from Black Comedy. Its origin can be traced back to Shakespeare's time. But now the term is used to refer to the literary trend that arose in the United Sates in the 1960s. Black humorists held that the world is harsh, absurd, full of uncomprehensible powers. People are suffering from such a world, but couldn't do anything about it, and therefore they may as well laugh. To stress the absurdity of the world, black humorists tended to narrate their stories in an anti-fictional manner, in which fantasy and reality are mixed up, and plot and time are presented in random order. Corresponding to the odd structure is the grotesque hero who has the converse of most of the traditional attributes of the hero. This hero is graceless, inept, sometimes stupid, sometimes dishonest. In fact, black humor is a substantial element in the anti-novel and the Theatre of the Absurd. Joseph Heller's *Catch-22* is an almost archetypal example. Other novelists working in the tradition of black humor include Gonter Grass, Mordecai Richler, Thomas Pynchon, and Kurt Vonnegut. Black humor is also found expression in the plays of Edward Albee, Harold Pinter, and Eugene Lonesco.

Kurt Vonnegut (1922-) was the most popular and widely read during the 1960s in the United States. His most famous novel *Slaughter House Five* (1969) is a typical example of the black humor. Based on the author's experience as a war prisoner in Dresden during World War Ⅱ, the novel is specially concerned with bombing of Dresden by the Allies, and offers ironic commentary on the modern inhumanity and the appalling opportunity for destruction provided by 20th-century technology. The insane conduct of modern warfare promoted by the modern technology is revealed and attacked through the life story of the anti-hero, Billy Pilgrim: Billy is a retired soldier, somewhat out of mind. He is dreaming and roaming among the four phases of his life: his childhood; his experiences in the war; his life after the war as a rich optometrist with his wife and children; and his experiences on the imagined planet Tralfamadore, where he is taken in a "flying saucer" to be exhibited in a zoo. Billy's random movement in these different parts of his life provides a dislocated sense of time and uncertainty for the reader as to what is real and as to what is not.

Joseph Heller (1923-), like Vonnegut, served in the US Army during World War Ⅱ. The war experience provided rich material for his anti-war novel *Catch-22* (1961), which firmly established his reputation as a novelist. The story is set in an air force base hospital on the fictional island of Pinosa during World War Ⅱ. Captain John Yossarian is determined to survive the war and will use any means at his disposal to do so. He hopes to get a medical discharge by pretending to be insane, but the "catch-22" ruling — that anyone rational enough to want to be grounded could not possibly insane, and is therefore capable of returning to flight duty — keeps him in the war. Finally, after all his friends are killed or missing, he decides to desert to Sweden. The novel is filled with lexical distortions and extravagant puns, incongruous details and misplaced events. It mocks the traditions of war fiction and the idealized concepts of patriotic heroism, mixing grisly horrors with comic absurdities to assail authority, hierarchies, and the madness of war.

CATCH-22
Chapter Forty-One Snowden
by Joseph Heller

"Cut," said a doctor.

"You cut," said another.

"No cuts," said Yossarian with a thick, unwieldy tongue.

"Now look who's butting in." complained one of the doctors.

"Another county heard from. Are we going to operate or aren't we?"

"He doesn't need an operation," complained the other. "It's a small wound. All we have to do is stop the bleeding, clean it out and a few stitches in."

"But I've never had a chance to operate before. Which one is the scalpel? Is this one the scalpel?"

"No, the other one is the scalpel. Well, go ahead and cut already if you're going to. Make the incision."

"Like this?"

"Not there, you dope!"

"No incisions," Yossarian said, perceiving through the lifting fog of insensibility that two strangers were ready to begin cutting him.

"Another county heard from," complained the first doctor sarcastically. "Is he going to keep talking that way while I operate on him?"

"You can't operate on him until I admit him," said a clerk.

"You can't admit him until I clear him," said a fat, gruff colonel with a mustache and an enormous pink face that pressed down very close to Yossarian and radiated scorching heat like the bottom of a huge frying pan. "Where were you born?"

The fat, gruff colonel reminded Yossarian of the fat, gruff colonel who had interrogated the chaplain and found him guilty. Yossarian stared up at him through a glassy film. The cloying scents of formaldehyde and alcohol sweetened the air.

"On a battlefield," he answered.

"No, no. In what state were you born?"

"In a state of innocence."

"No, no. You don't understand."

"Let me handle him," urged a hatchet-faced man with sunken acrimonious eyes and a thin, malevolent mouth. "Are you a smart clerk or something?" he asked Yossarian.

"He's delirious," one of the doctors said. "Why don't you let us take him back inside and treat him?"

"Leave him right here if he's delirious. He might say something incriminating."

"But he's still bleeding profusely. Can't you see? He might even die."

"Good for him!"

"It would serve the finky bastard right," said the fat, gruff colonel. "All right, John, let's speak out. We want to get to the truth."

"Everyone calls me Yo-Yo."

"We want you to co-operate with us, Yo-Yo. We're your friends and we want you to trust us. We're here to help you. We're not going to hurt you."

"Let's jab our thumbs down inside his wound and gouge it," suggested the hatchet-faced man.

Yossarian let his eyes fall closed and hoped they would think he was unconscious.

"He's fainted," he heard a doctor say. "Can't we treat him now before it's too late? He really might die."

"All right, take him. I hope the bastard does die."

"You can't treat him until I admit him." the clerk said.

Yossarian played dead with his eyes shut while the clerk admitted him by shuffling some papers, and then he was rolled away slowly into a stuffy, dark room with searing spotlights overhead in which the cloying smell of formaldehyde and sweet alcohol was even stronger. The pleasant, permeating stink was intoxicating. He smelled ether too and heard glass tinkling. He listened with secret, egotistical mirth to the husky breathing of the two doctors. It delighted him that they thought he was unconscious and did not know he was listening. It all seemed very silly to him until one of the doctors said:

"Well, do you think we should save his life? They might be sore at us if we do." "Let's operate," said the other doctor. "Let's cut him open and get to the inside of things once and for all. He keeps complaining about his liver. His liver. His liver looks pretty small on this X-ray."

"That's his pancreas, you dope, This is his liver."

"No it isn't. That's his heart. I'll bet you a nickel this is his liver. I'm going to operate and find out. Should I wash my hands first."

"No operations." Yossarian said, opening his eyes and trying to sit up.

"Another county heard from," scoffed one of the doctors indignantly. "Can't we make him shut up?"

"We could give him a total. The ether's right here."

"No totals," said Yossarian.

"Another county heard from." said a doctor.

"Let's give him a total and knock him out. Then we can do what we want with him."

They gave Yossarian total anesthesia and knocked him out. He woke up thirsty in a private room drowning in ether fumes. Colonel Korn was there at his bedside, waiting calmly in a chair in his baggy, wool, olive-drab shirt and trousers. A bland, phlegmatic smile hung on his brown face with its heavy-bearded cheeks. And he was buffing the facets of his bald head gently with the palms of both hands. He bent forward chuckling when Yossarian awoke, and assured him in the friendliest tones that the deal they had made was still on if Yossarian didn't die. Yossarian vomited, and Colonel Korn shot to his feet at the first cough and fled in disgust, so it seemed indeed that there was a silver lining to every cloud, Yossarian reflected, as he drifted back into a suffocating daze. A hand with sharp fingers shook him awake roughly. He turned and opened his eyes and saw a strange man with a mean face who curled his lip at him in a spiteful scowl and bragged.

We've got your pal, buddy. "We're got your pal. "

Yossarian turned cold and faint and broke into a sweat.

"Who's my pal?" he asked when he saw the chaplain sitting where Colonel Korn had been sitting.

"Maybe I'm you pal," the chaplain answered.

But Yossarian couldn't hear him and closed his eyes. Some-one gave him water to sip and tiptoed away. He slept and woke up feeling great until he turned his head to smile at the chaplain and saw Afarfy there instead. Yossarian moaned instinctively and screwed his face up with excruciating irritability when Afarfy chortled and asked how he was feeling. Afarfy looked puzzled when Yossarian inquired why he was not in jail. Yossarian shut his eyes to make him go away. When he opened them, Afarfy was gone and the chaplain was there. Yossarian broke into laughter when he spied the chaplain's cheerful grin and asked him what in the hell he was so happy about.

"I'm happy about you," the chaplain replied with excited can-dor and joy. I heard at Group that you were very seriously injured and that you would have to be sent home if you lived. Colonel Korn said your condition was critical. But I've just learned from one of the doctors that your wound is really a very slight one and that you'll probably be able to leave in a day or two. You're in no dan-ger. It isn't bad at all.

Yossarian listened to the chaplain's news with enormous re-lief. "That's good. "

"Yes," said the chaplain, a pink flush of impish pleasure creeping into his cheeks. "Yes, that is good. "

Yossarian laughed, recalling his first conversation with the chaplain. "You know, the first time I met you was in the hospital. And now I'm in the hospital again. Just about the only time I see you lately is in the hospital. Where've Leaves the area, so that he won't catch me. "

"Does it do any good?"

"It bakes my mind off my troubles," the chaplain answered with another shrug. "And it gives me something to do. "

"Well, that's good, then, isn't it?"

"Yes," agreed the chaplain enthusiastically, as though the idea had not occurred to him before. "Yes, I guess that is good. " He bent forward impulsively with awkward solicitude. "Yossarian, is there anything I can do for you while you're here, anything I can get you?"

Yossarian teased him jovially. "Like toys, or candy, or chewing gum?"

The chaplain blushed again, grinning self-consciously, and then turned very respectful. "Like books, perhaps, or anything at all. I wish there was something I could do to make you happy. You now, Yossarian, we're all very proud of you. "

"Proud?"

"Yes, of course. For risking your life to stop that Nazi assassin. It was a very noble thing to do. "

"What Nazi assassin?"

"The one that came here to murder colonel Cathcart and Colonel Korn. And you saved them. He might have stabbed you to death as you grappled with him on the balcony. It's lucky thing you're alive. "

Yossarian snickered sardonically when he understood. "That was no Nazi assassin. "

"Certainly it was. Colonel Korn said it was. "

"That was Nately's girl friend. And she was after me, not Colonel Cathcart and Colonel Korn. She's been trying to kill me ever since I broke the news to her that Nately was dead. "

"But how could that be?" the chaplain protested in livid and resentful confusion. "Colonel Cathcart and Colonel Korn both saw him as he ran away. The official report says you stopped a Nazi assassin from killing them."

"Don't believe the official report," Yossarian advised dryly. "It's part of the deal."

"What deal?"

"The deal I made with Colonel Cathcart and Colonel Korn. They'll let me go home a big hero if I say nice things about them to everybody and never criticize them to anyone for making the rest of the men fly more missions."

The chaplain was appalled and rose halfway out of his chair. He bristled with bellicose dismay. "But that's terrible! That's a shameful, scandalous deal, isn't it?"

"Odious," Yossarian answered, staring up woodenly at the ceiling with just the back of his head resting on the pillow. "I think 'odious' is the word we decided on."

"Then how could you agree to it?"

"Its that or a court-martial, chaplain."

"Oh," the chaplain exclaimed with a look of stark remorse, the back of his hand covering his mouth. He lowered himself into his chair uneasily "I shouldn't have said anything."

"They'd look me in prison with a bunch of criminals."

"Of course. You must do whatever you think is right, then." The chaplain nodded to himself as though deciding the argument and lapsed into embarrassed silence.

"Don't worry" Yossarian said with a sorrowful laugh after several moments had passed. "I'm not going to do it."

"But you must do it," the chaplain insisted, bending forward with concern. "Really, you must. I had no right to influence you, I really had no right to say anything."

"You didn't influence me." Yossarian hauled himself over onto his side and shook his head in solemn mockery. "Christ, Chaplain! Can you imagine that for a sin? Saving Colonel Cathcart's life!

That's one crime I don't want on my record. "

The chaplain returned to the subject with caution. "What will you do instead? You can't let them put you in prison. "

"I'll fly more missions, Or maybe I really will desert and let them catch me. They probably would. "

"And they'd put you in prison. You don't want to go to prison. "

"Then I'll just keep flying missions until the war ends, I guess. Some of us have to survive. "

"But you might get killed. "

"Then I guess I won't fly any more missions. "

"What will you do?"

"I don't know. "

"Will you let them send you home?"

"I don't know. Is it hot out? It's very warm in here. "

"You know," Yossarian remembered, "a very funny thing happened — maybe I dreamed it. I think a strange man came in here before and told me he's got me pal. I wonder if I imagined it. "

"I don't think you did," the chaplain informed him. "You started to tell me about him when I dropped in earlier. "

"Then he really did say it, 'We've got your pal, buddy,' he said, 'We've got your pal. ' He had the most malignant manner I ever saw. I wonder who my pal is. "

"I like to think that I'm your pal, Yossarian," the chaplain said with humble sincerity. "And they certainly have got me. They've got my number and they've got me under surveillance, and they've got me right where they want me. That's what they told me at my interrogation. "

"No, I don't think it's you he meant," Yossarian decided, "I think it must be someone like Nately or Dunbar. You know, someone who was killed in the war, like Clevinger, Orr, Dobbs, Kd Sampson or McWatt. " Yossarian emitted a startled gasp and shook his head. "I just realized it," he exclaimed, "They've got all my pals, haven't they? The only ones left are me and Hungry Joe." He tingled with dread as he saw the chaplain's face go pale. "Chaplain, what is it?"

"Hungry Joe was killed."

"God, no! On a mission?"

"He died in his sleep while having a dream. They found a cat on his face."

"Poor bastard," Yossarian said, and began to cry, hiding his tears in the crook of his shoulder. The chaplain left without saying good-bye. Yossarian ate something and went to sleep. A hand shook him awake in the middle of the night. He opened his eyes and saw a thin, mean man in a patient's bathrobe and pajamas who looked at him with a nasty smirk and jeered.

"We've got your pal, buddy. We've got your pal."

Yossarian was unnerved. "What the hell are you talking about?" he pleaded in incipient panic.

Yossarian longed for his tormentor's throat with one hand, but the man glided out of reach effortlessly and vanished into the corridor with a malicious laugh. Yossarian lay there trembling with a pounding pulse. He was bathed in icy sweat. He wondered who his pal was. It was dark in the hospital and perfectly quiet. He had no watch to tell him the time. He was wide-awake, and he knew he was a prisoner in one of those sleepless, bedridden nights that would take an eternity to dissolve into dawn. A throbbing chill oozed up his legs. He was cold, and he thought of Snowden, who had never been his pal but was a vaguely familiar kid who was badly wounded and freezing to death in the puddle of harsh yellow sunlight splashing into his face through the side gunport when Yossarian crawled into the rear section of the plane over the bomb bay after Dobbs had beseeched him on the intercom to help the gunner, please help the gunner. Yossarian's stomach turned over when his eyes first beheld the macabre scene; he was absolutely revolted, and he paused in fright few moments before descending, crouched on his hands and knees in the narrow tunnel over the bomb bay beside the sealed corrugated carton containing the first aid kit. Snowden was lying on his back on the floor with his legs stretched out, still burdened cumbersomely by his flak suit, his flak, helmet, his parachute harness and his Mae West. Not far away on the floor lay the small tail gunner in a dead faint. The wound Yossarian saw was in the outside of Snowden's thigh, as large and deep as a football, it seemed. It was impossible to tell where the shreds of his saturated coveralls ended and the ragged flesh began.

There was no morphine in the first-aid kit, no protection for Snowden against pain but the numbing shock of the gaping wound itself. The twelve syrettes of morphine had been stolen from their case and replaced by a cleanly lettered note that said: "What's good for M & M Engerprises is good for the country, Milo Minderbinder." Yossarian swore at Milo and held two aspirins out to ashen lips unable to receive them. But first he hastily drew a tourniquet around Snowden's thigh because he could not think what else to do in those first tumultuous moments when his senses were in turmoil, when he knew he must act competently at once and feared he might go to pieces completely. Snowden watched him steadily, saying nothing. No artery was spurting, but Yossarian pretended to absorb himself entirely into the fashioning of a tourniquet, because applying tourniquet was something he did know how to do. He worked with simulated skill and composure, feeling Snowden's lackluster gaze resting upon him. He recovered possession of himself before the tourniquet was finished and loosened it immediately to lessen the danger of gangrene. His mind was clear now, and he knew how to proceed. He rummaged through the first-aid kit for scissors.

"I'm cold," Snowden said softly, "I'm cold."

"You're going to be all right, kid", Yossarian reassured him with a grin. "You're going to be all right."

"I'm cold," Snowden said again in a frail, childlike voice. "I'm cold."

"There, there," Yossarian said, because he did not know what else to say. "There, there."

"I'm cold." Snowden whimpered. "I'm cold."

"There, there. There, there."

Yossarian was frightened and moved more swiftly. He found a pair of scissors at last and began cutting carefully through Snowden's coverallthigh up above the wound, just below the groin. He cut through the heavy gabardine cloth all the way around the thigh in a straight line. The tine tail gunner woke up while Yossarian was cutting with the scissors, saw him, and fainted again. Snowden rolled his head to the other side of his neck in order to stare at Yossarian, puzzled, tried not to look at him. He began cutting downward through the coveralls along the inside seam. The yawning wound — was that a tube of slimy bone he saw running deep inside the gory scarlet flow behind the twitching, startling fibers of weird muscle? — was dripping blood in several trickles, like snow melting on eaves, but viscous and red, already thickening as it dropped. Yossarian kept cutting through the coveralls to the bottom and peeled open the severed leg of the garment. It fell to the floor with a plop, exposing the hem of khaki undershorts that were soaking up blotches of blood on one side as though in thirst. Yossarian was stunned at how waxen and ghastly Snowden's bare leg looked, how loathsome, how lifeless and esoteric the downy, fine, curled blond hairs on his odd, white shin and alf. The wound, he saw now, was not nearly as large as a football, but as long and wide as his hand, and too raw and deep to see into clearly. The raw muscles inside twitched like live hamburger meat. A long sigh of relief escaped slowly through Yossarian's mouth when he saw that Snowden was not in danger of dying. The blood was already coagulating inside the wound, and it was simply a matter of bandaging him up and keeping him calm until the plane landed. Pie removed some packets of sulfanilamide from the first-aid kit. Snowden quivered when Yossarian pressed against him gently to turn him up slightly on his side.

"Did I hurt you?"

"I'm cold,"Snowden whimpered. "I'm cold."

"There, there,"Yossarian said. "There, there."

"I'm cold, I'm cold."

"There, there. There, there."

"It's starting to hurt me," Snowden cried out suddenly with a plaintive, urgent wince.

Yossarian scrambled frantically through the first-aid kit in search of morphine again and found only Milo's note and a bottle of aspirin. He cursed Milo and held two aspirin tablets out to Snowden. He had no water to offer. Snowden rejected the aspirin with an almost imperceptible shake of his head. His face was pale and pasty. Yossarian removed Snowden's flak helmet and lowered his head to the floor.

"I'm cold." Snowden moaned with half-closed eyes. "I'm cold."

The edges of his mouth were turning blue. Yossarain was petrified. He wondered whether to pull the rip cord of Snowden's parachute and cover him with the nylon folds. It was very warm in the plane. Glancing up unexpectedly, Snowden gave him a wan, cooperative smile and shifted the position of his hips a bit so that Yossarian could begin salting the wound with sulfanilamide. Yossarian worked with renewed confidence and optimism. The plane bounced hard inside an air pocket, and he remembered with a start that he had left his own parachute up front in the nose. There was nothing to be done about that. He poured envelope after envelope of the white crystallize powder into the bloody oval wound until nothing red could be seen and then drew a deep, apprehensive breath, steeling himself with gritted teeth as he touched his bare hand to the dangling shreds of drying flesh to tuck them up inside the wound. Quickly he covered the whole wound with a large cotton compress and jerked his hand away. He smiled nervously when his brief ordeal had ended. The actual contact with the dead flesh had not been nearly as repulsive as he had anticipated, and he found excuse to caress the wound with his fingers again and again to convince himself of his own courage.

Next he began binding the compress in place with a roll of gauze. The second time around Snowden's thigh with the bandage, he spotted the small hole on the inside through which the piece of flak had entered, a round, crinkled wound the size of a quarter with blue edges and a black core inside where the blood had crested. Yossarian sprinkled this one with sulfanilamide too and continued unwinding the gauze around Snowden's leg until the compress was secure. Then he snipped off the roll with the scissors and slit the end down the center. He made the whole thing fast with a tidy square knot. It was a good bandage, he knew, and he sat back on his heels with pride, wiping the perspiration from his brow, and grinned at Snowden with spontaneous friendliness.

"I'm cold." Snowden moaned. "I'm cold."

"You're going to be all right, kid," Yosearian assured him, patting his arm comfortingly, "Everything's under control."

Snowden shook his head feebly. "I'm cold," he repeated, with eyes as dull and blind as stone. "I'm cold."

"There, there," said Yossarian, with growing doubt and trepidation. "There, there. In a little while we'll be back on the ground and Doc Daneeka will take care of you."

But Snowden kept shaking his head and pointed at last, with just the barest movement of his chin, down toward his armpit. Yo-

西方文学

ssarian bent forward to peer and saw a strangely colored stain, seeping through the coveralls just above the armhole of Snowden's flak suit. Yossarian felt his heart stop, then pound so violently he found it difficult to breath. Snowden was wounded inside his flak suit. Yossarian ripped open the snaps of Snowden's flak suit and heard himself scream wildly as Snowden's insides slithered down to the floor in a soggy pile and just kept dripping out. A chunk of flak more than three inches big had shot into his other side just underneath the arm and blasted all the way through, drawing whole mottled quarts of Snowden along with it through the gigantic hole in his ribs it made as as it blasted out. Yossarian screamed a second time and squeezed both hands over his eyes. His teeth were chattering in horror as he stared — liver, lungs, kidneys, ribs, stomach and bits of the stewed tomatoes Snowden had eaten for lunch, Yossarian hated stewed tomatoes and turned away dizzily and began to vomit, clutching his burning throat. The tall gunner woke up while Yossarian was vomiting, saw him, and fainted again. Yossarian was limp with exhaustion, pain and despair when he finished. He turned back weakly to Snowden, whose breath had grown softer and more rapid, and whose face had grown paler. He wondered how in the world to begin to save him."

"I'm cold," Snowden whimpered. "I'm cold."

"There, there," Yossarian mumbled mechanically in a voice too low to be heard. "There, there."

Yossarian was cold, too, and shivering uncontrollably. He felt goose pimples chacking all over him as he gazed down despondently at the grim secret Snowden had spilled all over the messy floor. It was easy to read the message in his entrails. Man was matter, that was Snowden's secret. Drop him out a window and he'll fall. Set fire to him and he'll bum. Bury him and he'll rot like other kinds of garbage. The spirit gone, man is garbage, That was Snowden's secret. Ripeness was all.

"I'm cold." Snowden said. "I'm cold."

"There, there." said Yossarian. "There, there." He pulled the rip cord of Snowden's parachute and covered his body with the white nylon sheets.

"I'm cold."

"There, there."

12. Neo-Novel

Neo-novel, sometimes known as the anti-novel, was a kind of literary movement developed by a group of French writers in the mid-1950s. Rejecting such elements of the traditional novel as its social concerns, coherent plot construction, and psychological analysis of character by an omniscient author, the creators of the neo-novel function in the experimental tradition of Joyce, Kafka, and Faulkner. Unlike the Existential thinkers Sartre and Camus, who remained conventional stylists in their fiction, these novelists wanted the form of the work itself to express the postwar Existential vision of a world without order or ultimate destiny peopled by characters without innate psychological identity. The best known of the neo-novelists is Alain Robbe-Grillet who believes that the external world is objective and must be described without social or moral superstructures. He eschews all metaphorical language and employs a neutral, flat style. The refusal to allow order into their fictional world leads the neo-novelists to positions similar to some of those of a modern group to whom they seem opposed, the anti-realists. The most complete example of the anti-novel is probably Robb-Grillet's *Le Voyer*; other important writers in the school include Nathalie Sarraute, Michel

Butor, and Claude Simon.

Alain Robbe-Grillet (1922-) is a French author, literary theoretician, and representative of the nouveau roman — the new novel. His works lack the conventional elements, such as dramatic plotting, coherent concept of time, and psychological analysis of the character. The novels are composed largely of recurring images, impersonally depicted physical objects and random events of everyday life. From his first published novel, *Les Gommes* (1953, *The Erasers*), Robbe-Grillet has played with popular literary genres — several times with the traditional mystery novels, perhaps the most conventional literary form. *The Erasers* mixes a detective story with changing perspectives and abundant descriptions of natural objects such as a tomato wedge. The book received the Fénélon Prize in 1954. Robbe-Grillet was elected member of the prestigious Academie Francaise in 2004. *The Erasers* was followed by *Le Voyer* (1955, *The Voyeur*), *La Jalousie* (1957, *Jealousy*), which Nabokov called one of the greatest novels of the century, and *Dans le Labyrinthe* (1959, *In the Labyrinth*). His statement of how he thought of novels should be written was published in *Pour un Noveau Roman* (1963 *For a New Novel*). "If in many of the passages that follow, I readily employ the term New Novel, it is not to designate a school, nor even a specific and constituted group of writers working in the same direction; the expression is merely a convenient label applicable to all those seeking new forms for the novel, form capable of expressing (or creating) new relations between man and the world, to all those who have determined to invent the novel, in other words, to invent man. "

13. New-Realism

The Modernist movement, with its special emphasis on form and on fluidity in time and perspective has by no means displaced more realistic and less experimental kinds of story-telling. Modern writers like D. H. Lawrence, E. M. Forster in England, Ernest Hemingway, Sinclair Lewis, John Steinbeck in America, Roman Rolland in France, Thomas Mann in Germany, and Gorky in Russia, sticked to the traditional realistic doctrines: truthful representation of the actual world, integrity of plots, well-organized structure, typical character, and purity of language. However, in the modern context, these writers' realism has gone beyond what it was in that the neo-realistic writers cover wider subject matters, stress the exploration of the inner world, and exploit varieties of modern technical methods.

E. M. Forster (1879-1970) ranks high among the English novelists of this century. His high place is based on an unusually small output — *Where Angels Fear to Tread* (1905), *The Lonest Journey* (1907), *A Room with a View* (1908), *Howards End* (1910), *A Passage to India* (1924) and three collections of short stories. Forster's insistent theme was the human need to unify in personal relationships, expressed with characteristic verbal economy. His masterpiece, *A Passage to India* presented the deeply racial resentments between Indians and their overlords and overladies under British rule. Forster has been regarded as a novelists's novelist, for his ironical sub-humor, his muted prose style, and the largely unfictional nature of his fiction are perceived and appreciated more by other writers than by unprefessional readers.

D. H. Lawrence (1885-1930) was the son of a coalminer married to a schoolteacher who came to despise her uncultured and frequently drunken husband and forged an emotionally restrictive link with her son which was largely accountable for Lawrence's later inadequacy in intimate relationships with women, and for the sexual torments to which in imagination he was to subject many of his fictional characters. His *Sons and Lovers* (1913), the autobiographical novel, concerns the effect of mother-love upon the development of a son. Lawrence was a controversial figure because of his frank treatment of sex and his outspoken insistence upon a need for a readjustment in the relationship between the sexes. He is also often criticized for the didactic elements in his novels and the looseness in structure. However, as a prose writer he has few equals in that same field of natural description. Besides *Sons and Lovers*, *The White Peacock* (1910) and *The Rainbow* (1915) are Lawrence's more important works.

Ernest Hemingway (1899-1961) was the greatest American novelist in the 20th century. As a young man, he worked as a reporter and served in the Italian army in World War I, during which he was wounded. His war experience gave rise to the anti-war novels: *The Sun Also Rises* (1926), *A Farewell to Arms* (1929), and *For Whom the Bell Tolls* (1940). Herningway's last work is the well-known short novel, *The Old Man and the Sea*, which is a parable of inner strength and courage about a Cuban fisherman's struggle to bring home a great marlin he has caught. Hemingway's short stories are equally striking. The col-

lection Men Without Women (1927) highlights the characteristic Hemingway prose style with its clipped staccato dialogue and affectation of tough masculinity.

Sinclair Lewis (1885-1951) was the first American to be awarded the Nobel Prize. Lewis' novels are noted for their criticism of the provincial American life. His greatest works, *Main Street* (1920) and *Babbitt* (1922) are satirical portayal of small-town life in the Midwest. *Arrowsmith* (1925) is the story of an altruistic doctor who struggles to resist the temptations of a fashionable and profitable practice in order to pursue a scientific career. *Elmer Gantry* (1927), the story of a sham revivalist minister, was a satire on American religion.

John Steinbeck (1902-1968) was the most important American novelist during the Great Depression. His novels and short stories were largely sympathetic studies of the unhappy lot of California farm workers. *The Grapes of Wrath*, his best known work, is the story of a family fleeing from the dust bowl of Oklahoma to what they hope will be a better life in California. Reading it, one sees the Depression spreading devastation and desolation, the dispossessed and the wretched walking the earth like so many condemned souls in hell, and the worst human nature in its uncontrolled and uncontrollable manifestations. Steinbeck was awarded the Nobel Prize in 1962.

Roman Rolland (1866-1944) was a great French master of realism. In the late 19th century, he produced dramatic works about the French Revolution. Then he published *Michelangelo* (1915) and *Beethoven the Greater* (1929). Rolland's best known novel is *Jean-Christophe*, covering the life of a musical genius from birth to death.

Thomas Mann (1875-1955), the most influential and representative German novelist of the first half of the 20th century, was a writer of a great philosophical depth and originality. His masterpiece, *Buddenbrooks*, tracing a noble family from its prosperity to its deterioration. Among his other important works are *The Magic Mountain* (1924) and *Death in Venice* (1903). The former is a novel set in a mountain sanatorium in which those detained were personifications of different strains in prewar life, and the latter is an outstanding successful account of the conflict of sacred and profane love and the nexus of genius and disease whose fullest meaning extends to a philosophical investigation of the condition of the Teutonie psyche. He was awarded the Nobel Prize in 1929.

Maksim Gorky (1868-1936), the founder of the literary doctrine of socialist realism, was the greatest Russian writer of the 20th century. Early in his life, he began to do all kinds of jobs and saw a great deal of the brutal, unpleasant side of life. Most of his works are autobiographical, concerning the bitter life of the oppressed people of Russia, and he has been regarded as the spokesman of the uneducated masses. His greatest work of social realism, *Mother*, was published in 1908. This novel shows the beginnings of the revolutionary movement of the Russian working class. His trilogy containing *Childhood* (1912), *My Apprenticeship* (1915) and *My University* (1923) portrays the people he knew and his experience from boyhood to manhood.

Margaret Mitchell (1900-1949) was born in Atlanta and educated there and at Smith College, Massachusetts. Prevented by

西方文学

family responsibilities from qualifying as a doctor, she wrote for an Atlanta newspaper and married in 1925. From her family, all of whom were deeply interested in the history of the southern states, she had throughout her childhood and adolescence heard stories of the confederacy and the civil war, and from the knowledge thus acquired she created *Gone with the Wind* (1936), a thousand-page novel about a southern belle's (O'Hara) life and loves during and after the civil war, which was to become the most widely circulated of all best-sellers, while the film based on it was also record-breaking. Margaret wrote no other book.

Pearl Buck (1892-1973) was one of the most popular American authors of her day, humanitarian, crusader for women's rights, editor of Asia magazine, philanthropist, noted for her novels of life in China. Pearl S. Buck was awarded the Nobel Prize for literature in 1938, the third American to win the Nobel Prize in Literature, following Sinclair Lewis and Eugene O'Neil. Pearl S. Buck was born in Hillsboro, West Virginia. She spent her youth in China, in Chinkiang on the Yangtse River. She learned to speak Chinese before she could speak English. After being educated by her mother and by a Chinese tutor, who was a Confucian scholar, Buck was sent to a boarding school in Shanghai (1907-1909). Buck continued her education in the United States at Randolph-Macon Woman's College in Virginia, where she studied psychology. After graduating in 1914, she returned to China as a teacher for the Presbyterian Board of Missions. Buck married Dr. John Lossing Buck, an agricultural expert. They settled in a village in the North China. Buck worked as a teacher and interpreter for her husband and traveled through the countryside. In the 1920s the Bucks moved to Nanking, where she taught English and American literature at the university. In 1924 she returned to the United States to seek medical care for her first daughter, who was mentally retarded. In 1926 she received her M. A. in literature from Cornell University. As a writer Buck started with the novel *East Wind, West Wind* (1930), which received critical recognition. Her breakthrough novel, *The Good Earth*, appeared in 1931. Its style, a combination of biblical prose and the Chinese narrative saga, increased the dignity of its characters. The book gained a wide audience, and was made into a motion picture. The story follows the life of Wang Lung, from his beginnings as an impoverished peasant to his eventual position as a prosperous landowner.

Norman Mailer (1923-) was born in New Jersey, educated at Brooklyn and at Harvard, and served with the American forces in the Pacific during World War II, on which his first novel *The Naked and the Dead* (1948), a young man's panoramic version of life among the troops, was based. His *Barbary Shore* (1951) did not equal his realistic predecessor. In his later work Mailer became a complex embarrassment, falling under the spell of existentialism into attempting to rationalize his fascination with the hordes of psychopaths, protesting minorities, sexual neurotics and others that flooded some American cities. For his defense of much violence he was attacked as fascist. His later books include *An American Dream* (1965), *Why Are We in Vietnam?* (1967) and *The Armies of the Night* (1969).

J. D. Salinger (1919-) was born in New York and educated in Manhattan and Pennsylvania. He began to publish short stories during the early 1940s and served in the US infantry during World War Ⅱ. His only novel has been the highly successful *The Catcher in the Rye* (1951), narrated by a teenaged schoolboy in rebellion against the dubious values of the adult world. His stories, featuring the Glass family, as in *For Esme—with Love and Squalor* (1953), *Fanny and Zooey* (1962) and others were equally popular for their presentation of highly intelligent young Americans of the period. After his public was assured and gratified it was a matter of regret that he then fell virtually silent.

Saul Bellow (1915-2005) was born in Quebec and educated at Chicago and North western universities. His earliest novels, such as *Dangling Man* (1944), placed the concepts of Kafka and Camus in an American World. In *Adventures of Augie March* (1953) he explored Chicago life and won him his first National Book Award. *Herzog* (1964), *Mr Sammler's Planet* (1970), *Humboldt's Gift* (1975), and *The Deau's December* (1982) put him in the forefront of interpreters of the struggles of urban dwellers to define their roles and responsibilities in the modern world. He was awarded the Nobel Prize for Literature in 1976. He also wrote *The Last Analysis* (1965) and other plays.

Isaac Bashevis Singer (1904-1988) was one of the great storytellers of the 20th century. His writing is a unique blend of religious morality and social awareness combined with an investigation of personal desires. Though his work often took the form of parables or tales based on a 19th century tradition, he was deeply concerned with the events of his time and the future of his people and their culture. Throughout the 1940s, Singer's reputation began to grow among the many Yiddish-speaking immigrants. In

1950 Singer produced his first major work, *The Family Moskat* — the story of a 20th century Polish Jewish family before the war. He followed this novel with a series of well-received short stories, including his most famous, "Gimpel, The Fool."

By the 1970s, he had become a major international writer. After World War Ⅱ there were few Yiddish writers remaining and Singer was not only a vocal proponent of Yiddish writing, but the major figure in Yiddish letters. Throughout the 1970s he wrote dozens of stories that were eventually collected into books, and published in Yiddish and English as well as many other languages. He branched out, writing memoirs and children's books as well as two other major novels set in the 20th century, *The Penitent* (1974) and *Shosha* (1978). The same year as his publication of *Shosha*, Singer won the Nobel Prize in literature. After being awarded the Nobel Prize, Singer gained a monumental status among writers throughout the world. He continued to write during the last years of his life, often returning to Polish history which so entranced him throughout his early life. In 1988 he published *The King of the Fields* and three years later, *Scums*. That same year, Isaac Bashevis Singer died at the age of eighty-seven in Surfside, Florida. Incredibly prolific, Singer created an insightful and deep body of work that will forever remain an important part of literary history.

西方文学

333

CAT IN THE RAIN
by Ernest Hemingway

There were only two Americans stopping at the hotel. They did not know any of the people they passed on the stairs on their way to and from their room. Their room was on the second floor facing the sea. It also faced the public garden and the war monument. There were big palms and green benches in the public garden. In the good weather there was always an artist with his easel. Artists liked the way the palms grew and the bright colors of the hotels facing the gardens and the sea. Italians came from a long way off to look up at the war monument. It was made of bronze and glistened in the rain. It was raining. The rain dripped from the palm trees. Water stood in pools on the gravel paths. The sea broke in a long line in the rain and slipped back down the beach to come up and break again in a long line in the rain. The motor cars were gone from the square by the war monument. Across the square in the doorway of the cafe a waiter stood looking out at the empty square.

The American wife stood at the window looking out. Outside right under their window a cat was crouched under one of the dripping green tables. The cat was trying to make herself so compact that she would not be dripped on.

"I'm going down and get that kitty," the American wife said.

"I'll do it," her husband offered from the bed.

"No, I'll get it. The poor kitty out trying to keep dry under a table."

The husband went on reading, lying propped up with the two pillows at the foot of the bed.

"Don't get wet," he said.

The wife went downstairs and the hotel owner stood up and bowed to her as she passed the office. His desk was at the far end of the office. He was an old man and very tall.

"Il piove,"[1] the wife said. She liked the hotel-keeper.

"Si, si, Signora. Brutto tempo.[2] It's very bad weather."

He stood behind his desk in the far end of the dim room. The wife liked him. She liked the deadly serious way he received and complaints. She liked his dignity. She liked the way he wanted to serve her. She liked the way he felt about being a hotel-keeper. She liked his old, heavy face and big hands.

Liking him she opened the door and looked out. It was raining harder. A man in a rubber cape was crossing the empty square to the cafe. The cat would be around to the right. Perhaps she could go along under the eaves. As she stood in the doorway an umbrella opened behind her. It was the maid who looked after their room.

"You must not get wet," she smiled, speaking Italian. Of course, the hotel-keeper had sent her.

With the maid holding the umbrella over her, she walked along the gravel path until she was under their windows. The table was there, washed bright green in the rain, but the cat was gone. She was suddenly disappointed. The maid looked up at her.

"Ha perduto qualque cosa, Signora?"[3]

"There was a cat," said the American girl.

"A cat?"

"Si, il gatto."[4]

"A cat?" the maid laughed. "A cat in the rain?"

"Yes," she said, "under the table." Then, "Oh, I wanted it so much. I wanted a kitty."

When she talked English the maid's face tightened.

"Come, Signora," she said. "We must get back inside. You will be wet."

"I suppose so," said the American girl.

They went back along the gravel path and passed in the door. The maid stayed outside to close the umbrella. As the American girl passed the office, the padrone[5] bowed from his desk. Something felt very small and tight inside the girl. The padrone made her feel very small and at the same time really important. She had a momentary feeling of being of supreme importance. She went on up the stairs. She opened the door of the room. George was on the bed, reading.

"Did you get the cat?" he asked, putting the book down.

"It was gone."

"Wonder where it went to," he said, resting his eyes from reading.

She sat down on the bed.

"I wanted it so much," she said. "I don't know why I wanted it so much. I wanted that poor kitty. It isn't any fun to be a poor kitty out in the rain."

George was reading again.

She went over and sat in front of the mirror of the dressing table looking at herself with the hand glass. She studied her profile, first one side and then the other. Then she studied the back of her head and neck.

"Don't you think it would be a good idea if I let my hair grow out?" she asked, looking at her profile again.

George looked up and saw the back of her neck, clipped close like a boy's.

"I like it the way it is."

"I get tired of it," she said. "I get so tired of looking like a boy."

George shifted his position in the bed. He hadn't looked away from her since she started to speak.

"You look pretty darn nice," he said.

She laid the mirror down on the dresser and went over to the window and looked out. It was getting dark.

"I want to pull my hair back tight and smooth and make a big knot at the back that I can feel," she said. "I want to have a kitty to sit on my lap and purr when I stroke her."

"Yeah?" George said from the bed.

"And I want to eat at a table with my own silver and I want candles. And I want it to be spring and I want to brush my hair out in front of a mirror and I want a kitty and I want some new clothes."

"Oh, shut up and get something to read," George said. He was reading again.

His wife was looking out of the window. It was quite dark now and still raining in the palm trees.

"Anyway, I want a cat," she said, "I want a cat. I want a cat now. If I can't have long hair or any fun, I can have a cat."

George was not listening. He was reading his book. His wife looked out of the window where the light had come on in the square. Someone knocked at the door.

"Avanti,"[6] George said. He looked up from his book.

In the doorway stood the maid. She held a big tortoise-shell cat pressed tight against her and swung down against her body.

"Excuse me," she said, "the padrone asked me to bring this for the Signora."

Notes

1. Il piove: It's raining.
2. Si ... brutto tempo: Yes madam, the weather is very bad.
3. Ha perduto ... Signora: Have you lost something, madame?
4. Si, il gatto: Yes, a cat.
5. padrone: inn keeper.
6. Avanti: come in.

Considerations

1. What is the connection between the wife's complaints and her desire for a cat?
2. What is the function of rain in the story? How does it contribute to the story's tone?
3. What is the significance of the fact that George and his wife are the only Americans in the hotel?

14. *Writers of Contemporary Explorations*

Katherine Anne Porter (1890-1980) was an American essayist, a short story writer, and a journalist, whose only novel was *The Ship of Fools* (1962), a disillusioned story set in a little purgatory on the sea. Porter spent twenty years with the book before it was finished. It made her rich and famous. However, Porter is also remembered as one of America's best short-story writers. Porter's literary production can be divided into three stages: her early writings done in Mexico, the rediscovery of her southern identity, and the last period of cynicism. Porter's first collection of short stories was *Flowering Judas*. The limited edition of 600 copies appeared in 1930. The collection was enlarged in 1935. Porter's *Pale Horse*, *Pale Rider* (1939) received widespread critical acclaim. It consisted of three short novels: 'Old Mortality', 'Noon Wine', a study of evil, set on a Texas farm circa 1900, and the titlepiece, which tells of a short-lived love affair between a soldier and a young Southern newspaperwoman during the influenza epidemic of World War I. The central character in the stories is Miranda, whose background is roughly parallel to Porter's — she runs away from a convent, and in the last story she is working as a reporter on a western newspaper. In *The Leaning Tower* (1944) there are six related stories dealing with Miranda and the background of her family. Her *Collected Stories* (1965) was awarded in 1966 the Pulitzer Prize and the National Book Award.

The Ship of Fools, a bitterly ironic novel, appeared when Porter was 72. The book was made into an Oscar winning film in 1966. It is set in 1931 aboard a German passenger ship, returning to Germany from Mexico. Mixed bag of passengers, Germans, Americans, Spaniards, Gypsies, and Mexicans represent a microcosmos of peoples, whose life are characterized by jealousy, cruelty, hatred, love and duplicity. In the first part the reader becomes acquainted with the various characters. The second part contains the torment of the passengers in steerage, their attempts to love and their struggle for detachment. In part three a bacchanalian fiesta brings out all the hidden fears and guilts. Porter explores the origin of human evil through the allegorical use of characters, who represent various national and moral types.

Doris Lessing(1919-) is one of the most celebrated and distinguished writers of the present time. Her most recent books include *The Sweetest Dream*, *The Grandmothers*, and the two volumes of her autobiography, *Under My Skin* and *Walking in the Shade*. She has recently been awarded the David Cohen Memorial Prize for British Literature, Spain's Prince of Asturias Prize, and the S. T. Dupont Golden PEN Award for a Lifetime's Distinguished Service to Literature, as well as a whole host of other prestigious international awards. She lives in north London.

Doris Lessing grew up in South Africa, the daughter of British citizens. She left school and home at an early age, finally moving to England in 1949. There she began her career as a novelist, publishing *The Grass is Singing* in 1950. During the 1950s she worked on what was to become 5 novels in the Children of Violence series, and in 1962 she gained international notice for her novel *The Golden Notebook*. Often cited as a heroic figure to feminists, Lessing has continued to write novels, graphic novels, librettos and essays, including works influenced by science fiction and Sufi mysticism.

Toni Morrison (1931-) is widely considered to be one of the leading black novelists. She is the recipient of numerous awards and in 1993 she was awarded the Nobel Prize for literature (the first African American to have the honor).

Morrison has written several novels. Although each is distinctive in terms of theme, setting, historical situation and prose style, taken together they form an incisive interrogation of American history and of the relation of African Americans to historical circumstance. Often her focus is particularly on female experience, and she frequently explores the tensions involved in the conflict between "African" and "American." Morrison has also focused on inescapable tensions within primarily black communities, as in *Jazz* (1992) and *Paradise* (1998). She is also a creative and sophisticated user of existing narratives as in her masterpiece *Beloved* (1987), which utilizes the slave narrative.

Morrison's prose style is complex, intricate and sometimes dense, having affinities with that of Faulkner, though she also

西方文学

makes occasional use of Magic Realism. In 1991 she published *Playing in the Dark: Whiteness and the Literary Imagination*, an important work of criticism in which she eloquently argues for the presence of a potentially destabilizing blackness in white American literature.

Beloved was awarded the 1988 Pulitzer Prize. Set in Ohio during Reconstruction the novel concerns the rehabilitation of Sethe, who as a runaway slave attempts to murder her four children rather than allow them to go into slavery. She succeeds in killing her unnamed elder daughter, referred to as "Beloved", whose ghost 18 years later arrives at Sethe's home, where she lives with her other daughter Denver. Having been ostracized by her community because of the killing, Sethe gradually dedicates herself to Beloved as reparation for the killing, and this further isolates her until Denver initiates contact with the community. In a symbolic repetition of the scene of the original killing, Beloved is expelled and the restoration of Sethe begins. The novel includes references back to slavery at Sweet Home in Kentucky and the experiences of other slaves on the farm, especially Sethe's lover Paul D. and her preacher mother-in-law Baby Suggs. Thematically, the novel's major concern is with finding a livable negotiation between the need to forget or suppress a wounding past in order to function in the present, and the necessity of remembering a past without being paralyzed by it. Although Morrison makes use of the slave narrative and also refers to an actual case of slave infanticide, *Beloved's* narrative is fragmented and nonlinear, reflecting the problems that the characters must confront in creating order and coherence in their lives.

Alice Walker (1944-) is a novelist and poet, born in Eatonton, Georgia, the eighth child of a family of sharecroppers, educated at Spelman College and Sarah Lawrence College. Alice Walker soon became committed to the civil rights movement. She worked for voter registration in Georgia, welfare rights and Head Start in Mississippi, and the Welfare Department in New York City. She taught for a time in Mississippi, first at Jackson State University (1968-1969) and then at Tougaloo College (1969-1970).

Her first publications were two collections of poetry: *Once: Poems* (1968), which reflects her experience of the civil rights movement and her travel in Africa; *Revolutionary Petunias and Other Poems* (1973), which is a tribute to those who struggle against racism and oppression. Her first novel, *The Third Life of Grange Copeland* (1970), is the story of three generations of black tenant farmers from 1900 to the 1960s. A book of short stories, *In Love and Trouble: Stories of Black Women* (1973), explores the experience and heritage of black women, a theme to which Walker returns in a second collection, *You Can't Keep a Good Woman Down* (1981). The epistolary novel, *The Color Purple* (1982), which won a Pulitzer Prize, centers on the life of Celie, a black woman who has been raped by the man she believed to be her father. She bears his children, and then is forced to marry an older man whom she despises. The novel is made up of Celie's despairing letters to God and to her sister Nettie who has gone to Africa as a missionary, and of Nettie's letters to Celie. Walker's other publications include a biography for children, *Langston Hughes, American Poet* (1974); *Meridian* (1977), a novel about the lives of civil rights workers in the South during the 1960s; and two collections of poems, *Good Night, Willie Lee, I'll See You in the Morning* (1979) and *Horses Make a Landscape Look More Beautiful: Poems* (1984). A volume of essays appeared in 1983 entitled *In Search of My Mothers Garden: Womanist Prose*.

In her early novels and short stories particularly, Walker demonstrates a sophisticated management of narrative technique, especially in the fragmented narrative of *Meridian* and the epistolary style of *The Color Purple*. Thematically her work is united by the project of raising the visibility of black women.

Jane Smiley (1951-) turned fifty just in time for the new millennium. She lives in California with her three children, three dogs, and her sixteen horses. Born in Los Angeles, California, Jane moved to the suburbs of St. Louis, Missouri, as an infant, and lived there through grammar school and high school (The John Burroughs School). After getting her BA at Vassar College in 1971, she traveled in Europe for a year, working on an archeological dig and sight-seeing, then returned to Iowa for graduate school at the University of Iowa. MFA and Ph. D. in hand, she went to work in 1981 at Iowa State University, in Ames, where she taught until 1996. She has been married three times. Jane is the author of ten works of fiction, including *The Age of Grief*, *The Greenlanders*, *Ordinary Love and Good Will*, *A Thousand Acres*, which won the Pulitzer Prize in 1992 and *Moo*, as well as many essays for magazines. She has written on politics, farming, horse training, child-rearing, literature, impulse buying, getting dressed, marriage, and many other topics. Her new novel *Horse*

Heaven was being published in April 2000, and *Good Faith* in April 2003.

Smiley's novel, *A Thousand Acres* (*King Lear*), portrays the enduring violence of incest to body and spirit. The narrative voice describes the family — a wealthy farmer and his three daughters. Family relationships are explored, especially the hidden roots that shape and define behaviors and conflicts, some lasting a lifetime. The disclosure of a horribly dark secret explains the personalities of the three daughters and, for two, their metaphoric afflictions (infertility and breast cancer). The novel is layered with rich complexities, but none more powerful and astonishing than the core event, the sexual victimization of two vulnerable teenage girls who, as the story unfolds, are permanently scarred. Through a reinterpretation of Lear, Smiley demonstrates the cost of this hideous form of male domination and female victimization.

John Maxwell Coetzee (1940-), the 2003 Nobel Laureate in Literature, was born in Cape Town, South Africa. Coetzee entered the University of Cape Town in 1957, and in 1960 and 1961 graduated successively with honours degrees in English and mathematics. He spent the years 1962-1965 in England, working as a computer programmer while doing research for a thesis on the English novelist Ford Madox Ford. In 1965 Coetzee entered the graduate school of the University of Texas at Austin, and in 1968 graduated with a PhD in English, linguistics, and Germanic languages. His doctoral dissertation was on the early fiction of Samuel Beckett.

Coetzee began writing fiction in 1969. His first book, *Dusk-*

lands, was published in South Africa in 1974. *In the Heart of the Country* (1977) won South Africa's then principal literary award, the CNA Prize, and was published in Britain and the USA. *Waiting for the Barbarians* (1980) received international notice. His reputation was confirmed by *Life & Times of Michael K* (1983), which won Britain's Booker Prize. It was followed by *Foe* (1986), *Age of Iron* (1990), The *Master of Petersburg* (1994), and *Disgrace* (1999), which again won the Booker Prize. Coetzee also wrote two fictionalized memoirs, *Boyhood* (1997) and *Youth* (2002). In 2002 Coetzee emigrated to Australia. He lives with his partner Dorothy Driver in Adelaide, South Australia, where he holds an honorary position at the University of Adelaide.

Seamus (Justin) Heaney (1939-) is an Irish poet who was awarded the Nobel Prize for Literature in 1995. According to Heaney, poetry balances the "scales of reality towards some transcendent equilibrium." From the early collections, Heaney has combined in his work personal memories with images of Irish heritage and the landscape of Northern Ireland. There are also references to English-Irish and Catholic-Protestant conflict.

Heaney's first book, *Eleven Poems*, appeared in 1965. At the age of 27 he won in 1966 the Eric Gregory Award with *Death of a Naturalist*. With these works Heaney established his reputation as a poet. After *North* (1975), in which Heaney addressed the ongoing civil strife in Northern Ireland, he was considered the finest Irish poet since W. B. Yeats, and with Ted Hughes among the leading poets in the English-speaking world. Among its much anthologized poems is 'Punishment', in which the poet de-

西方文学

345

picts a tribal revenge of adultery, but confesses his own powerlessness in front of ancient, violent forces. "I almost love you / but would have cast, I know, / the stones of silence. I am the artful voyeur / your brain's exposed and darkened combs ... " Heaney's works are rooted in Northern Irish rural life, and draw on myth and unique aspects of the Irish experience. Reflections on his childhood have given way to darker commentaries on the social and political problems in Northern Ireland. In *The Government of the Tongue* (1988) Heaney questioned the role of poetry in modern society. The central symbol in his work is the bog, the wide unfenced county, that reaches back millions of years. The bog is the starting point for the exploration of the past, and in several works Heaney has returned to the "bog people", bodies preserved in the soil of Denmark and Ireland.

Strong individualistic, meditative mood, marks Heaney's later works, including *Station Island* (1984), *The Haw Lantern* (1987), and *Seeing Things* (1991). *The Haw Lantern* contains poems in memory of Heaney's mother, who died in 1984. In *Electric Light* (2001) Heaney's childhood memories mix with his sense of fleeting time and death. Heaney's poems have often been allegorical. He has drawn on the *Divine Comedy* of Dante and on the work of such contemporary central European writers as Czeslaw Milosz. In his Nobel lecture in 1995 Heaney defended poetry "as the ship and the anchor" of our spirit within an ocean of violent, divisive world politics.

Harold Pinter (1930-) is an English playwright who achieved international success as one of the most complex post-World War II dramatists. His plays are noted for their use of silence to increase tension, understatement, and cryptic small talk. Equally recognizable are the 'Pinteresque' themes — nameless menace, erotic fantasy, obsession and jealousy, family hatred and mental disturbance. In 2005, Pinter was awarded the Nobel Prize for literature.

Pinter's plays can be associated with the Theatre of the Absurd, and clearly owe a debt to Beckett. Pinter's first play *The Room*, was performed in 1957, followed by *The Birthday Party* (1958), in which Stanley, an out-of-work pianist in a seaside boarding house, is mysteriously threatened and taken over by two intruders, an Irishman and a Jew, who present him with a Kafkaesque indictment of unexplained crimes, *The Caretaker* in 1960, and *The Homecoming* in 1965. Other plays have followed, but it is these early plays that are generally recognized as Pinter's special contribution to modern drama, in which menace and violence constantly threaten the characters' lives.

Pinter's major plays originate often from a single, powerful visual image. They are usually set in a single room, whose occupants are threatened by forces or people whose precise intentions neither the characters nor the audience can define. The struggle for survival or identity dominates the action of his characters. Language is not only used as a means of communication but as a weapon. Beneath the words, there is a silence of fear, rage and domination, fear of intimacy.

The Homecoming (1965) is perhaps the most enigmatic of all Pinter's early works. In the story an estranged son, Teddy, brings his wife Ruth home to London to meet his family, his father Max, a nagging, aggressive ex-butcher, and other tough members of the all-male household. At the end Teddy returns a-lone to his university job in America. Ruth stays as a mother or whore to his family. Everyone needs her. Similar motifs — the battle for domination in a sexual context — recur in *Landscape* and *Silence* (both 1969), and in *Old Times* (1971), in which the key line is "Normal, what's normal?" After *Betrayal* (1978) Pinter wrote no new full-length plays until *Moonlight* (1994). In the 1990s Pinter became more active as a director than as a play-wright, and has been becoming more active in human rights is-sue. In February 2005 Pinter announced in an interview that he has decided to abandon his career as a playwright and put all his energy into politics. "I've written 29 plays. Isn't that enough?"

Wole Soyinka (1934-) , the 1986 Nobel Prize winner, was born on 13 July 1934 at Abeokuta, near Ibadan in western Niger-ia. After preparatory university studies in 1954 at Government College in Ibadan, he continued at the University of Leeds, where, later, in 1973, he took his doctorate. During the six years spent in England, he was a dramaturgist at the Royal Court Theatre in London 1958-1959. In 1960, he was awarded a Rocke-feller bursary and returned to Nigeria to study African drama. At the same time, he taught drama and literature at various univer-sities in Ibadan, Lagos, and Ife, where, since 1975, he has been professor of comparative literature. In 1960, he founded the the-atre group, "The 1960 Masks" and in 1964, the "Orisun Theatre Company", in which he has produced his own plays and taken part as actor. He has periodically been visiting professor at the u-niversities of Cambridge, Sheffield, and Yale.

Soyinka has published about 20 works: drama, novels and

poetry. He writes in English and his literary language is marked by great scope and richness of words. As dramatist, Soyinka has been influenced by, among others, the Irish writer, J. M. Synge, but links up with the traditional popular African theatre with its combination of dance, music, and action. He bases his writing on the mythology of his own tribe — the Yoruba — with Ogun, the god of iron and war, at the centre. He wrote his first plays during his time in London, *The Swamp Dwellers* and *The Lion and the Jewel* (a light comedy), which were performed at Ibadan in 1958 and 1959 and were published in 1963. Later, satirical comedies are *The Trial of Brother Jero* (1963) with its sequel, *Jero's Metamorphosis* (1973), *A Dance of the Forests* (1963), *Kongi's Harvest* (1967) and *Madmen and Specialists* (1971) Soyinka's latest dramatic works are *A Play of Giants* (1984) and *Requiem for a Futurologist* (1985). Soyinka has written two novels, *The Interpreters* (1965), a complicated work which has been compared to Joyce's and Faulkner's, in which six Nigerian intellectuals discuss and interpret their African experiences, and *Season of Anomy* (1973) which is based on the writer's thoughts during his imprisonment in the civil war in Nigeria and confronts the Orpheus and Euridice myth with the mythology of the Yoruba.

15. Modern Criticism

With the flowering of the modern literary works came the flourish of modern literary criticism. In fact, the 20th century has been called an age of criticism. Its major types, as far as pure criticism is concerned, include New Humanism, Marxism, New

Criticism, Structuralism, Feminism, Post-structuralism, Reader-Response criticism, Dialogism, Psychological criticism, New Historitism, Queer theory, and Post-colonialism.

New Humanism refers to the American movement of 1910-1933, which, under the leadership of Irving Babbitt (1865-1933) and Paul Elmer More (1864-1937), formulated a critical position resting on the traditional moral and critical standards of the humanists. The movement collapsed under the impact of the Depression and the rise of Marxist criticism. Its social conservatism and its enmity toward recent literary trends ensured its demise, and today one has the impression that it is being forgotten.

Marxist Criticism is supposed to have dominated the years of the Great Depression. Marxism usually did not mean an actual grasp of Marxist doctrine but merely a generalized anticapitalism, sympathy for the working class, acceptance of the class struggle and hope for a radical social revolution and for a new proletarian art. The major English and American Marxist critics were Christopher Caudwell and Granville Hicks, who urged the reading of literature in the light of radical social views. The Marxist movement collapsed with Pearl Harbor and the war. But Marxist motifs in literary criticism remained prominent in such critics as Edmund Wilson, Kenneth Burke, Lionel Trilling and F. O. Matthiessen.

New Criticism, also referred to as Formalism, is a term derived from Ranson's book *The New Criticism*, published in 1941. In a strict sense the term is applied to the criticism written by John Crowe Ranson, Allen Tate, R. P. Blackmur, Robert Penn Warren, and Cleanth Brooks. Generally the term is applied to the whole body of criticism that protests literary critics' prevailing concern with the lives and psychology of authors and with literary history, concentrates on the work of art as an object in itself, examines it through a process of close analysis, and discovers its intrinsic worth. The New Critics constitute the school in contemporary criticism that most completely employs the objective theory of art.

Structuralism, primarily a European and particularly a French movement reaching its first flowering in the 1960s, represented at one time a growing interest among American critics. As a revolt against literary history and biographical criticism, it is a return to the text, but unlike the New Criticism it seeks to see the text in terms of the methods of modern structural linguistics. Following Ferdinand de Saussure's linguistic theory, structuralists such as Roman Jackobson and Roland Barthes insisted on the decisive importance of structural relations and attempted to develop a "semiotics" (science of signs). There are two basic types of structuralism. One concentrates its study on the patterns formed by linguistic elements in the work and examines these patterns to find which ones unify the text and throw certain elements in relief. The other sees literary conventions and forms as constituting a system of codes that contribute to and convey meaning. The special interest here is on the organization and function of distinctively literary elements, on how a literary device or even genre functions rather than how it imitates an external reality or expresses an internal feeling, and on how meaning is conveyed rather than what meaning is conveyed.

Feminist Criticism is an aspect of the feminist movement which has a long history with its practice in the works of the 18th-century women writers and it flourished in the 1960s and 1970s, when appeared a large number of feminist works such as Elaine Showalter's *A Literature of Their Own* (1977) and Santa M. Gilbert and Susan Gubar's *The Madwoman in the Attic* (1979). The purpose of the movement is the recognition of the claims of women for rights equal to those possessed by men. In literary criticism, its aims are remembering forgotten women writers, explaining why their achievement has not seemed great to established criticism, and evaluating the better known women writers in the light of their position as women.

Post-Structuralism is the kind of literary criticism which attempts to contest and subvert structuralism. Whereas structuralists, using linguistics as a model and employing semiotic theory, posit the possibility of systematically knowing a text and revealing the "grammar" behind its form and meaning, post-structuralists argue against the possibility of such knowledge and description. They have suggested that structuralism rests on distinctions between "signifier" and "signified", texts and other texts, and text and world are overly simplistic. Influenced by the writings of the philosopher Jacques Derrida, post-structuralists have shown how all signifieds are also signifiers, and they have treated texts as "intertexts", in which meaning is undecidable.

Psychological Criticism The assumption of psychological criticism is that literature is the expression of the author's psyche, often his or her unconscious, and, like dreams, needs to be interpreted. Psychological Criticism can be subdivided into Freudian criticism, Lacanian criticism and Jungian criticism.

Freudian Criticism The dominant school is the Freudian, based on the work of Sigmund Freud (1856-1939). Many of its practitioners assert that the meaning of a literary work does not tie on its surface but in the psyche (some would even claim, in the neuroses) of the author. The value of the work, then, lies in how powerfully and convincingly it expresses the author's unconscious and how universal the psychological elements are. A well-known Freudian reading of *Hamlet*, for example, insists that Hamlet is upset because he is jealous of his uncle, for he, like all male children, unconsciously wants to go to bed with his mother. The ghost may then be a manifestation of Hamlet's unconscious desire; his madness is not just acting but is the result of this frustrated desire; his cruelly gross mistreatment of Ophelia is a deflection of his disgust at his mother's being "lecherous, unfaithful" in her love for him. A Freudian critic may assume then that Hamlet is suffering from an Oedipus complex, a Freudian term for the desire of the son for his mother, its name derived from the Greek myth that is the basis of Sophocles' play *Oedipus the King*.

Some Freudian critics stress the author's psyche and find *Hamlet* the expression of Shakespeare's own Oedipus complex. Others stress the effect on the reader, the work having a purgative or cleaning effect by expressing in socially and morally acceptable ways unconscious desires that would be unacceptable if expressed directly.

Lacanian Criticism As it absorbs the indeterminacies of post-structuralism under the influence of thinkers such as Jacques Lacan, psychological criticism has become increasingly complex.

Accepting the Oedipal paradigm and the unconscious as the realm of repressed desire, Lacanian psychology (and the critical theory that comes from that psychology) conflates these concepts with the deconstructionist emphasis on language as expressing absence — you use a word to represent an absent object but you cannot make it present. The word, then, like the unconscious desire, is something that cannot be fulfilled. Language, reaching out with one word after the other, striving for but never reaching its object, is the arena of desire.

Jungian Criticism Just as a Freudian assumes that human psyches have similar histories and structures, the Jungian critic assumes that we all share a universal or collective unconscious (as well as having a racial and individual unconscious). According to Carl Gustav Jung (1875-1961) and his followers, in the collective and in our individual unconscious are universal images, patterns, and forms of human experiences or archetypes. These archetypes can never be known directly, but they surface in art in an imperfect, shadowy way, taking the form of archetypal images — the snake with its tail in its mouth, rebirth, mother, the double, the descent into Hell. To get a sense of the archetype beneath the archetypal images or shadows in the characters, plot, language, and images of a work, to bring these together in an archetypal interpretation, is the function of the Jungian critic. He is guided by his belief that there is a central myth common to all literature. Just as, for the Freudian literary critic, the "family romance," out of which the Oedipus story comes, is central, so the Jungian assumes there is a monomyth that underlies the archetypal images and gives a clue as to how they can be related to suggest the archetypes themselves. The myth is that of the quest. In that all-encompassing myth the hero struggles to free himself (the gender of the pronoun is specific and significant) from the Great Mother, to become a separate, self-sufficient being who is then rewarded by union with his ideal mother, the feminine *anima*.

Reader-Response Criticism The formalists focus on the text. Though the psychological critics focus most frequently on the author, their assumptions about the similarity or universality of the human mind make them consider as well the role of the reader. There is another approach that, though not psychological in the usual sense of the word, also focuses on the reception of the text, on reader response. The conventional notion of reading is that a writer or speaker has an "idea", encodes it — that is, turns it into words and the reader or listener decodes it, deriving when successful, the writer / speaker's "idea." What the reader-response critic assumes, however, is that such equivalency between sender and receiver is the text. The text becomes a work only when it is read, just as a score becomes music only when it is played. And just as every musical performance, even of exactly the same notes, is somewhat different, a different interpretatton, so no two readers read or perform exactly the same work from identical texts. Besides the individual differences of readers, space is made for different readings or interpretations by gaps in a text itself. Some of these are temporary — such as the withholding of the name of the murderer until the end — and are closed by the text sooner or later, though each reader will in the meantime fill them differently. But others are permanent, and can never be filled with certainty; the result is a degree of uncertainty or indeterminacy in the text.

The reader-response critic's focus on the reading process is especially useful in the study of long works such as novels. The critic follows the text sequentially, observing what expectations are being aroused, how they are being satisfied or modified, how the reader recapitulates "evidence" from the portion of the text he has read to project forward a configuration, a tentative assumption of what the work as a whole will be and mean once it is done. The expectations are in part built by the text and in part by the repertoire of the reader, i. e. , the reader's reading experience plus his or her social and cultural knowledge.

Dialogism is another critical approach that gives a significant role to the reader and is particularly useful for long fiction, largely identified with the work of Mikhail Bakhtin (1895-1975). The dialogic critic bases the study of language and literature on the individual utterance, taking into account the specific time, the place, the speaker and the listener or reader. Such critics thus see language as a continuous dialogue, each utterance being a reply to what has gone before. Even thought, which they define as inner speech, is a dialogue between utterances that you have taken in. Even your own language (and thus thought) is itself dialogic, for it is made up of the dialogue in which you are engaged, that which you have heard from parents and peers, teachers and television, all kinds of social and professional discourse and reading. Indeed, you speak many "languages" — those of your ethnic, social, economic, national, professional, gender, and other identities. Your individual language consists in the combination of those languages. The literary form in which the dialogic is most interesting, complex, and significant is the novel, for there you have the languages not only of the characters (as you do in drama), but also that of a mediator or narrator and passages of description of analysis or information that seem to come from other voices — newspapers, whaling manuals, legal cases, and so on. Because the world is growing more interrelated and we have multiple voices rather than one dominant voice or language, the novel has become the most appropriate form for the representation of that world.

Because the dialogic sees utterances, including literary utterances or works, as specific to a time and place, one of its dimensions, unlike formalist, struchuralist, or psychological criticism, is *historical*. 19th-century historical criticism took the obvious fact that a work is created in a specific historical and cultural context and that the author is a part of that context in order to treat literature as a product of the culture. Formalists and others emphasizing the aesthetic value of literature saw this as reducing the literary work to the status of a mere historical document and the abandonment of literary study to history. The dialogic critic sees the work in relation to its host context, a part of the dialogue of the culture. The work in turn helps to create the context for other utterances, literary and otherwise. Some consider dialogic criticism a form of sociological criticism.

New Historicism has less obvious ideological commitments than Marxism or feminism, but it shares their interest in the investigation of how power is distributed and used in different cultures. Drawing on the insights of modern anthropology (and especially on the work of Clifford Geertz), new historicism wishes to isolate the fundamental values in texts and cultures, and it regards text both as evidence of basic cultural patterns and as forces in cultural and social change. Many of the most influential practitioners of the new historicism come out of the ranks of Marxism and feminism, and new historicists are usually knowledgeable about most varieties of literary theory. Like Marxists and feminists, they are anxious to uncover the ideological commitments in texts, and they care deeply about historical and cultural difference and the way texts represent it. But personal commitments and specific political agendas usually are less important — at least explicitly — to new historicists, and one of the main contentions between feminists and new historicists or between Marxists and new historicists — involves disagreement about the role that one's own politics should play in the practice of criticism. Many observers regard new historicism as politically to the left in its analysis of traditional cultural values, but critics on the left are suspicious of new historicism, especially of its reluctance to state its premises openly, and they generally regard its assumptions as conservative. Whatever its fundamental political commitments, however (or whether its commitments can be fairly described as having a consistent and specifiable bias), new historicism is far more interested than any other literary approach in social groups generally ignored by literary historians, and it refuses to privilege "literature" over other printed, oral, or material texts. "Popular literature" often gets major attention in the work of new historicists, who see all texts in a culture as somehow expressive of its values and directions and thus as equally useful in determining the larger intellectual, epistemological, and ethical system of which any text is a part. Texts here are thus seen as less specifically individual and distinctive than in most objective criticisms, and although new historicists are sometimes interested in the psychology of authors or readers their main concern is with the prevailing tendencies shared across a culture and thus shared across all kinds of texts, whatever their class status, literary value, or political aim.

Pluralism can be considered as a mixture of various criticism. The classifications of criticism are not pigeonholes, and you will notice that many of the approaches overlap: many feminists, especially French feminist critics, are Lacanian or post-structuralist as well, while British feminists often lean toward sociological, especially Marxist criticism; dialogic critics accept many of the starting points and methods of reader-response and sociological critics, and so on. These crossovers or combinations are generally enriching; they cause problems only when the critic seems to be operating out of contradictory assumptions.

There is a lively debate among critics and theorists at present involving the question of whether readers should bring together the insights and methods of different schools (practitioners of the mixing of methods are usually called pluralists) or whether they should commit themselves wholeheartedly to a single system. Pluralists contend that they make use of promising insights or methods wherever they find them and argue that putting together the values of different approaches leads to a more fair and balanced view of texts and their uses. Opponents — those who insist on a consistency of ideological commitment — argue that pluralism are simply unwilling to state or admit their real commitments, and that any mixing of methods leads to confusion, uncertainty, and inconsistency rather than fairness. Readers, conscious or not of their assumptions and their methods, make this basic choice — to follow one lead or many — and the kind of reading they do and the conclusions they come to depend not only on this basic choice but many others suggested by the dominant strands of recent criticism that have been described here. Not all critics are aware of their assumptions, methodologies, or values, and some would even deny that they begin with any particular assumptions or biases, but is often useful, especially to readers newly learning to practice literary criticism, to sort out their own beliefs carefully and see exactly what kind of difference it makes in the way they read literature and ask questions of it.

Queer theory is often used to designate the combined area of gay and lesbian studies and criticism, as well as theoretical and critical writings concerning all modes of variance (such as cross-dressing) from the normative model of biological sex, gender identity, and sexual desires. The term "queer" was originally derogatory, used to stigmatize male and female same-sex love as deviant and unnatural; since the early 1990s, however, it has been increasingly adopted by gays and lesbians themselves as a non-invidious term to identify a way of life and an area for scholarly inquiry.

Both lesbian studies and gay studies began as "liberation movement" — in parallel with the movements for African-American and feminist liberation — during the anti-Vietnam War, anti-establishment, and counter-cultural ferment of the late 1960s and

1970s. Since that time these studies have maintained a relation to the political activities to achieve, for gays and lesbians, political, legal, and economic rights equal to those of the heterosexual majority. Through the 1970s, the two movements were primarily separatist: gays often thought of themselves as quintessentially male, while many lesbians, aligning themselves with the feminist movement, characterized the gay movements as sharing the anti-female attitudes of the reigning patriarchal culture. Recently, however, there has been a growing recognition (signalized by the adoption of the joint term "queer") of the degree to which the two groups share a history as a despised and suppressed minority and posses common political and social goals.

In the 1970s, researchers for the most part assumed that there was a fixed, unitary identity as a gay man or as a lesbian that has remained stable through human history. A major endeavor was to identify and reclaim the works of non-heterosexual writers from Plato to Walt Whitman, Proust, Gide, Auden, James Baldwin, Virginia Woolf, Adrienne Rich, and Andre Lorde. The list included writers (Shakespeare and Christina Rossetti are examples) who represented homoerotic subject matter, but whose own sexuality the available biographical evidence leaves uncertain. In the 1980 and 1990s, however — in large part because of the assimilation of the viewpoints and analytic methods of Derrida, Foucault, and other poststructualists — the earlier assumptions about a unitary and stable gay or lesbian identity were frequently put to question, and historical and critical analyses became increasingly subtle and complex.

Postcolonial criticism emerged as a distinct category only in the 1990. It has gained currency through the influence of such books as: *In Other Worlds* (Gayatri Spivak, 1987); *The Empire Writes Back* (Bill Ashcroft, 1989); *Nation and Narration* (Homi Bhabha, 1990) and *Culture and Imperialism* (Edward Said, 1993).

One significant effect of postcolonial criticism is to further undermine the universalist claims once made on behalf of literature by liberal humanist critics. If we claim that great literature has a timeless and universal significance we thereby denote or disregard cultural, social, regional, and national differences in experience and outlook, preferring instead to judge all literature by a single, supposedly "universal", standard. Thus, for example, a routine claim about the "Wessex" setting of Hardy's novels is that it is really a canvas on which Hardy depicts and examines fundamental, universal aspects of the human condition. Thus, Hardy's books are not thought of as primarily regional or historical, or masculine or white or working-class novels — they are just novels, and built into this attitude is the assumption that this way of writing and presenting reality is the unquestioned norm, so that the situations depicted can stand for all possible forms of human interaction. This universalism is rejected by postcolonial criticism; whenever a universal signification is claimed for a work, then, white, Eurocentric norms and practices are being promoted by a sleight of hand to this elevated status, and all others correspondingly relegated to subsidiary, marginalized roles.

The ancestry of postcolonial criticism can be traced to Frantz Fanon's *The Wretched of the Earth*, published in French in 1961, and voicing what might be called "cultural resistance" to

France's African empire. Fanon (a psychiatrist) from Martinique argued that the first step for colonialized people in finding a voice and identity is to reclaim their own past. For centuries the European colonizing power will have devalued the nation's past, seeing its pre-colonial era as a pre-civilised limbo, or even as a historical void. Children, both black and white, will have been taught to see history, culture and progress as beginning with the arrival of the Europeans. If the first step towards a postcolonial perspective is to reclaim one's own past, then the second is to begin to erode the colonialist ideology by which that past had been devalued.

Hence, another major work, which can be said to inaugurate postcolonial criticism proper is Edward Said's *Orientalism* (1978), which is a specific exposition of the Eurocentric universalism which takes for granted both the superiority of what is European or Western, and the inferiority of what is not. Said identifies a European cultural tradition of "Orientalism", which is a particular and long-standing way of identifying the East as "Other" and inferior to the West. The Orient, he says, features in the Western mind "as a sort of surrogate and even underground self" (*Literature in the Modern World*, ed. Dennis Walder, p. 236). This means, in effect, that the east becomes the repository or projection of those aspects of themselves which Westerners do not choose to acknowledge (cruelty, sensuality, decadence, laziness, and so on). At the same time, and paradoxically, the East is seen as a fascinating realm of the exotic, the mystical and the seductive. It also tends to be seen as homogenous, the people there being anonymous masses, rather than individuals, their actions determined by instinctive emotions (lust, terror, fury, etc.) rather than by conscious choices or decisions. Their emotions and reactions are always determined by racial considerations (they are like this because they are Asiatics or blacks or orientals) rather than by aspects of individual status or circumstance (for example, because they happen to be a sister, or an uncle, or a collector of antique pottery).

Glossary

Accent: the emphasis or stress placed on a particular syllable in a poetic foot.

Allegory: a type of extended symbolism in which abstract ideas or concepts (truth, beauty, evil) are made concrete through personification.

Alliteration: a series of words that begin with the same letter or sound ("now or never").

Allusion: an indirect reference to a person, an object, or an action.

Alexandrine: *See* Hexameter.

Ambiguity: a multiple meaning in a poem or story. (When used accidentally as a result of faulty diction, it can be confusing; when used on purpose and skillfully, it enhances the work.)

Anachronism: a misplacing of persons, objects, or events in time.

Analogy: an extended comparison of two things that resemble each other but are not exactly alike.

Analysis: division of a literary work into its basic parts to show their relationships and functions.

Anapest: a metrical foot consisting of two unaccented syllables followed by an accented one.

Anecdote: a short, usually personal, narrative often used to illustrate a particular characteristic.

Annotation: a note supplied in the margin or at the end of a text.

Antagonist: the adversary of the protagonist (hero).

Anthropomorphism: attributing human traits to nonhuman things.

Anticlimax: a continuation of the plot after the story's climax. Its intent is to relieve or detract from the tension of the climax, or to present further complications of the plot.

Aphorism: a concise saying that illustrates or defines a general principle or statement.

Apocopated rhyme: rhyme in which the unaccented syllable of one of the rhyming words is ignored ("flight", "lightly").

Apologue: a brief, contrived allegory (such as a fable or parable) that illustrates a moral.

Apology: in literature, a justification of a particular action or belief.

Archetype: a basic pattern of human values, such as the stock plot archetypes of romantic love, the overthrow of a tyrant, and death and resurrection or rebirth.

Argumentation: one of the four basic types of discourse; the attempt to convince the reader of the truth or relevance of the author's position by presenting objective evidence and using logic.

Assonance: imperfect rhyme in which the stressed vowels correspond (e. g. :"cloud" and "shout").

Atmosphere: the pervasive mood or feeling of a literary work.

Autobiography: an account of a person's life, or parts thereof, written by himself. Basically, autobiographical literary categories are *letters*, *diaries*, *journals*, and *memoirs*.

Balance: (1) the equilibrium achieved through the proportionate arrangement of the basic elements in a literary work; (2) in rhetoric, the parallel structure of similar or opposing elements, used for contrast.

Ballad: a simple poem that tells a story and is usually meant to be sung.

Ballade: A verse form consisting of three stanzas, an envoy, and an identical refrain. (*See* Envoy.)

Ballad stanza: the stanza used in ballads, usually consisting of four lines rhyming *abcb* with the first and third lines in iambic tetrameter and the second and fourth lines in iambic trimeter.

Baroque: an elaborate, ornate style used especially by poets (the 17th-century English metaphysical poets in particular) who stress the bizarre. The baroque style is characterized by extravagant comparisons and unbalanced structure.

Bathos: the ludicrous or ridiculous description of emotions or feelings.

Beast fable: a fable in which real or imaginary animals assume human characteristics. (*See* Fable.)

Biography: an account of a person's life written by another person.

Blank verse: unrhymed iambic pentameter, the most popular of all verse lines for English poetry.

Broken rhyme: rhyme in which a word is broken off at the end of one line and continued in the next for the sake of the rhyme.

Burlesque: a mocking, satiric imitation of another work. (*See also* Parody.)

Cacophony: a combination of discordant sounds sometimes used deliberately for emphasis in poetry.

Caricature: a form of ridicule that exaggerates and distorts one's worst faults and physical features.

Catastrophe: resolution of the conflict of the plot by disaster.

Catharsis: the emotional release or spiritual exaltation resulting from reading or seeing a tragedy.

Characterization: the development of a character within a particular work.

Classicism: a form of literary criticism that emphasizes the classic qualities of form, reason, restraint, and is based on distinguished artistic models of the past.

Climax: the point in the plot of a story at which the conflict and interest are highest and the resolution of the conflict is determined or at least begun.

Coherence: in literary composition, the clear relationship of the various parts (sentences, paragraphs) that form an integrated, connected whole.

Collequy: a formal conversation or discourse between two or more characters.

Comic relief: a device by which tensions in a serious work are relaxed by a humorous or farcical episode or scene.

Compactness: density of prose or poetic style.

Complication: the intensification of conflict leading to more complex entanglements of plot.

Conceit: an elaborate extended simile or figurative comparison within a poem; used especially by the metaphysical poets.

Conflict: the element of the plot around which all other elements

西方文学

revolve.

Connotation: the nonliteral meanings a word conveys because of its suggested or implied meanings.

Consistency: the agreement of the parts to form a unified, believable whole.

Consonance: a rhyme scheme in which only consonant sounds correspond (e. g. :"food" and "fad").

Convention: a device that is universally accepted; especially any practice that is improbable (such as the soliloquy in drama) or unrealistic (such as flashbacks in literature or the theater) but is accepted as part of the art.

Couplet: two successive verse lines that are alike in meter and rhyme.

Criticism: a judgment or evaluation of a literary work. Some important aspects of critical approaches are: *Historical* — evaluating a work in the light of the milieu from which it arose; *Freudian* — emphasizing the unconscious intent of the author; the *New Criticism* — focusing entirely on the work itself, its merits and shortcomings, not upon the author's intentions or salient facts about him or his environment; *Impressionistic* — emphasizing the critic's own reactions to the work; *Textual* — analyzing the text itself and the extraneous facts pertinent to an understanding of it; *Theoretical* — emphasizing general principles of literature as they relate to a particular work; *Relativistic* — comparing how the work stands up to a given set of standards; *Comparative* — comparing one work with another that shares comparable qualities.

Critique: a critical evaluation of a work based on predetermined principles.

Dactyl: a metrical foot of three syllables, one accented syllable followed by two unaccented ones: heavenly.

Decasyllabic: a ten-syllable line, most common in iambic pentameter verse.

Deduction: in logic, the form of reasoning that moves from the general to the specific; in literature and exposition, the conclusion that follows from the premises presented.

Denotation: the literal or "dictionary" definition of a work.

Denouement: the point following the climax of a plot at which the complications begin to unravel and are resolved.

Description: one of the four basic kinds of discourse (argumentation, exposition, and narration are the others). Descriptive prose conveys feelings or creates images by presenting qualities, appearances, and facts about someone or something.

Dialect: a local or regional variation of a language.

Dialogue: conversation between the characters in a work of literature.

Diction: the particular way in which words are used in a literary work.

Didactic literature: literature that teaches or moralizes.

Discourse: any formal communication of ideas. (In rhetoric there are four basic classes of discourse: argumentation, description, exposition, and narration.)

Disyllable: any word of two syllables (e. g. : es-say).

Doggerel: inferior poetry in which the verse is poorly composed; sometimes intentionally used for satiric or humorous effects.

Double entendre: double meaning (French words).

西方文学

Drama: (1) a play intended for performance in a theater; (2) the genetic term applied to a body of plays, as Restoration drama.

Dramatic irony: allowing the audience to know something in order to create tension before a character becomes aware of it.

Dramatic monologue: a one-sided conversation of one person with another.

Ecologue: a pastoral poem involving (usually) shepherds' conversation that may conceal satire or allegory.

Elegiac stanza: a verse form named after Thomas Gray's "Elegy in a Country Churchyard" (1750). The rhyme scheme is *abab*, and the meter an iambic pentameter and concerning grief or a lament. Example: Auden's "In Memory of W. B. Yeats."

Elision: dropping a vowel preceding a consonant (isn't, can't); often used in poetry to maintain meter.

Elizabethan: referring to the reign of Queen Elizabeth I (1558-1603) [and often to the Jacobean period of James I (1603-1625)].

Emotive language: language selected for its express connotative value to arouse emotional response.

Empathy: the ability to identify oneself with another person or literary figure.

End-stopped: referring to a line of verse that is complete in itself in structure and sense. (*See* Couplet.)

Envoy: a short, summarizing stanza of a ballade.

Epic: a long narrative poem in which the characters and the action are of heroic proportions. Example: Homer's *Odyssey*.

Epigram: a short, pointed statement, often humorous or satiric.

Epilogue: the concluding statement of a prose work (except drama).

Epiphany: a term borrowed from religion by James Joyce to describe a moment of sudden spiritual insight into the meaning and essence of a thing or situation.

Episode: a unified event within a narrative.

Epithet: a word or short phrase that aptly describes and labels a person or thing.

Essay: a prose composition of undefined length that (usually) treats a single subject or theme.

Etymology: the study of the history of words.

Eulogy: a written or spoken expression of praise, generally formal in style.

Euphemism: a mild or inoffensive word substituted for one that is considered gross, indelicate, or taboo.

Euphony: the harmonious combination of sounds.

Existentialism: a philosophy that asserts that existence precedes essence; it denies the existence of absolute principles or objective meanings and insists that man is responsible for himself and acts with free will. The themes of existential literary work stress man's isolation, his loneliness, his sense of futility, and the irrevocability of his actions. Examples: works of Albert Camus, Jean-Paul Sartre, and Samuel Beckett.

Explication: a close reading of a literary text and the analysis of its structure and meaning.

Expressionism: a literary school that stresses the internal, or subjective, rather than the external, or objective, reality.

Examples: works of Dostoyevsky, Joyce, and Kafka.

Fable: a short tale that relates a moral.

Farce: a type of low comedy or burlesque that features extreme exaggeration of action.

Feminine ending: a line of verse in which the final syllable is unstressed.

Feminine rhyme: two-sylllable rhyme ("flatter" and "scatter"); also called *double rhyme*.

Figurative language: figures of speech and word combinations that go beyond literal (denotative) meanings.

Flashback: a literary technique that involves interrupting the story line to relate events that happened at a previous time.

Flat character: usually, a minor character in a story who is a stereotype or a ploy for the major characters.

Folklore: customs, songs, tales, and sayings that are transmitted within a culture from one generation to the next.

Foot: the basic unit of rhythm in verse.

Foreshadowing: hinting at events yet to come in the plot.

Foreword: an introduction to a literary work, often written by someone other than the author.

Form: (1) the general term for the main genres of literature (poetry, novel, tragedy, and so forth); (2) the structure of a work as opposed to its content.

Free verse: verse that does not follow a set metrical pattern but flows like natural speech patterns. In free-verse poetry, the stanza gives the poem form or structure. Example: Eliot's "The Wasteland. "

Genre: A literary classification or type, such as drama, short story, and so forth.

Gothic novel: a genre of novel that features morbidity, horror, and (often) elements of the supernatural.

Haiku: a popular form of Japanese verse that consists of seventeen syllables in a tercet of five, seven, and five syllables per line.

Hedonism: a philosophical belief that pleasure constitutes man's highest good.

Heptameter: a seven-foot line of verse (also called the *fourteener* when the feet are iambic).

Hero: the protagonist or main character.

Heroc couplet: two consecutive lines of end-rhymed iambic pentameter verse.

Hexameter: a six-foot line of verse.

Historical novel: a novel set in the past with either real or fictional historical figures as characters.

Homeric (or epic) simile: a lengthy figurative comparison that parallels a number of similarities.

Humanism: a philosophical doctrine that emphasizes the perfectibility of man; it originated during the Renaissance period and held that man was not inherently wicked or fallen from grace, as the medieval view had proclaimed, but that human values are good and should be the center of the study of man himself.

Humanities: the general term describing the areas of learning that are culturally oriented: art, music, literature, philosophy, and so forth.

Hyperbole: the use of extravagant exaggeration for emphasis.

Iamb (or iambus): a two-syllable foot with an unaccented syllable, followed by an accented one (about).

Iambic pentameter: a metrical line consisting of five iambic feet.

Ictus: an unnatural accent in a line of verse; i. e., an accent that does not correspond with the spoken stress.

Idiom: an expression in a language with a meaning that cannot be derived from the words involved.

Idyll: a pastoral poem describing the idealized life of shepherds in picturesque terms; also, a short epic that depicts heroic events of the past.

Image: the impression elicited by a word or phrase.

Imagery: figurative language that conveys sensory impressions.

Imagism: a poetic movement, chiefly among American poets, that reached its height during the pre-World War I years; it sought to produce visual imagery that was clear, definite, and concentrated. Examples: works of Ezra Pound, Amy Lowell, William Carlos Williams.

Impressionism: in literature, the attempt to present experience without formal, structured analysis or by evoking an emotional effect without factual, detailed description; in criticism, a school wherein the critic analyzes his reactions to a literary work rather than the work itself.

In media res: the practice of plunging the reader into a narrative account at a point well along in the chronological sequence of events.

Internal rhyme: rhyming of sounds within a line of verse.

Invective: biting, abusive language that is not tempered by wit or humor.

Inversion: reordering normal sentence order; used in poetry for rhyme.

Irony: a statement in which the intended meaning is the opposite of the literal meaning.

Jacobean: referring to the period of the reign of James I of England (1603-1625).

Jargon: a set of special terms peculiar to a certain group or activity.

Jangleur: the French counterpart of the English *jester*, a wandering entertainer whose repertoire included playing musical instruments, singing, performing magic tricks and acrobatics, telling stories, and so forth.

Journalism: the writing and publishing of information in a newspaper or periodical issued at regular intervals.

Kenning: a compound metaphor used in place of a single noun, as "ring-giver" for "king"; associated primarily with Anglo-Saxon and Old Norse poetry.

Lay: a short epic or romantic story set to music, especially popular with the English wandering minstrels (11th to 15th centuries).

Lament: a poem that expresses deep sorrow, such as a dirge or elegy.

Lampoon: a caricature, usually malicious, of a literary or political figure; Lampoons fall under the general category of satire.

Legend: a traditional story that has some basis in fact, but is embellished with fictitious detail.

Lexicon: a dictionary or specialized listing of words.

Libretto: The verbal text of an opera or lyrics of a musical comedy.

Linguistics: the formal study of language.

Lipogram: the complete avoidance of a certain letter or the use of a single letter for a certain effect in a composition, particdarly in a poem.

Litany: a liturgical form in which the clergymen and the congregation alternate responses.

Literal meanng: the exact meaning (denotation).

Literature: (for our purposes) imaginitive writing-fiction, prose, poetry, drama, essays, mythology, folklore, legend.

Litotes: a figure of speech that affirms the validity of something by denying its opposite (also called *understatement*).

Liturgical drama: drama that grew out of church ritual in the 10th century.

Locale: the setting of a work of literature.

Logic: the study of arguments and reasoning to determine their validity.

Lyric poetry: (usually) non-narrative poetry that expresses personal emotion.

Macrocosm: the whole universe or entire realm of human existence. (*See* Microcosm.)

Macrology: excessive wordiness that detracts from a literary style.

Magnum opus: an artist's greatest, or major, work.

Malapropism: a comic substitution of words.

Malediction: an invocation to bring ill-fortune or death to an adversary; the opposite of *benediction*.

Mannerism: the identifying stylistic marks of an individual writer or school of writers; (also, a 16th-century art style).

Masculine ending: ending a line of poetry on an accented final syllable.

Masculine rhyme: rhyme in which the final syllable of one line rhymes with the final syllable of another (also called *single rhyme*).

Masque (mask): a lavishly produced pageant of simple drama, dance, and music popular in the Renaissance court.

Materialism: a philosophy that stresses the reality of material things (physical objects) and states that spiritual or ideal forms are products of the imagination and have no real force or value.

Maxim: a general truth stated in concise form.

Memoir: an autobiographical narrative that focuses on events and characters other than the writer's own.

Metachronism: the postdating of events in narrative fiction. (*See also* Anachronism.)

Metaphor: a figure of speech that implies a direct likeness between two unlike things.

Metaphysical poetry: in literature, a term applied to the poetry of a group of 17th-century poets who emphasized the intellectual and psychological aspects of emotion and religion. Examples: Donne, Marvell, and Herbert.

Meter: the rhythmic pattern in poetry determined by the number of accents in the lines of the poem (accentual-syllabic rhythm). Most English poetry is classified according to the following rhythmic units (feet): iambic, trochaic, dactylic, anapestic, spondaic, and pyrrhic. The number of feet determines the meter; the standard meters for English verse are: monometer (one foot), dimeter (two feet), trimeter (three feet), tetrameter (four feet), pentameter (five feet), hexameter (six feet) and heptameter (seven feet).

Metonymy: the use of one name for something closely associated with it, as "the crown" for "the king. " (*See* Synecdoche.)

Metrical romance: a medieval tale of romantic love and idealized courtly traditions in a remote and exotic setting. Example: "Sir Gawain and the Green Knight. "

Middle English: the English language as spoken and written between the Norman Conquest (1066) and the beginning of the 16th century.

Microcosm: a small portion of the whole. In literature, often used to represent greater reality, as man's experience is seen in terms of the greater universe in which he operates.

Miles gloriosus: a stock character in literature, usually a cowardly braggart, often victim of the practical jokes of others. Example: Sir John Falstaff in Shakespeare's *Henry IV*.

Milieu: the intellectual and sociological climate of a period.

Mime: originally a low form of vulgar comedy — developed in Italy in the 5th century B C.

Minnesinger: a German lyric poet of the medieval period (1200-1300), similar to the French *troubadour*.

Minstrel: a 13th or 14th-century musical entertainer who carried news from town to town, performed on the harp, sang, and recited romances.

Miracle play: a type of play developed in the 12th century that dealt with the lives of saints; today, almost synonymous with *mystery play*, which designates a play that dealt with Biblical themes.

Mock epic (or mock heroic): a literary form that burlesques the "grand style" of epic poetry by treating a subject of trivial importance with pretended seriousness. Example: Pope's "The Rape of the Lock."

Modulation: a deliberate variation in the metrical pattern of a poem to prevent monotony.

Monody: a lament or song of grief sung by an individual singer.

Monologue: a speech or written composition presented wholly by one person.

Monometer: a one-foot line of verse.

Mood: the prevailing atmosphere or tone of a literary work.

Moral: the ethical lesson of a literary work.

Morality play: a post-14th-century type of allegorical drama that depicted the conflict between virtue and vice. Example: *Everyman.*

Mosaic rhyme: rhyme in which one or more of the rhyme partners is made up of more than one word.

Motif: a narrative element that serves as the basis for an expanded poem, tale, song.

Movement: a literary trend that is distinguished by identifiable characteristics, such as impressionism or the free verse movement.

Mummery: a dumb show or simple dramatic presentation acted by performers wearing masks and disguised in costume.

Muses: the nine Greek goddesses represented as patrons of music, literature, and the liberal arts.

Musical comedy: a type of drama developed in England and the United States in the early 12th century that features songs to carry the story line, but the dialogue is spoken, not sung.

Mysticism: the philosophy or theory that God — or the controlling deity — can be known immediately and personally through a natural human faculty that transcends intellect. (*See* Transcendentalism.)

Myth: an anonymous, traditional story that grows out of the universal human need to explain the "unknowable;" myths differ from legends in that they are not based on historical facts.

Narration: the recounting of an event or series of events.

Narrative: the story that is related in the process of narration.

Narrator: the teller of a story or poem: first-person ("I") and third-person ("he") narration is conventional. (*See* Point of view.)

Naturalism: in literature, a 19th-century movement that espouses determinism: man is not a creature of free will, but a pawn in the hands of his environment and his heredity. Examples: works of Stephen Crane, Jack London, and Emile Zola.

Neoclassicism: a late-17th and 18th-century school of literature that attempted to revive the principles of classicism. Man is viewed as imperfect and dualistic; a sense of order and reason prevails; restrained emotion dominates the writing; intellectual art is fostered. Example: works of Dryden, Milton, Pope, and Dr. Johnson.

Neologism: a newly coined word or phrase.

New Criticism: the name given to a modern school of literary critics concerned primarily with analyzing a work of art as an object in and of itself. Example: works of John Crowe Ransom, Robert Penn Warren, and Allen Tate.

Nom de plume: a pseudonymn or pen name.

Novel: a form of complex fictitious prose that contains the three elements of plot, characters, and setting.

Novelette: a work of prose fiction that is longer than the short story and shorter than the novel.

Novella: a significant influence upon the formation of the English novel, the *novelle* were realistic Italian tales. Example: Boccaccio's *Decameron*.

Objective correlative: defined by T. S. Eliot as "a set of objects, a situation, a chain of events which shall be the formula of that particular emotion, such that when the external facts, which must terminate in sensory experience, are given, the emotion is mediately evoked." Thus when an author has in mind a certain emotion he wishes to convey, he presents a situation or a set of external objects that, hopefully, trigger a precise emotional response in the reader. The objective correlative is a symbol or set of symbols, then, that can assure the emotional validity of a poem or work of prose.

Objective theory of art: a critical view that judges the work of art as an object in itself independent of any external facts of its composition.

Occasional verse: poetry written to commemorate a special event, such as a marriage song or verse.

Octameter: an eight-foot line of verse.

Octave: an eight-line stanza of poetry.

Ode: an elaborate lyric poem of complicated verse form with an exalted or dignified theme.

Omniscient narrator: a narrator who has unlimited scope in his presentation and is not limited to reporting external events through the eyes of a single character.

One-act play: a modern dramatic form stressing unity of effect, focusing on dialogues and characters, and not developing too much narrative background and details.

Onomatopoeia: the use of words whose sounds suggest their meanings ("hiss", "buzz", "murmur").

Opera: a dramatic form in which the dialogue is sung instead of spoken.

Operetta: an 18th-century forerunner of musical comedy, originally a parody or burlesque of grand opera.

Oration: an elaborately structured formal speech, intended to arouse the audience to action.

Otiose: a term used in literary ctiticism to denote a style that is ornate and redundant.

Ottava rima: eight iambic pentameter lines rhyming *abababcc*.

Oxford movement: a 19th-century religious movement led by Cardinal Newman corresponding to the romantic movement in literature.

Oxymoron: a rhetorical combination of contradictory terms for special emphasis, as in "eloquent silence."

Paean: (1) a hymn of praise of joy; (2) an uncommon (although frequently used by Hopkins) metrical foot consisting of one stressed (accented) syllable and three unstressed syllables.

Pageant: (1) a scaffold or stage, often constructed on wheels, upon which medieval plays were performed, and those plays performed on such stages; (2) a dramatic spectacle designed to celebrate a special event.

Paleography: the study of ancient writing materials, and written symbols.

Palindrome: a word, phrase or sentence that reads the same from right to left as from left to right, as in "noon" and "deified".

Palinode: a written retraction of a previous writing, particularly such a recanting in verse form of an earlier ode.

Panegyric: a eulogy or other formal written or oral composition praising a person.

Pantheism: a religous-philosophic attitude that asserts that God exists in everything (finite objects) and finite objects are what make up the glory of God, so that nature reveals God and, at the same time, is God.

Pantomime: a dramatic art depending on silent motion, facial expression, gesturing, and costuming to express emotional or narrative situations.

Parable: a short, fictional story that teaches a moral lesson, usually in the form of an extended metaphor or allegory.

Paradox: a statement that is seemingly self-contradictory or silly, but in fact is true.

Parallelism: a structural arrangement of syntactically similar words, phrases, or clauses so that one element is developed equally with another.

Paraphrase: to restate the ideas of a composition in completely different words.

Pararhyme: rhyme in which the first and final consonants are the same but the vowels differ ("small, smell").

Parody: a composition that deliberately burlesques or imitates another in order to ridicule or criticize.

Pastoral verse: poems dealing with rustic life, particularly that of shepherds, and elegies in which a death is lamented in pastoral imagery.

Pathetic fallacy: a term coined by John Ruskin to express the practice of attributing human emotions to inanimate objects. Examples: "the harsh winter," "cruel fate." The best poets use the pathetic fallacy consciously for good effect.

Pathos: the quality that elicits sorrow, pity, or sympathy in the reader.

Pedantry: a critical term of reproach applied to writing or speech that displays an excessive amount of foreign phrases and superfluous verbiage.

Pentameter: a five-foot line of verse.

Perfect rhyme: rhyme in which the rhymed syllables are identical (flew, blew); also called *identical or true rhyme*.

Peripety: an Aristotelian term designating the protagonist's change of fortune.

Periphrasis: a deliberate use of indirect or circumlocutious writing to get to the point.

Peroraliom: a conclusion and summing up of ideas in an oration, or a recapitullation of the major points of any discourse.

Persiflage: a flippant, chatty manner of treating a subject or theme.

Persona: a character used by an author as the narrative voice.

Personification: a figure of speech that attributes human characteristics to animals, inanimate objects, or philosophical abstractions and ideas.

Philippic: in modern usage, pertaining to invective speech or writing.

Philistinism: worship of material prosperity and technological success.

Philology: the study of language and literature in all its manifestations, including language theory and literary criticism.

Picaresque novel: a 16th-century form of the novel (orginally Spanish) that features an episodic account of the life of a *picaro*, a roguish, rascally fellow whose life is a series of misadventures.

Pindaric ode: a form of ode characterized by a three-part division.

Plagiarism: the stealing of another's text, language, idea, or plot, and presenting it as one's own.

Plaint: a lament or verse expressing sorrow.

Platonism: The idealistic philosophies of the Creek philosopher Plato (4th century B C). Basically he is known for the doctrine of ideas ("forms"), which states that true reality is found in the spiritual realm of ideal forms or images of which earthly objects are simple reflections.

Pleiade: A group of 16th-century French poets and critics who attempted to refine and enrich the French language and to strive for classicism in their literature.

Pleonasm: a superfluous use of words, redundancy.

Plot: the arrangement of events in a narrative.

Poem: a rhythmic, unified composition characterized by imagination and the use of figurative language.

Poetic justice: in literature, the term implies "just due;" i. e. , the virtuous are rewarded, the evil are punished.

Poetic license: the privilege to depart from normal logic, diction, or rhyme in order to achieve a particular desired effect.

Point of view: in narrative fiction, the author's attitude toward his story.

Polemic: a harsh argument against a religious, social, or political stance or ideology.

Polysyllabic rhyme: the rhyming of three or more syllables at the end of two or more words ("lightly pursues / brightly renews").

Portmanteau word: a word formed by deliberately fusing together two words (as James Joyee did in *Ulysses* and *Finnegan's Wake*).

Poulter's measure: the poetic combination (rarely used) of the twelve-syllable Alexandrine line of verse with a heptameter (fourteen syllable) line.

Pragmatic theory of art: according to literary critic M. H. Abrams, a theory of art in which the effect the work of art produces in its audience is the factor in judging its success.

Preciosity, precious: a critical term applied to writing that is affected or consciously "pretty" in style.

Preface: a short introductory statement at the beginning of a prose work in which the author states his purpose and intent.

Pre-Raphaelite movement: a movement of group of 19th-century English artists and writers who believed in a return to a simple, straightforward pressentation in art and literature of nature and man as a natural animal, as they felt was characteristic of Italian art before Raphael.

Prolepsis: the foreshadowing or predicting of a future event as if it were already affecting the present.

Prolixity: inclusion of excessive detail.

Prologue: an introduction to a play or literary work that prepares the reader for what is to follow.

Proscenium: in the modern theater, the front area of the stage between the orchestra pit and the curtain.

Prose: writing that does not have a regular rhythmic pattern.

Prosody: the technical study of versification.

Protagonist: the chief character in a narrative play or story.

Prototype: the original or first form of a thing or species.

Proverb: a saying, usually symbolic, that expresses a truth or recognized observation.

Pseudonym: a fictitious name.

Psychological novel: a novel that emphasizes the interior motivations of its characters. Examples: works of James, Faulkner, and Joyce.

Pun: play on words.

Purist: a person who is excessively devoted to absolute correctness in use of the English language.

Pyrrhic foot: a metrical foot of two unaccented syllables.

Qualitative verse: verse whose basic rhythm is determined by the length of time allowed for the pronunciation of sounds (syllables). Example: classical poetry.

Quatrain: a stanza of four lines; also a stanza composed of four verses.

Quintain (or quintet): a five-line stanza.

Quip: a witty, sarcastic, or jesting remark. Puns are examples of quips.

Rabelaisian: referring to lusty, irreverent humor in the manner of the 16th-century author Francois Rabelais.

Rationalism: a system of thought that holds as its authority reason rather than sense perception, intuition, revelation, or traditional authority.

Realism: a general term meaning accuracy of detail and true presentation of actuality.

Realisic movement: a mid-19th and early 20th-century movement that emphasized everyday experience and the immediate, pressing details of daily experience in literature. Examples: Balzac, George Eliot, and Mark Twain.

Rebuttal: a term from forensics (debating, public speaking) that denotes a final summing up of answers to the opposition in an argument.

Redundant: repetitive.

Refrain: a group of words, phrases, or lines that are repeated at intervals in a poem or song.

Regionalism: in literature, an emphasis on the history, folklore, speech, manners, dress, and so forth, of a particular geographical area.

Renaissance: the period in western European history between the medieval and the modern ages (approximately 1350-1650) marked by a growing sense of the importance of the individual.

Repartee: a quick, clever rejoinder or response.

Repetend: a poetical device in which a word or phrase is repeated at irregular intervals throughout a stanza or poem.

Repetition: the recurrent use of words, phrases, or sound patterns for emphasis.

Requiem: a chant or poem offering a prayer for the repose of the dead.

Restoration Age: 1660-1688, the period in English history after the Stuarts returned to the throne.

Reversal: the change of fortune for the protagonist in a dramatic or fictional plot. (*See* Peripety.)

Rhetoric: the principles and theory dealing with the logical, clear, convincing presentation of facts and ideas in a speech or written composition.

Rhetorical question: a question that does not require, or intend to require, an answer.

Rhyme: the similarity or duplication of sounds, usually in corresponding positions in lines of verse. There are two general types of rhyme: true, or perfect, rhyme in which vowels and consonants rhyme; and approximate rhyme, which consists of assonance, consonance, and alliteration. Rhyme can be classified according to the position of rhymed syllables in the lines or according to the number of syllables in which the identity of sound occurs. The first group consists of end, internal, or beginning rhyme; the second contains masculine, feminine, and triple rhyme (*See also* Apocopated rhyme, Broken rhyme, Mosaic rhyme, Pararhyme, Slant rhyme, Visual rhyme.)

Rhyme royal: a seven-line stanza of iambic pentameter verse, rhymed *ababbcc*.

Rhyme scheme: the rhyme pattern or sequence in a stanza or poem.

Rococo: in literature, designating a style that is overdone, precious, pretentious, and ornate.

西方文学

Rodomontade: a term derived from the name of a bragging Moorish king in Ariosto's *Orlando Furioso*, meaning braggadocio or vain boasting.

Roman a clef: a novel in which real persons are depicted disguised as fictional characters.

Romanesque: in literature, denoting the fanciful or fabulous, or the presence of romance.

Romantic movement: an 18th and 19th-century reaction against formality in art and literature; it stressed individualism, a love of nature, the imagination, and a revived interest in the past. Example: Wordsworth, Coleridge, Shelley, Keats, Byron, and Scott; Hawthorne, Melville, and Emerson.

Rondeau: a French verse form consisting of thirteen to fifteen lines, eight syllables to a line, with two end rhymes repeated over and over.

Rondel: a thirteen or fourteen-line variation of the rondeau, using only two rhymes and repeating complete lines in the refrain.

Roundel: an eleven-line verse with a refrain taken from words in the first line repeated in the 4th and 11th lines.

Run-on-lines: in poetry, the opposite of end-stopped lines; the grammatic structure and sense of a line is carried over from one line to the next; also called enjambement.

Saga: originally, an Icelandic or Scandinavian tale narrative legendary and historical accounts of heroic adventures.

Sapphic form: a verse form consisting of three verses of eleven syllables each.

Sarcasm: a form of irony denoting strong disapproval.

Satire: a type of writing that ridicules human frailties.

Scansion: the method used to determine meter and rhyme in English poetry; it consists of dividing verse into feet by counting accented syllables and indicating rhyme schemes with letter names. (*See* Meter, Foot, etc.)

Scenario: the plot outline of a drama.

Scene: in drama, the division of action and setting within an act.

Scholasticism: the name given to the system of thinking and writing of 11th to 16th-century philosopher-teachers who attempted to prove everything by syllogistic reasoning. Example: St. Thomas Aquinas.

School plays: classical and early English plays performed in England in the 16th century at the universities, foreshadowing many of the forms and techniques of Elizabethan drama.

Scientific method: basically, inductive reasoning, proceeding from the specific to the general.

Scop: an Anglo-Saxon (500-1100 A D) bard or court poet who composed and recited heroic lyric poetry.

Semantics: the study of the meanings of words, in particular, and of meaning, *per se*, in all forms of communication.

Sentimentalism: an emphasis on feeling, often expressed as expressive emotionalism in literature.

Sestet: a six-line stanza or poem, particularly the last six lines of the Petrarchian sonnet.

Sestina: a complex French lyrical form consisting of six-line stanzas and a three envoy (*q. v.*) with a pattern of end-words in place of a refrain.

Sextain: a six-line stanza or poem; it is a sestet, except that the term does not apply to the sonnet.

Short story: a short (1,000-to 10,000-word), carefully constructed literary form consisting of plot, setting, characters, and theme.

Sigmatism: the repetitive use of sibilant letters — x, z, soft c and sounding combinations (sh, tion, etc.) — to produce a certain consonant effect.

Simile: a figure of speech in which two basically unlike objects or things are directly compared.

Skald (scald): the Norse counterpart of the Anglo-Saxon scop; a singing poet-minstrel.

Skeltonic verse: a form of metrically irregular verse characterized by short lines of two or three stresses with irregular rhymed couplets; used by John Skelton (1460-1529) for his satiric poetry.

Slang: vernacular speech, usually unacceptable in formal usage and compositions.

Slant rhyme: rhyme in which the sounds are similar but not exactly the same; also called approximate or near rhyme. Example: "name", "gain".

Slice of life: a technique that presents an interchange between characters as it might happen in real life with no commentary; no problems are solved and no specific alternatives for action are presented.

Socratic irony: the dialectic device of pretending ignorance and humility in order to lead an opponent into contradicting himself.

Solecism: a violation of grammatical structure in speech or composition.

Soliloquy: a speech that reveals a character's innermost feelings and plans while other characters remain unaware of what he is saying.

Sonnet: a lyric poem of fourteen Lines with a definite rhyme scheme; Petrarchian: *abba abba cdc cde*; Shakespearean: *ab ab cd cd ef ef gg*.

Spenserian stanza: a nine-verse stanzaic pattern in which the first eight verses are iambic pentameter and the 9th is iambic hexameter; the rhyme scheme is *ababbcbcc*.

Spondee: a metrical foot of two accented syllables.

Spoonerism: an interchange of syllables in two or more words usually resulting in a humorous verbal blunder.

Sprung rhythm: meter based on the number of accented (stressed) syllables with no regard for the unstressed syllables in a line of verse.

Stanza: the recurring group of lines of a poem forming the largest division in terms of metrical form, unified thought, and rhyme scheme.

Stave: A stanza or set of verses (often written to be sung.)

Stock character: a conventional, stereotyped character.

Stream-of-consciousness novel: the type of psychological novel made popular by James Joyce and William Faulkner in which the consciousness of one or more characters is explored (consciousness in this context meaning all levels of awareness from pre-speech to highly articulated rational thought.)

Strophe: a stanzaic unit of poetry specifically associated with the Pindaric ode.

Sturm und Drang: a late 18th-century German literary movement characterized by elements of nationalism, folklore, and expression of emotion. Examples: works of Goethe and Schiller.

Style: the distinguishable characteristics of an author's writing.

Surrealism: a modern literary and artistic movement that attempts to depict objects "beyond reality" (surreal) — man's imagination, dreams, visions, etc.

Syllabic verse: verse in which meter is determined by the number of syllables, not by accents or quantitative values.

Symbol: an object or image that stands for or suggests something else.

Symbolism: a modern literary movement that began in reaction to realism, replacing the objectivity and directness of the realists' method with new techniques that attempted to present a true reality beyond objective reality. Examples: certain works of Eliot, Yeats, and Rilke.

Syncopation: a temporary shift in regular metrical accent.

Syncope: the deletion of a letter or a syllable in a word, as in "heavn'ly" and "e'er".

Synecdoche: the use of a part of one thing to signify the whole.

Synesthesia: a device used by symbolic writers in which the responses of two or more senses are aroused by a blending of sensuous imagery.

Synonym: words that are alike or closely associated in meaning.

Synopsis: a summry of the main points of a composition.

Syntax: the orderly arrangement of words into phrases and sentences.

Tail-rhyme stanza: a form in which short rhyming lines are placed

西方文学

after the longer lines; the "tail" rhymes serve as links between the stanzas.

Tall tale: an early American folk tale recounting the fantastically exaggerated heroic exploits of frontier heroes such as Paul Bunyan and Davy Crockett.

Tanka: a form of Japanese syllabic verse consisting of thirty-one syllables arranged in five lines.

Tautology: useless repetition of words.

Tenor (and vehicle): in criticism, tenor is the subject which the vehicle represents; or, the tenor is the real subject and the vehicle is the figurative subject, the image, according to critic I. A. Richards.

Tension: in 20th-century criticism, designating the integral unity of a poem.

Tercet: a three-line stanza; the rhyme scheme may be *aaa*, *bbb*, *ccc*, etc., or it may be interwoven with the following stanza.

Terza rima: an interlooking rhyme scheme: *aba*, *bcb*, *cdc*, *ded*, etc.

Tetrameter: a four-foot line of verse.

Threnody: a dirge or funeral song, shorter than an elegy.

Tone: (1) in literary criticism, the total effect of a work; (2) the mood or attitude expressed by the author toward his subject matter; (3) the mood of the work itself.

Tract: an agumentative pamphlet that sets forth the views and positions of its author(s).

Tragedy: a dramatic form that recounts the life story of a protagonist, usually ending in his downfall through his tragic flaw, moving the audience to "pity and fear" (Aristitolean definition) in the process.

Tragic flaw: the fatal weakness of character in the hero that leads to his downfall.

Tragi-comedy: a play that contains both tragic and comic elements.

Transcendentalism: a belief that intuition and the human conscience transcend external experience to put man in touch with higher forms of reality.

Transcendental movement: an American mid-19th-century literary movement based on principles of transcendentalism. Examples: Emerson's "Nature" (1836) and *Thoreau's Walden* (1854).

Travesty: a grotesque, mocking burlesque of another work of literature.

Trilogy: a three-part literary work in which each part is a complete unit in and of itself but is also vitally connected to the other parts.

Trimeter: a three-foot line of verse.

Triolet: a French verse form of eight lines in which the first line recurs three times; the rhyme scheme is *abaaabab*.

Triple rhyme: rhyme in which three consecutive syllables rhyme.

Triplet: a three-line stanza or a sequence of three rhyming verses.

Trochee: a two-syllable metrical foot with the first syllable accented and the second unaccented.

Trope: in rhetoric, the use of a word in a sense that is different from its literal meaning, as in ironic expressions, metaphors and similes.

Troubadour: an aristocratic lyric poet of southern France in the 12th and 13th centuries.

Trouvere: a member of a group of northern French lyric poets who corresponded to the troubadours of southern France. (Chretien de Troyes, a famous trouvere, is credited with writing some of the early Arthurian legends.)

Tudor: referring to the period in England between 1485 and 1603; the kings of this family were Henry Ⅶ, Henry Ⅷ, Edward Ⅵ, Mary, and Elizabeth (1558-1603).

Ubi sunt motif: an oft-repeated poetic theme that poses the question "where are" the good things of yesterday.

Understatement: a form of verbal irony that implies much more than is stated, or which affirms an idea by denying its opposite.

Unities principles: (Aristotelian unities of time, place, and action): (1) The events of a play must not exceed more than the length of one day (Time); (2)only one setting is permitted (Place); and (3) a play should have a beginning, middle and end, and should not mix tragic and comic elements (Action).

Unity: the literary concept that a work should have an organizing principle that unifies all parts to produce a single total effect.

Variorum edition: an edition of an author's work with complete notations and variations.

Universality: in literature, having universality means appealing to readers of all times and all places.

Vehicle: (*See* Tenor.)

Verisimilitude: the portrayal of truth and actuality by use of realistic detail.

Virgule: the diagonal mark / used to mark off metrical feet in scansion. //marks the caesura.

Visual rhyme: words that have a similar spelling but are not pronounced alike ("bead", "thread").

Weak ending: the final syllable of a line in poetry that is stressed to fit the metric pattern, but would not be stressed in normal speech.

Wit (and humor): in literature, wit denotes intellectual prowess or wisdom; humor designates eccentricity or the laughable.

Zeugma: a rhetorical device in which one word links two other words unlike in sense and grammatically incorrect as in "flying birds and hearts".

西方文学

References

Abrams M H. *The Norton Anthology of English Literature*. New York,London: W. W. Norton & Company, 1986

Branet Sylvan. *An Introduction to Literature*. New York: Harper Collins College Publishers, 1993

Bradbry M, McFarlane J. *Modernism*. London: Penguin Books, 1978

Cary F Hanry. *The Divine Comedy of Dante Alighieri*. New-York: P. F. Collier & Son Corporation, 1937

Cook Albert. *An Anthology of Greek Tragedy*. Indianapolis & New York: The Bobbs-Merrill Company, Inc. 1972

Greenouch J B. *Virgil and Other Latin Poets*. Boston: Ginn and Company,1930

GUI Yangqing. *Selected Readings in English and American Literature*. Shanghai: China Translation and Publishing Corp, 1985

Harris L Stephen. *The New Testament*. London: Mayfield Publishing Company, 1995

Hart James. *The Oxford Companion to American Literature*. New York:Oxford University Press, 1965

Hebel J William. *Poetry of the English Renaissance*. New York: Meredith Corporation, 1975

Hough G. *The Romantic Poets*. London: Hutchinson University Library, 1966

西方文学

Hurtik. *An Introduction to Poetry and Criticism*. Lexington:
  Xerox College Publishing, 1972

Lodge D. *20th Century Literary Criticism*. London: Longma,
  1983

MA Qingfu. *Introduction to the Western Literary Criticism*.
  Shenyang: Liaoning University Publishing House, 1986

Mc Michael G. *Anthology of American Literature*. New York:
  Macmillan Publishing Company, 1980

Mc Nulty, Bard J. *Modes of Literature*. Boston: Houghton Mif-
  flin Company, 1977

Mack Maynard. *The Norton Anthology of World Masterpieces*.
  New York: W. W. Norton & Company, 1977

O'Connor Van William. *Modern American Novelists*. New
  York: Washington Square Press, 1973

Pritchett S V. *The Oxford Book of Short Stories*. Oxford: Oxford University Press, 1981

Rosenberg Donna. *World Literature*. Lincolnwood: National
  Textbook Company, 1994

Salzman Jack. *The Cambridge Handbook of American Literature*. London: Cambridge University Press, 1986

Seldon R. *Practicing Theory and Reading Literature*. New
  York: OUP, 1989

Shaw Harry. *Concise Dictionary of Literary Terms*. New York:
  McGraw-Hill Book Company, 1976

Ward C A. *Longman Companion to 12th Century Literature*.
  Hong Kong: Longman Group Limited, 1981

Wellek Rent. *A History of Modern Criticism*. New York, London: Yale University Press, 1896

西方文学

Winsatt & Brooks. *Neo-Classical Criticism*. London: Routledge & Kegan Paul, 1970

YANG Qishen, SUN Zhu. *Selected Readings in English Literature*. Shanghai: Translation and Publishing Corp, 1991